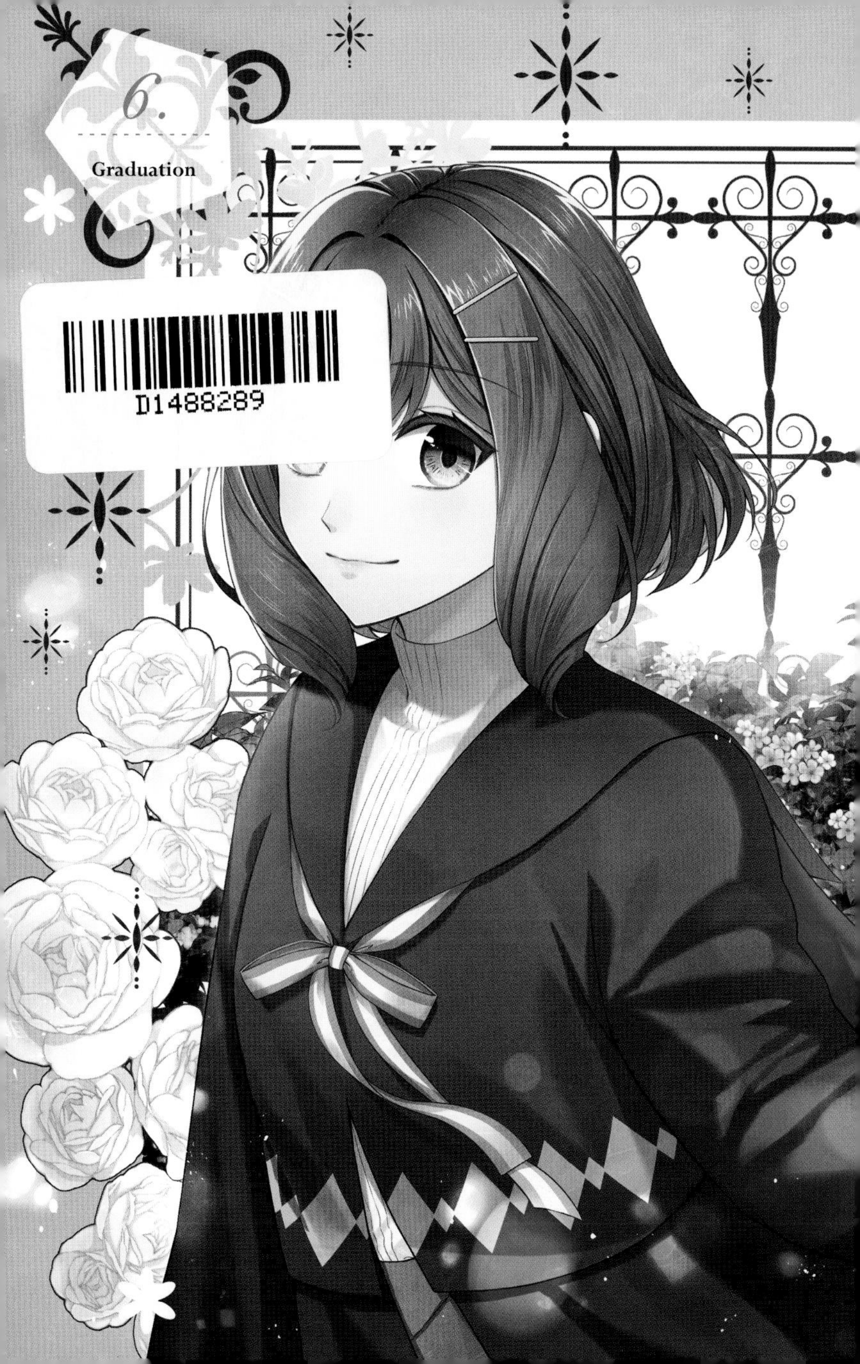
6.
Graduation

Contents

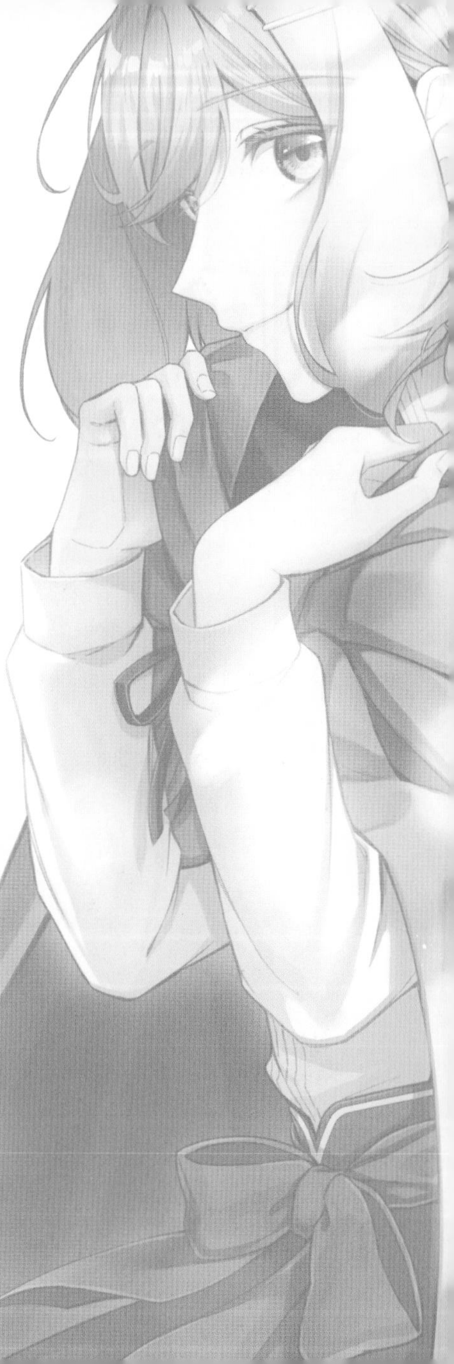

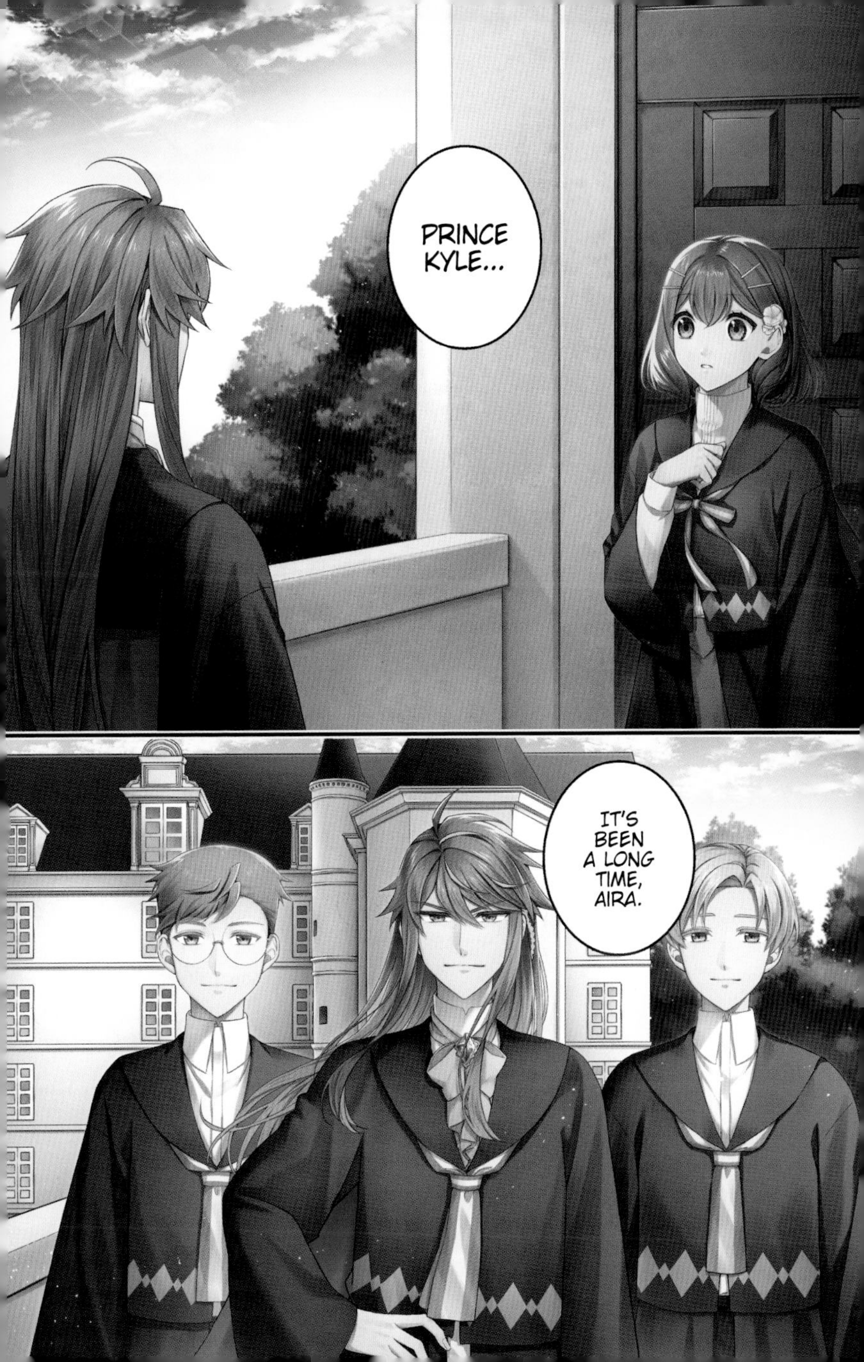
PRINCE KYLE...
IT'S BEEN A LONG TIME, AIRA.

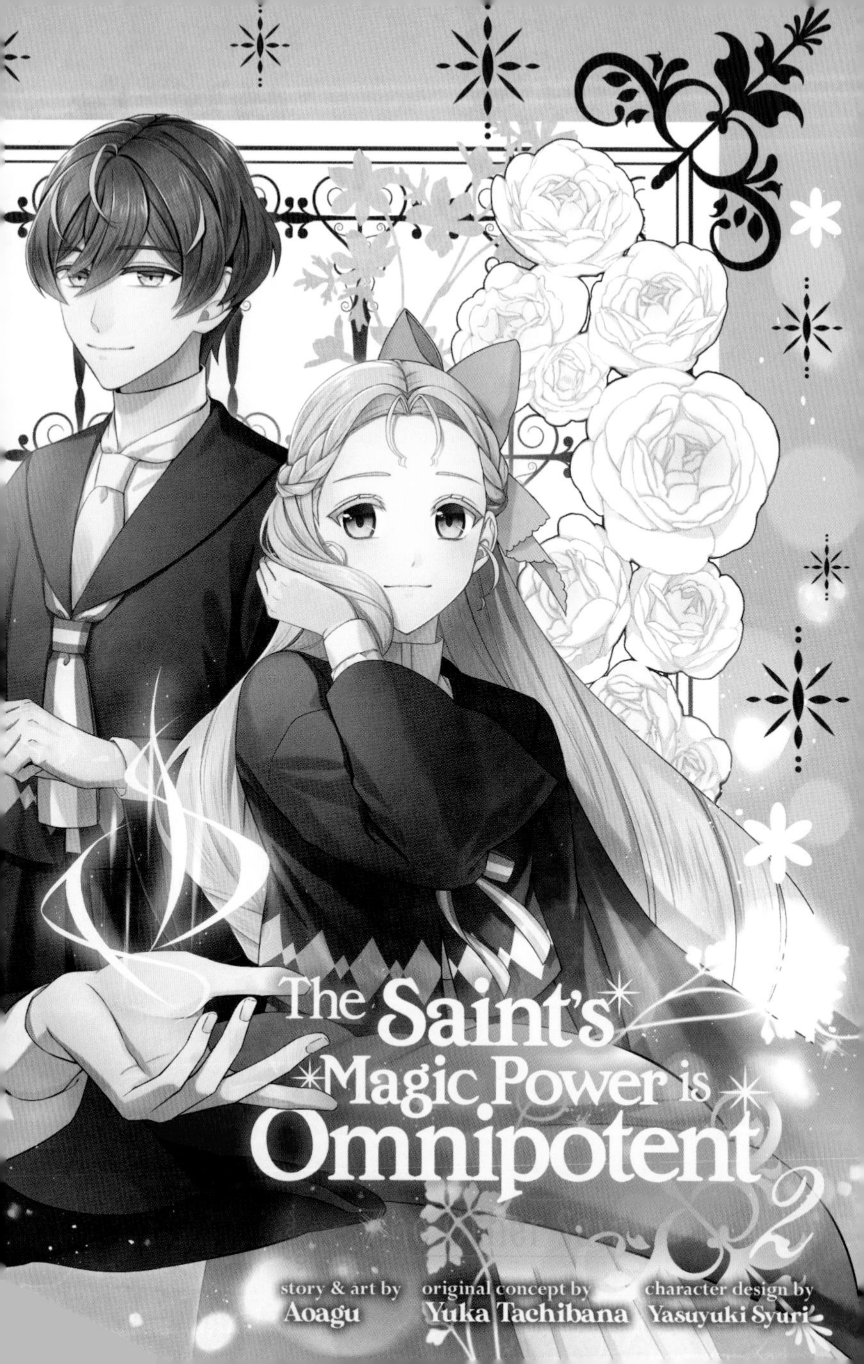
The Saint's Magic Power is Omnipotent
2
story & art by
Aoagu
original concept by
Yuka Tachibana
character design by
Yasuyuki Syuri

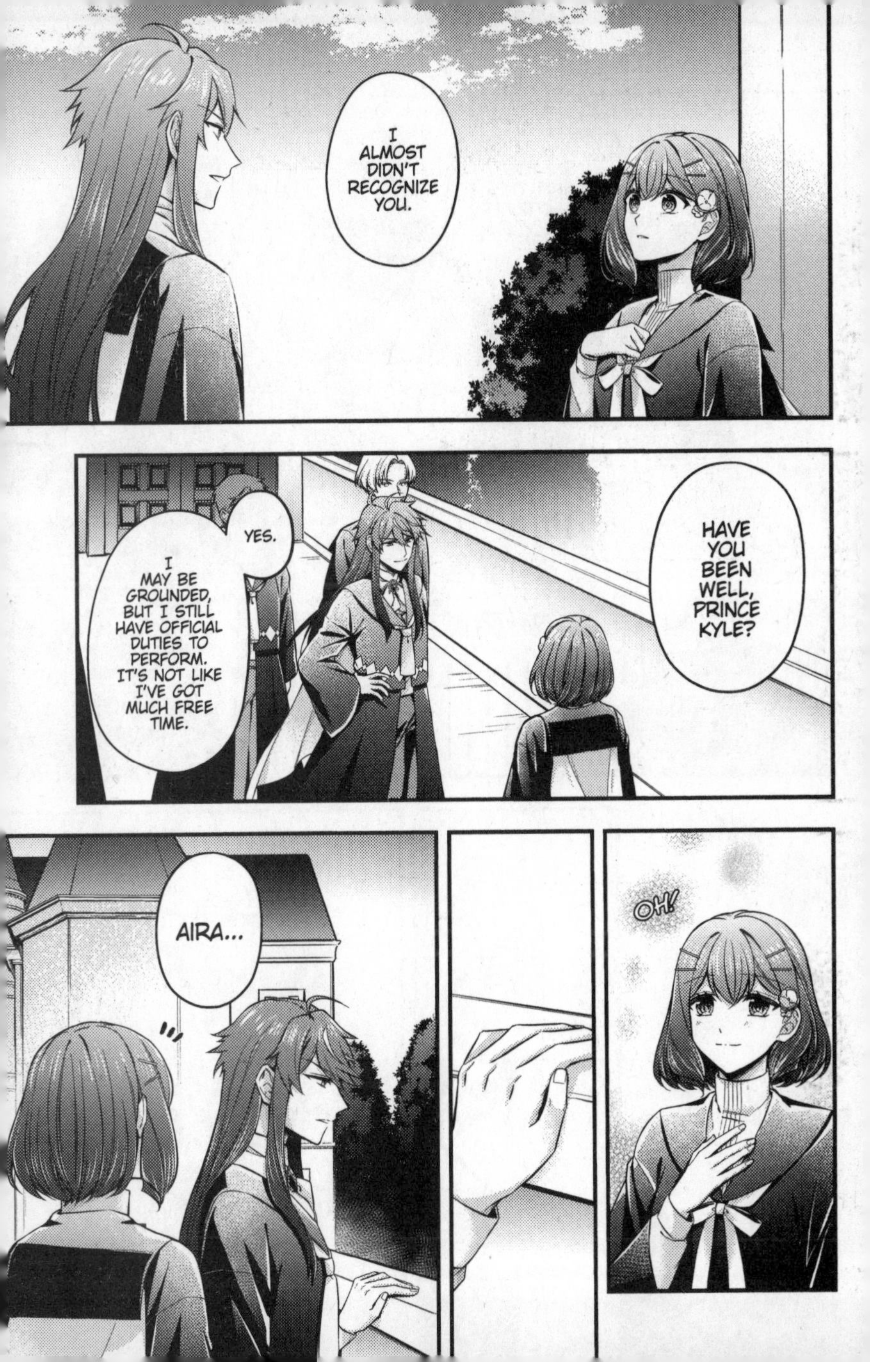
I ALMOST DIDN'T RECOGNIZE YOU.
HAVE YOU BEEN WELL, PRINCE KYLE?
YES.
I MAY BE GROUNDED, BUT I STILL HAVE OFFICIAL DUTIES TO PERFORM. IT'S NOT LIKE I'VE GOT MUCH FREE TIME.
OH!
AIRA...

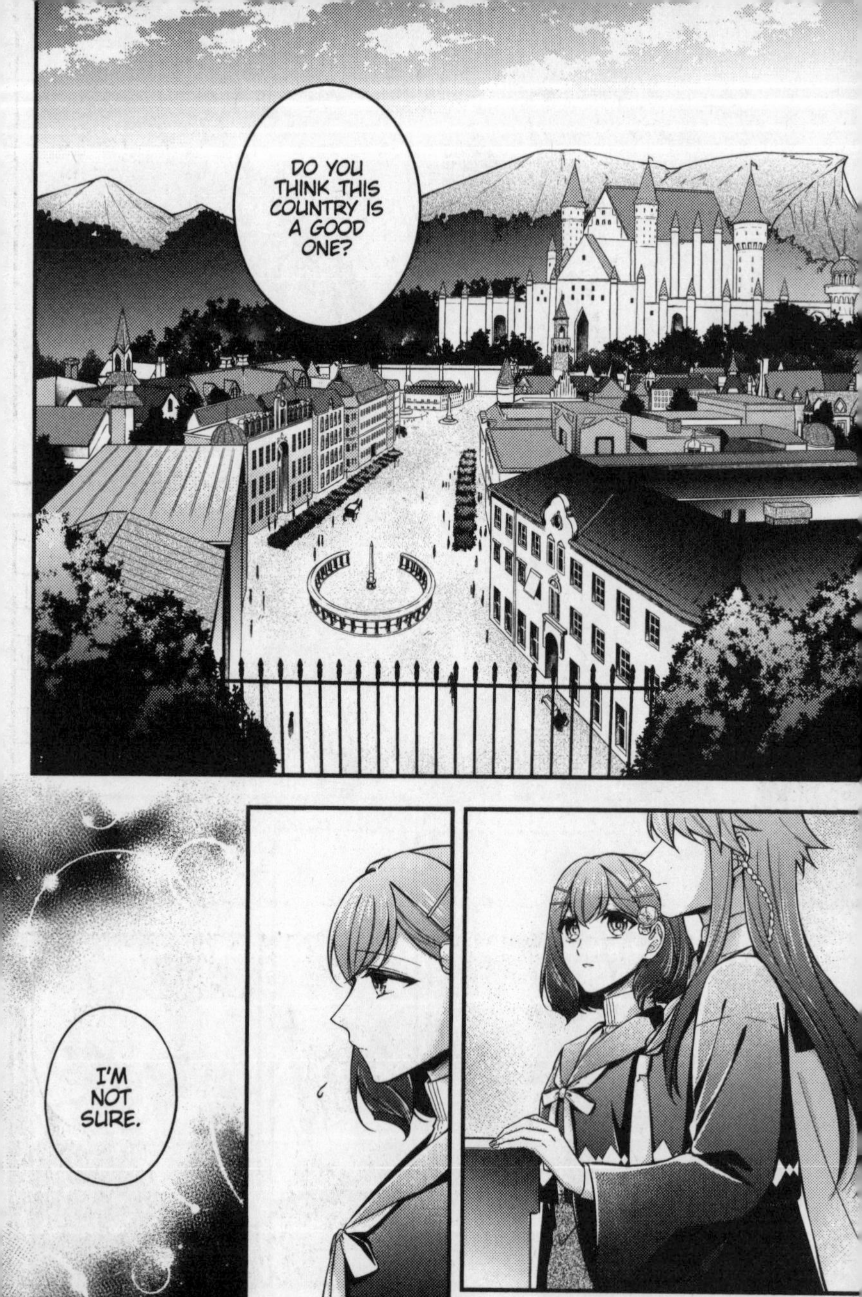
DO YOU THINK THIS COUNTRY IS A GOOD ONE?
I'M NOT SURE.

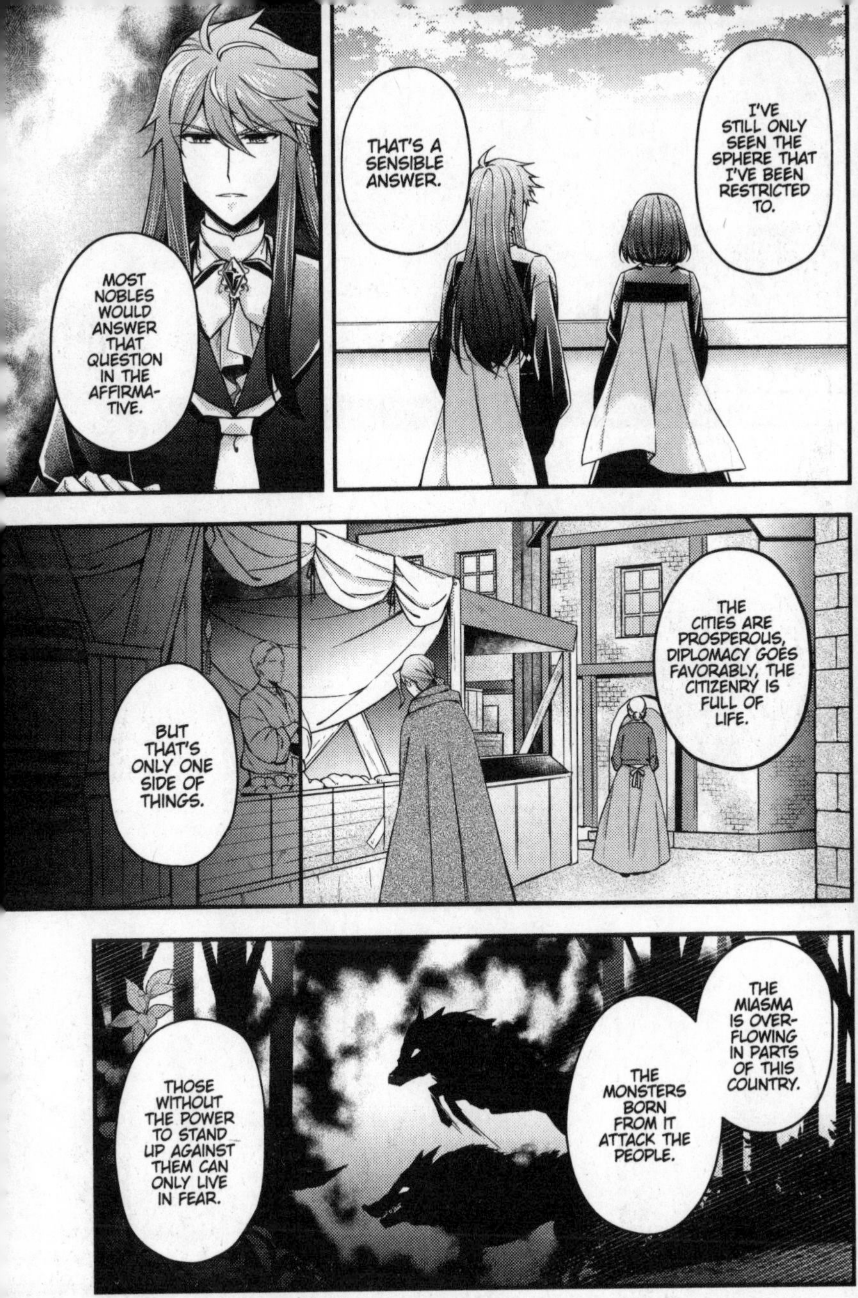
I'VE STILL ONLY SEEN THE SPHERE THAT I'VE BEEN RESTRICTED TO.
THAT'S A SENSIBLE ANSWER.
MOST NOBLES WOULD ANSWER THAT QUESTION IN THE AFFIRMA-TIVE.
THE CITIES ARE PROSPEROUS, DIPLOMACY GOES FAVORABLY, THE CITIZENRY IS FULL OF LIFE.
BUT THAT'S ONLY ONE SIDE OF THINGS.
THE MIASMA IS OVER-FLOWING IN PARTS OF THIS COUNTRY.
THE MONSTERS BORN FROM IT ATTACK THE PEOPLE.
THOSE WITHOUT THE POWER TO STAND UP AGAINST THEM CAN ONLY LIVE IN FEAR.

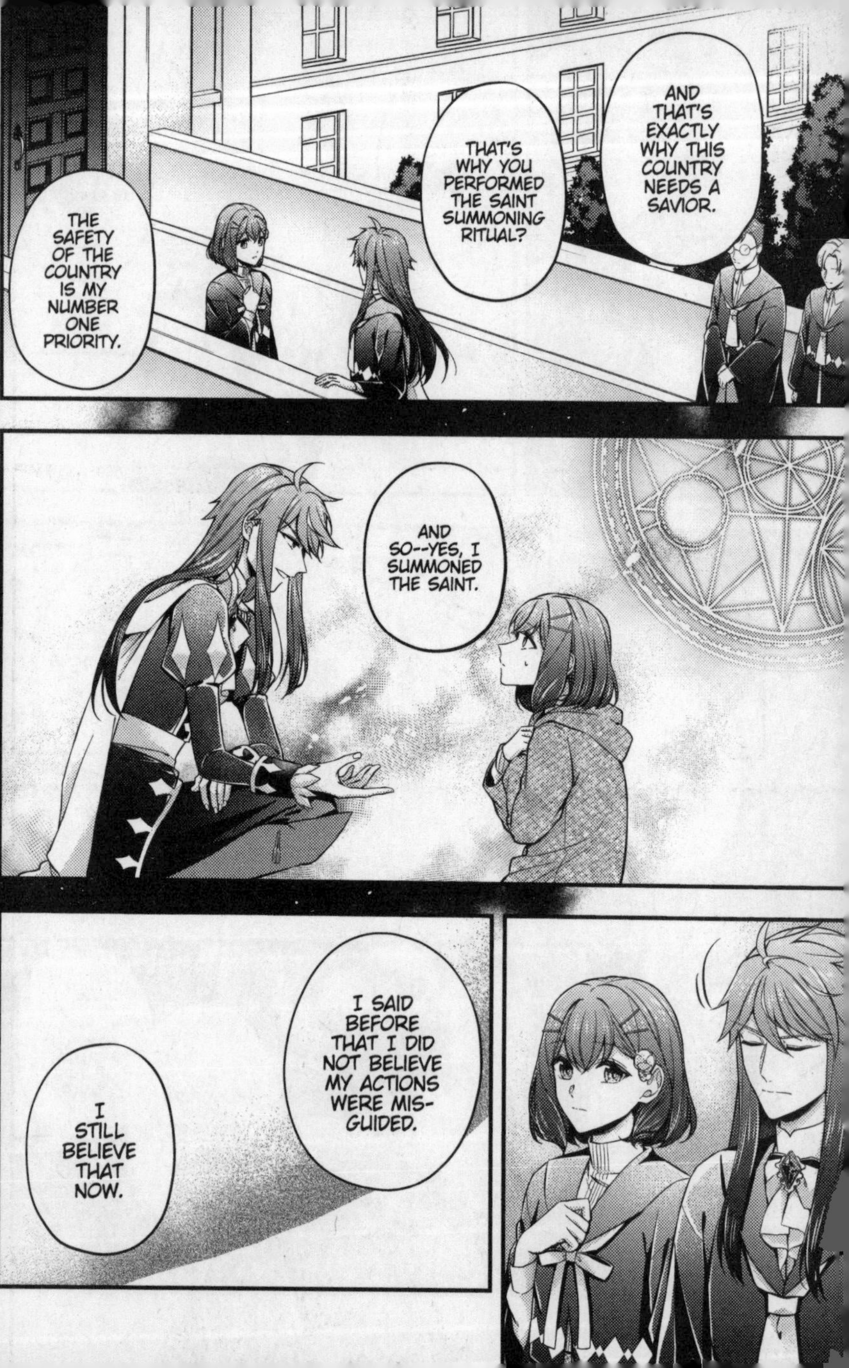
AND THAT'S EXACTLY WHY THIS COUNTRY NEEDS A SAVIOR.
THAT'S WHY YOU PERFORMED THE SAINT SUMMONING RITUAL?
THE SAFETY OF THE COUNTRY IS MY NUMBER ONE PRIORITY.
AND SO--YES, I SUMMONED THE SAINT.
I SAID BEFORE THAT I DID NOT BELIEVE MY ACTIONS WERE MIS-GUIDED.
I STILL BELIEVE THAT NOW.

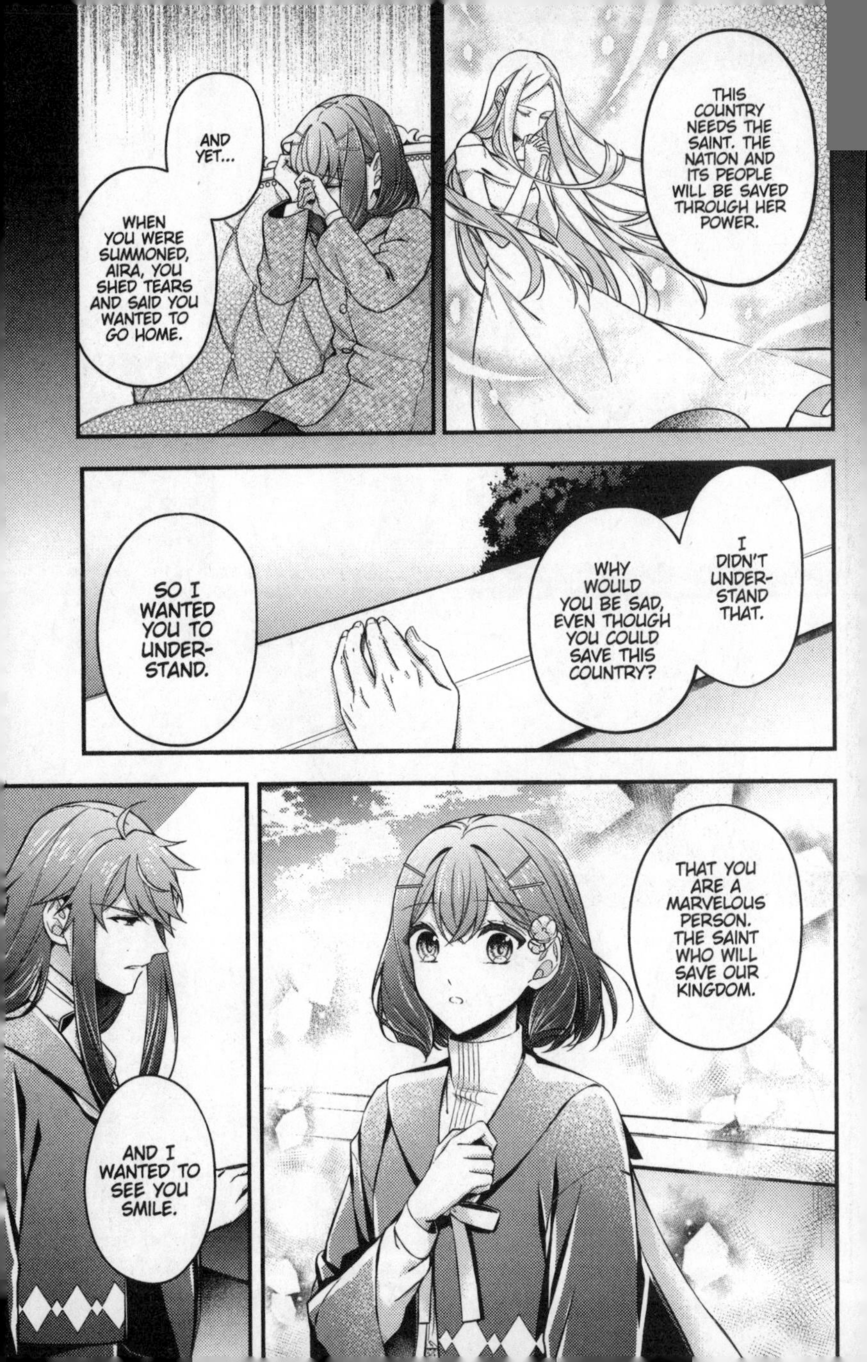
THIS COUNTRY NEEDS THE SAINT. THE NATION AND ITS PEOPLE WILL BE SAVED THROUGH HER POWER.
AND YET...
WHEN YOU WERE SUMMONED, AIRA, YOU SHED TEARS AND SAID YOU WANTED TO GO HOME.
I DIDN'T UNDER-STAND THAT.
WHY WOULD YOU BE SAD, EVEN THOUGH YOU COULD SAVE THIS COUNTRY?
SO I WANTED YOU TO UNDER-STAND.
THAT YOU ARE A MARVELOUS PERSON. THE SAINT WHO WILL SAVE OUR KINGDOM.
AND I WANTED TO SEE YOU SMILE.

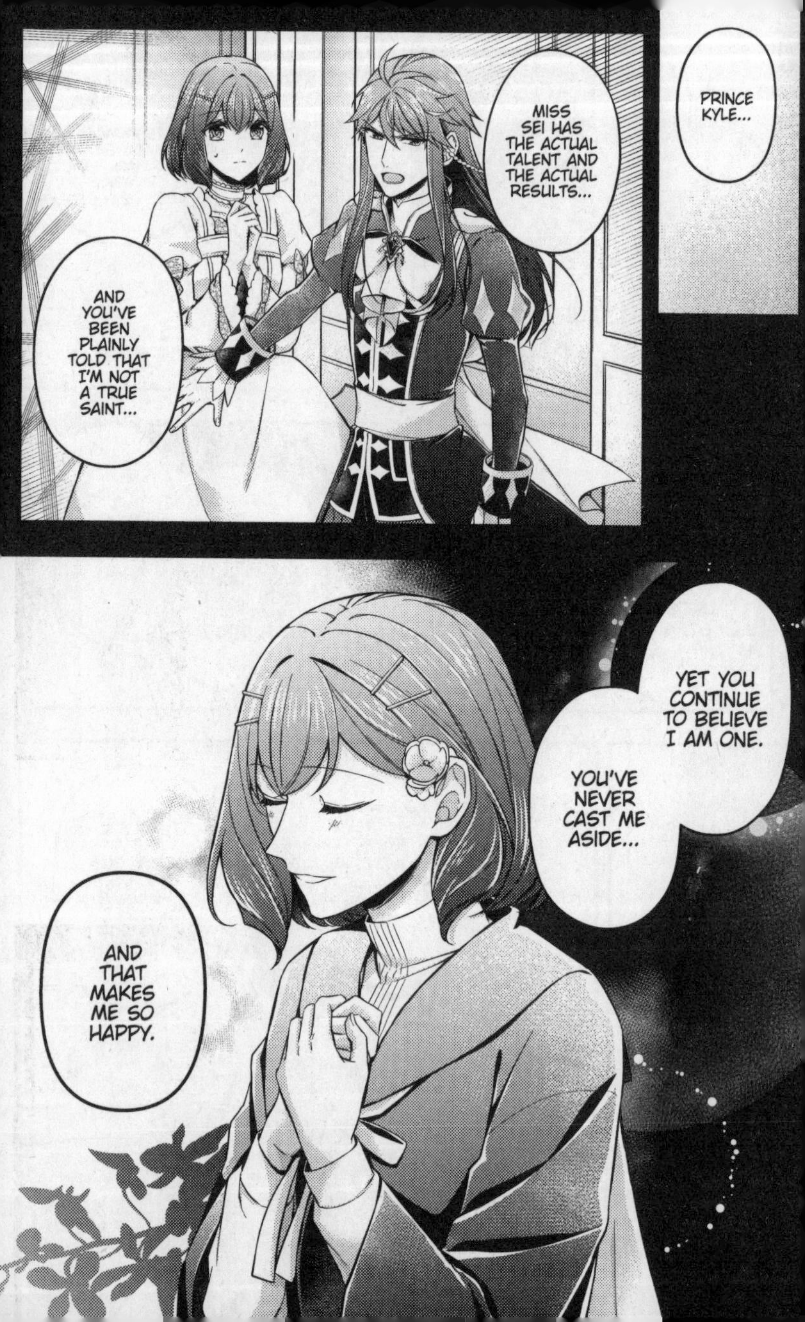
PRINCE KYLE...
MISS SEI HAS THE ACTUAL TALENT AND THE ACTUAL RESULTS...
AND YOU'VE BEEN PLAINLY TOLD THAT I'M NOT A TRUE SAINT...
YET YOU CONTINUE TO BELIEVE I AM ONE.
YOU'VE NEVER CAST ME ASIDE...
AND THAT MAKES ME SO HAPPY.

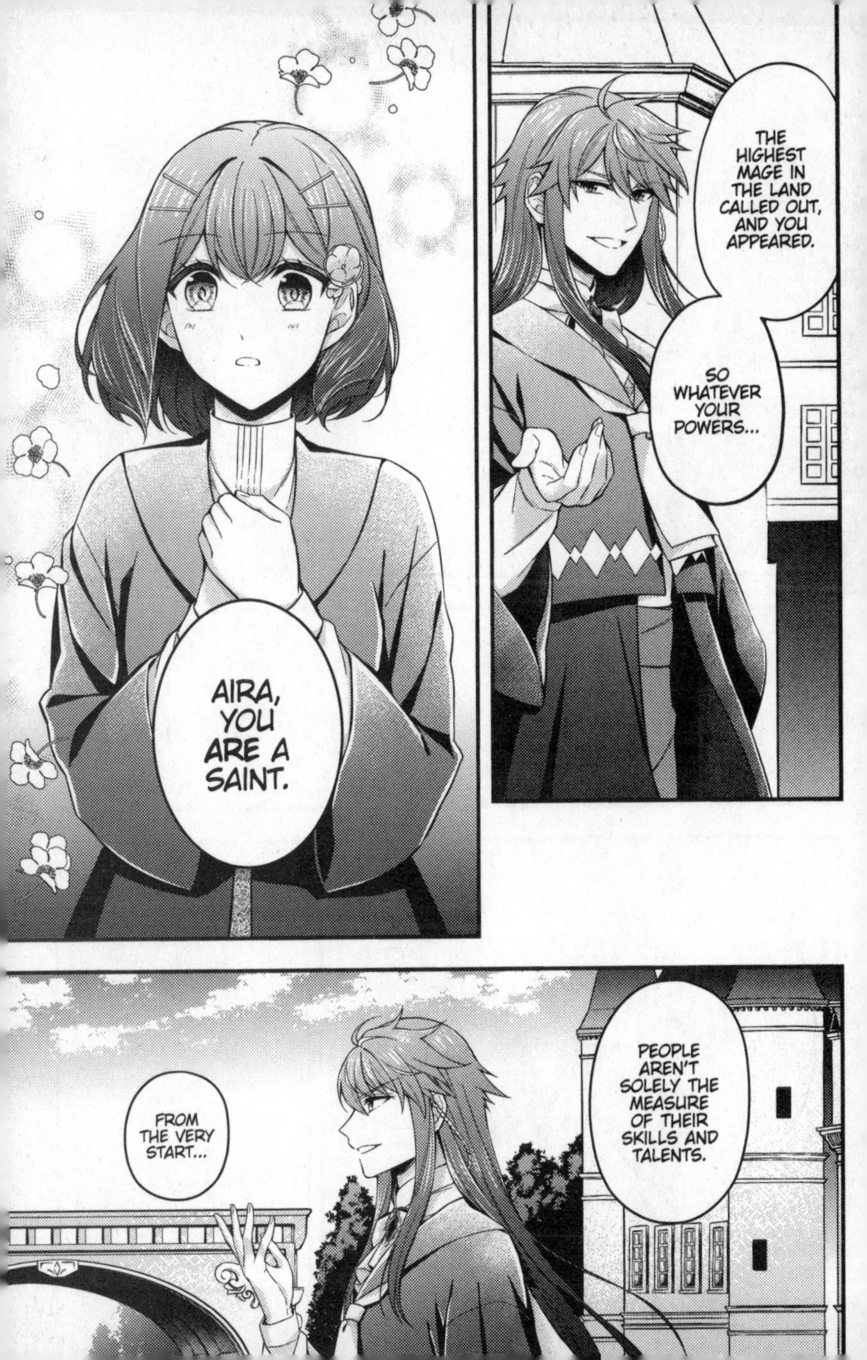
THE HIGHEST MAGE IN THE LAND CALLED OUT, AND YOU APPEARED.
SO WHATEVER YOUR POWERS...
AIRA, YOU ARE A SAINT.
PEOPLE AREN'T SOLELY THE MEASURE OF THEIR SKILLS AND TALENTS.
FROM THE VERY START...

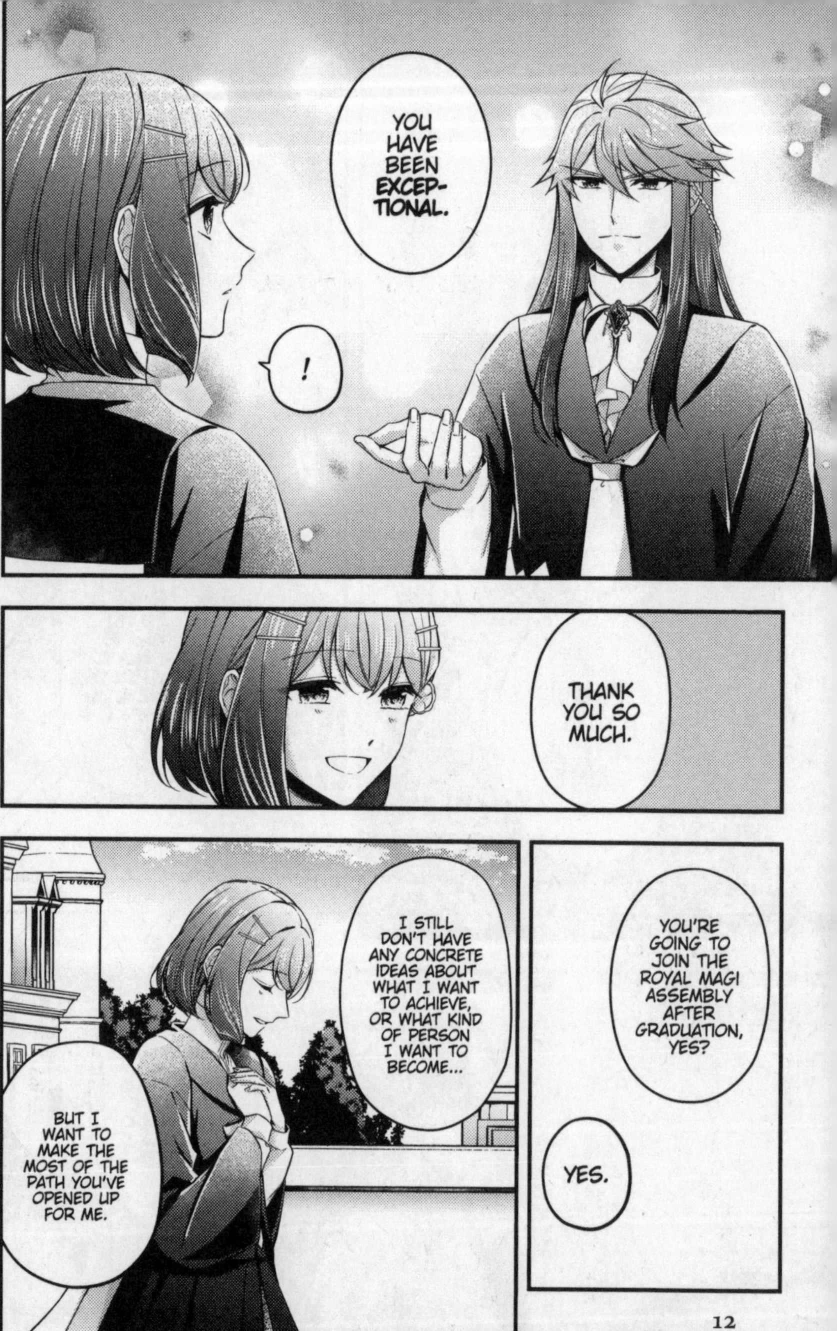
YOU HAVE BEEN EXCEP-TIONAL.
!
THANK YOU SO MUCH.
YOU'RE GOING TO JOIN THE ROYAL MAGI ASSEMBLY AFTER GRADUATION, YES?
YES.
I STILL DON'T HAVE ANY CONCRETE IDEAS ABOUT WHAT I WANT TO ACHIEVE, OR WHAT KIND OF PERSON I WANT TO BECOME...
BUT I WANT TO MAKE THE MOST OF THE PATH YOU'VE OPENED UP FOR ME.

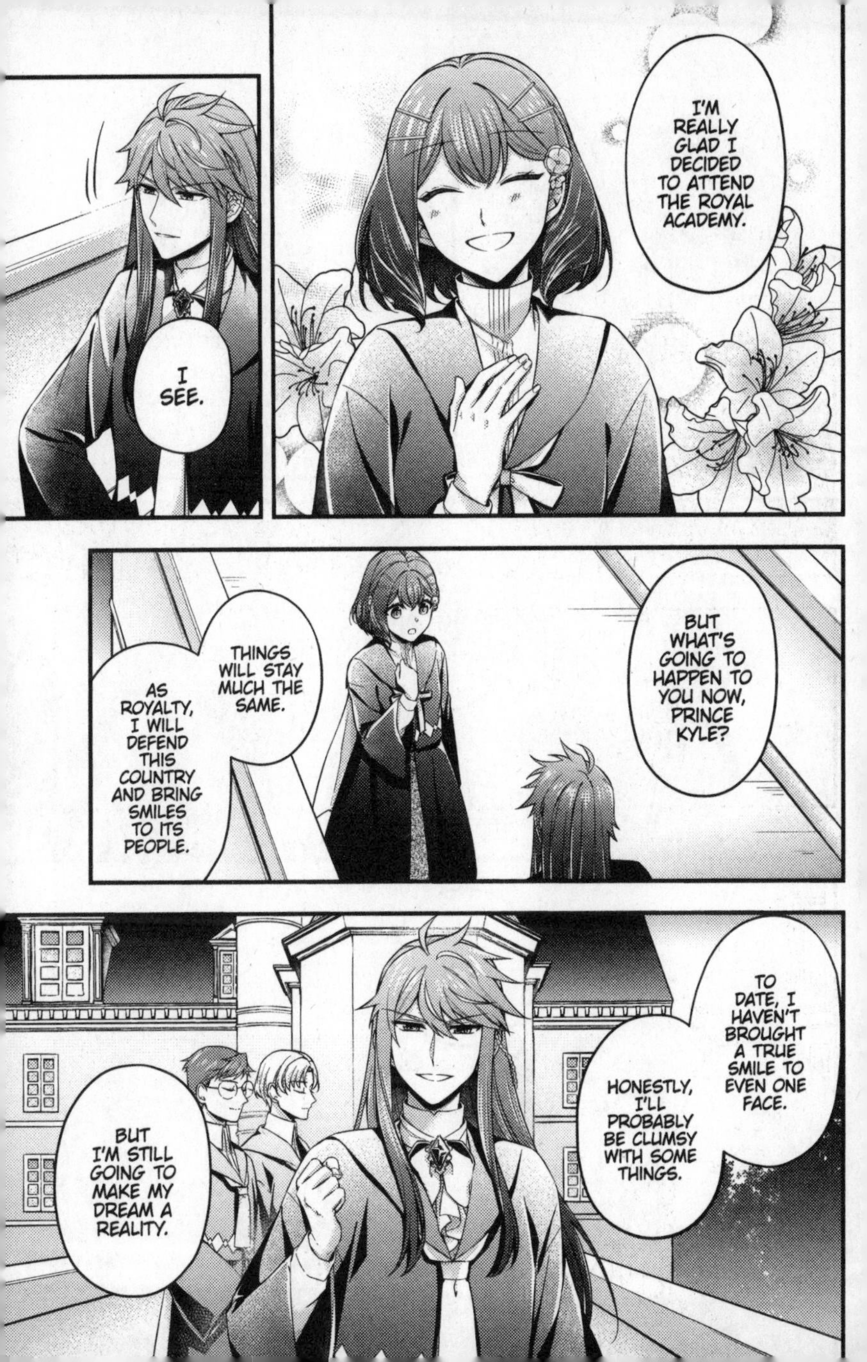
I'M REALLY GLAD I DECIDED TO ATTEND THE ROYAL ACADEMY.
I SEE.
BUT WHAT'S GOING TO HAPPEN TO YOU NOW, PRINCE KYLE?
THINGS WILL STAY MUCH THE SAME.
AS ROYALTY, I WILL DEFEND THIS COUNTRY AND BRING SMILES TO ITS PEOPLE.
TO DATE, I HAVEN'T BROUGHT A TRUE SMILE TO EVEN ONE FACE.
HONESTLY, I'LL PROBABLY BE CLUMSY WITH SOME THINGS.
BUT I'M STILL GOING TO MAKE MY DREAM A REALITY.

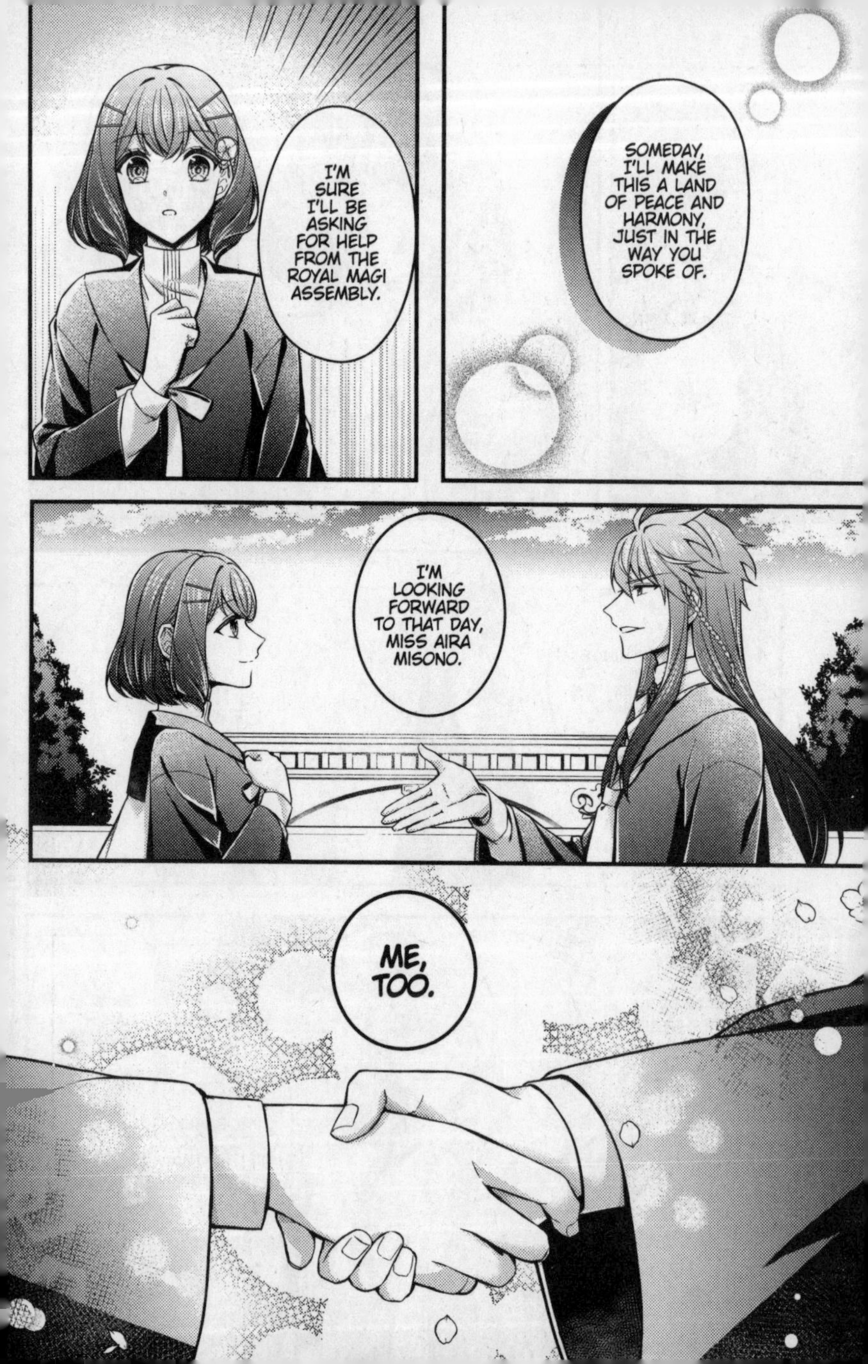
SOMEDAY, I'LL MAKE THIS A LAND OF PEACE AND HARMONY, JUST IN THE WAY YOU SPOKE OF.
I'M SURE I'LL BE ASKING FOR HELP FROM THE ROYAL MAGI ASSEMBLY.
I'M LOOKING FORWARD TO THAT DAY, MISS AIRA MISONO.
ME, TOO.

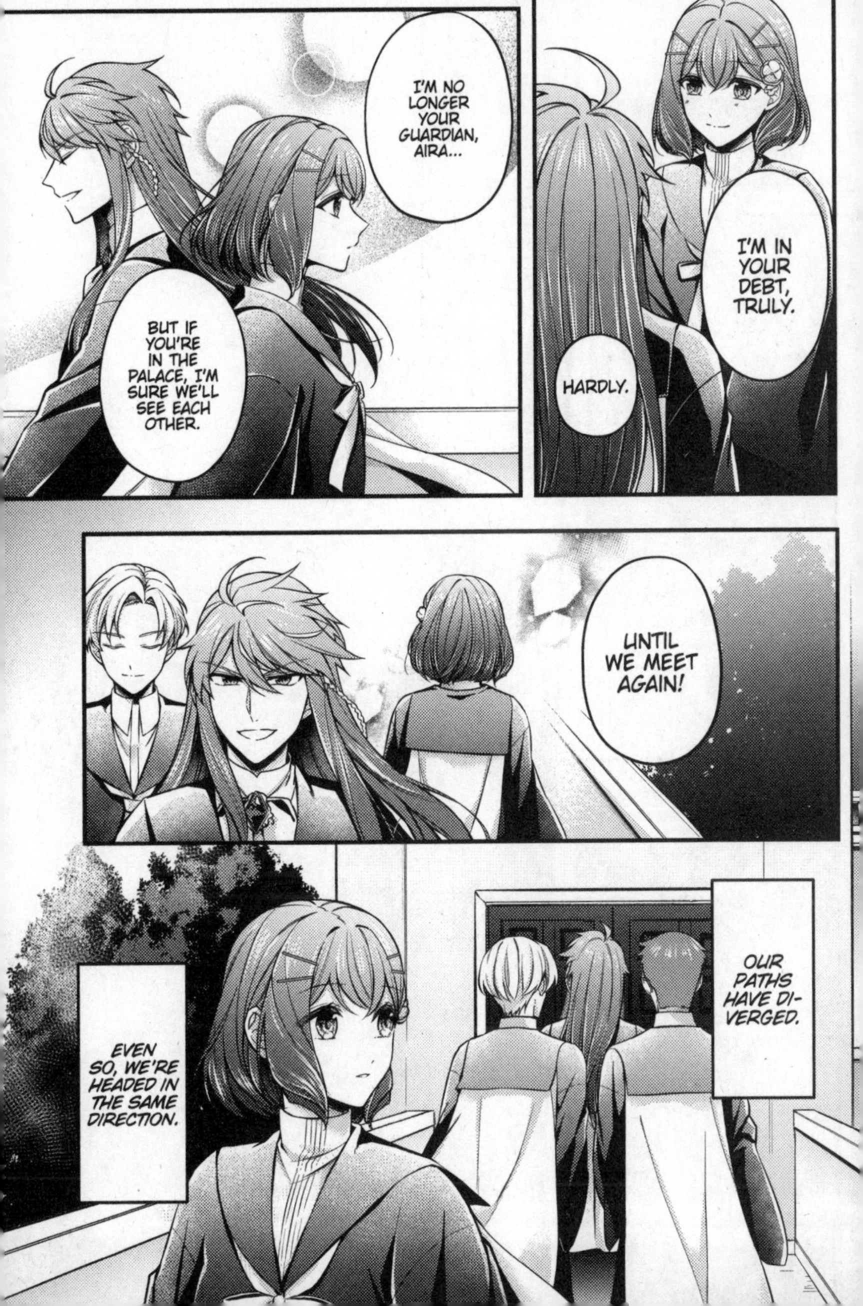
I'M IN YOUR DEBT, TRULY.
HARDLY.
I'M NO LONGER YOUR GUARDIAN, AIRA...
BUT IF YOU'RE IN THE PALACE, I'M SURE WE'LL SEE EACH OTHER.
UNTIL WE MEET AGAIN!
OUR PATHS HAVE DI-VERGED.
EVEN SO, WE'RE HEADED IN THE SAME DIRECTION.

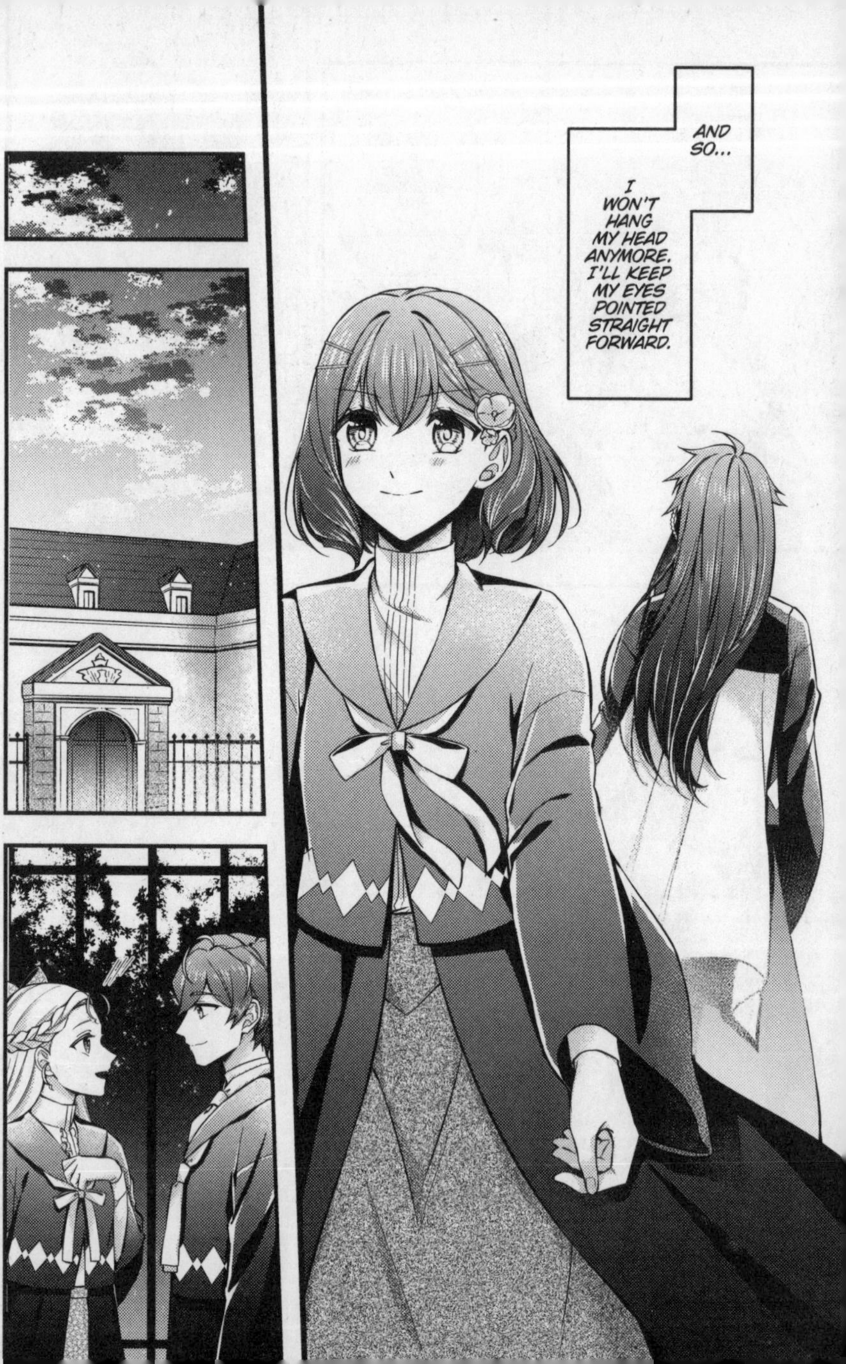
AND SO...
I WON'T HANG MY HEAD ANYMORE. I'LL KEEP MY EYES POINTED STRAIGHT FORWARD.

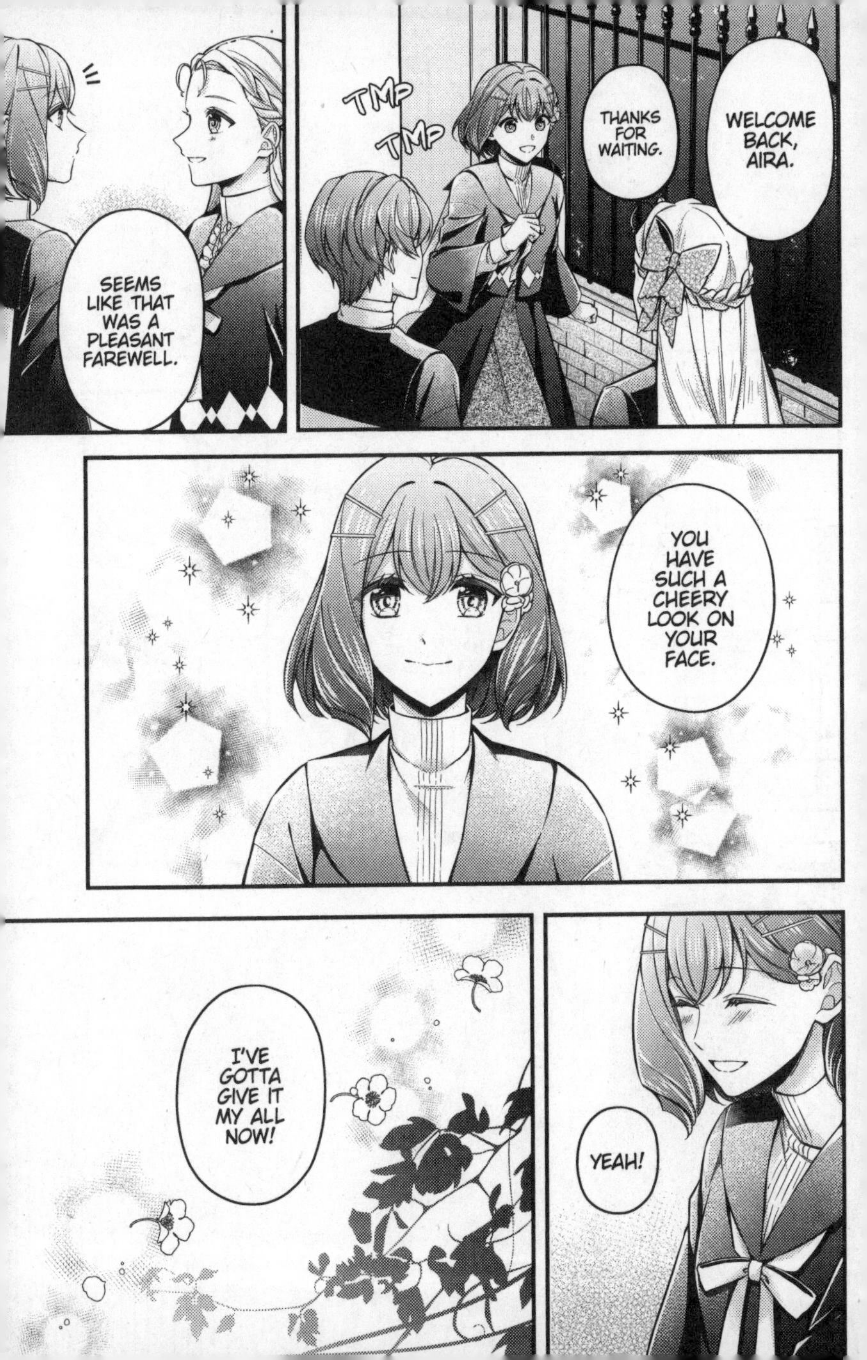
WELCOME BACK, AIRA.
THANKS FOR WAITING.
TMP
TMP
SEEMS LIKE THAT WAS A PLEASANT FAREWELL.
YOU HAVE SUCH A CHEERY LOOK ON YOUR FACE.
YEAH!
I'VE GOTTA GIVE IT MY ALL NOW!

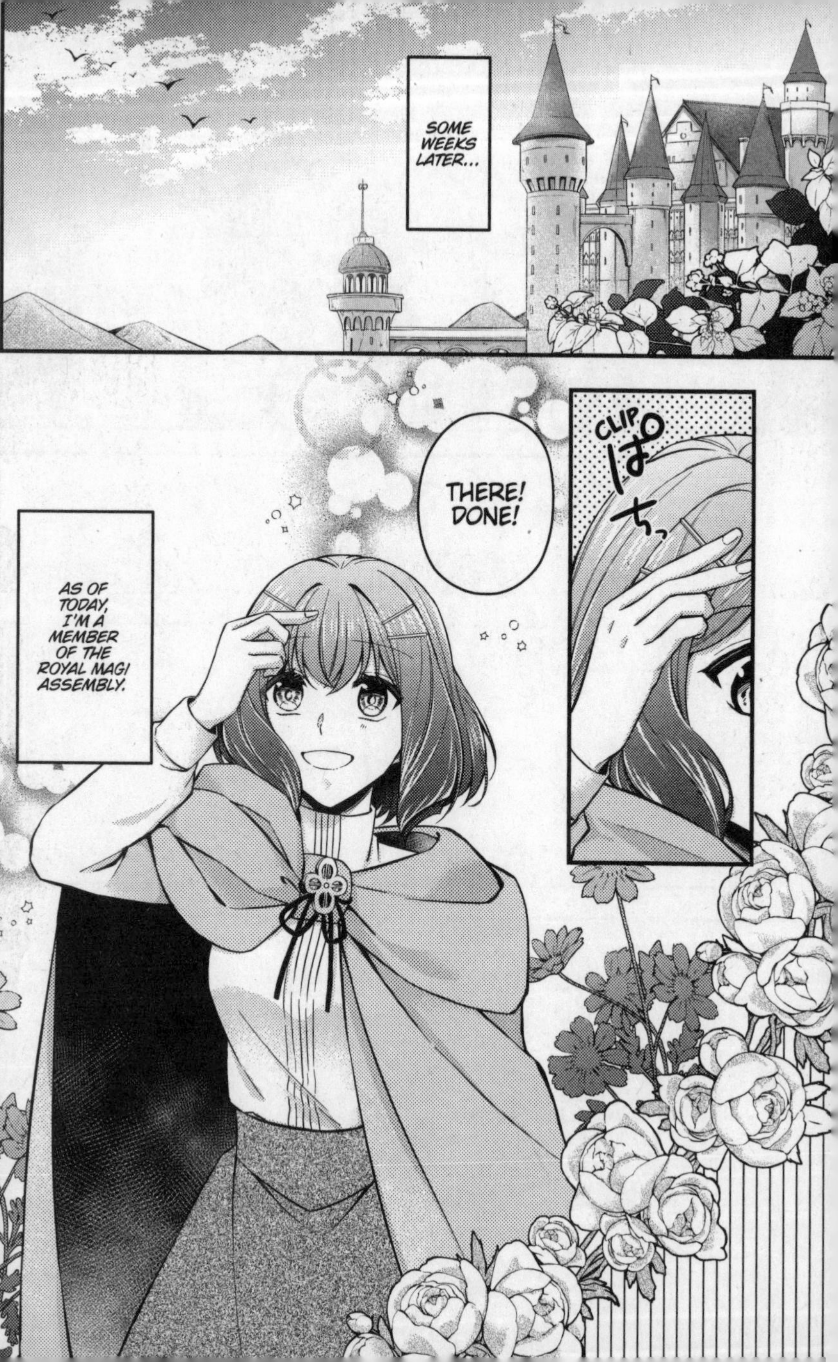
SOME WEEKS LATER...
CLIP
ぱちっ
THERE! DONE!
AS OF TODAY, I'M A MEMBER OF THE ROYAL MAGI ASSEMBLY.

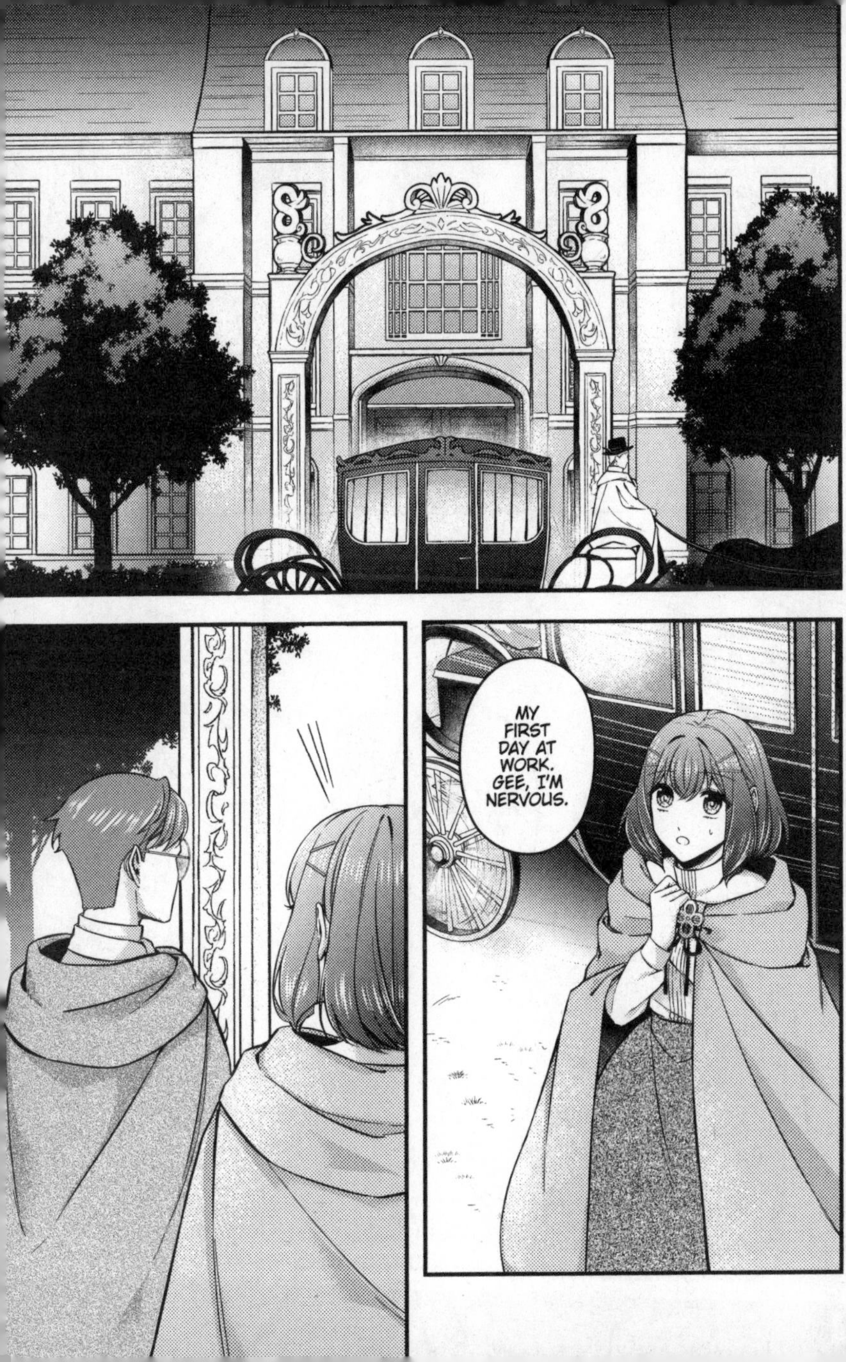
MY FIRST DAY AT WORK. GEE, I'M NERVOUS.

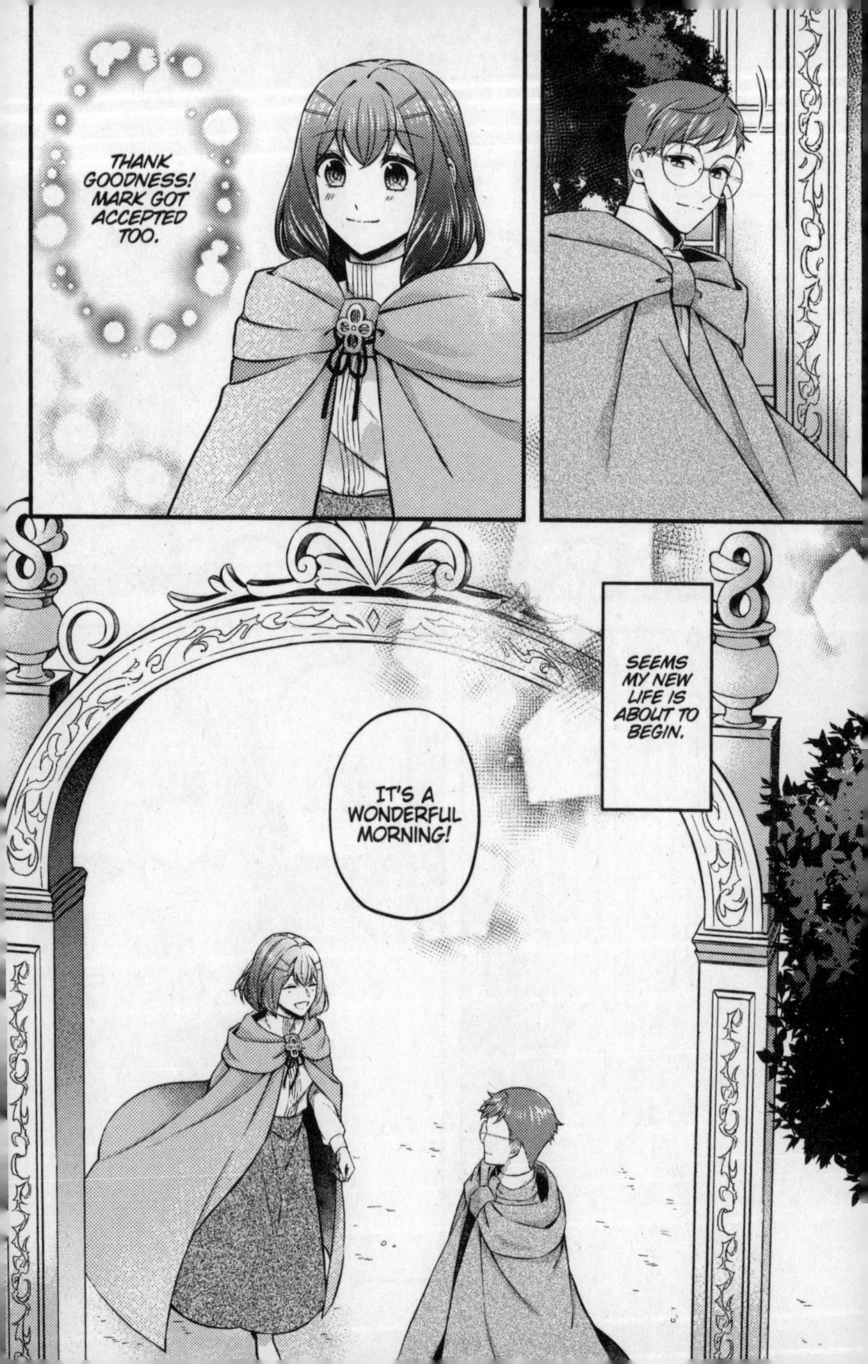
THANK GOODNESS! MARK GOT ACCEPTED TOO.
SEEMS MY NEW LIFE IS ABOUT TO BEGIN.
IT'S A WONDERFUL MORNING!

The Saint's *Magic Power is * Omnipotent
The Other Saint

The Saint's Magic Power is Omnipotent

~ The Other Saint ~

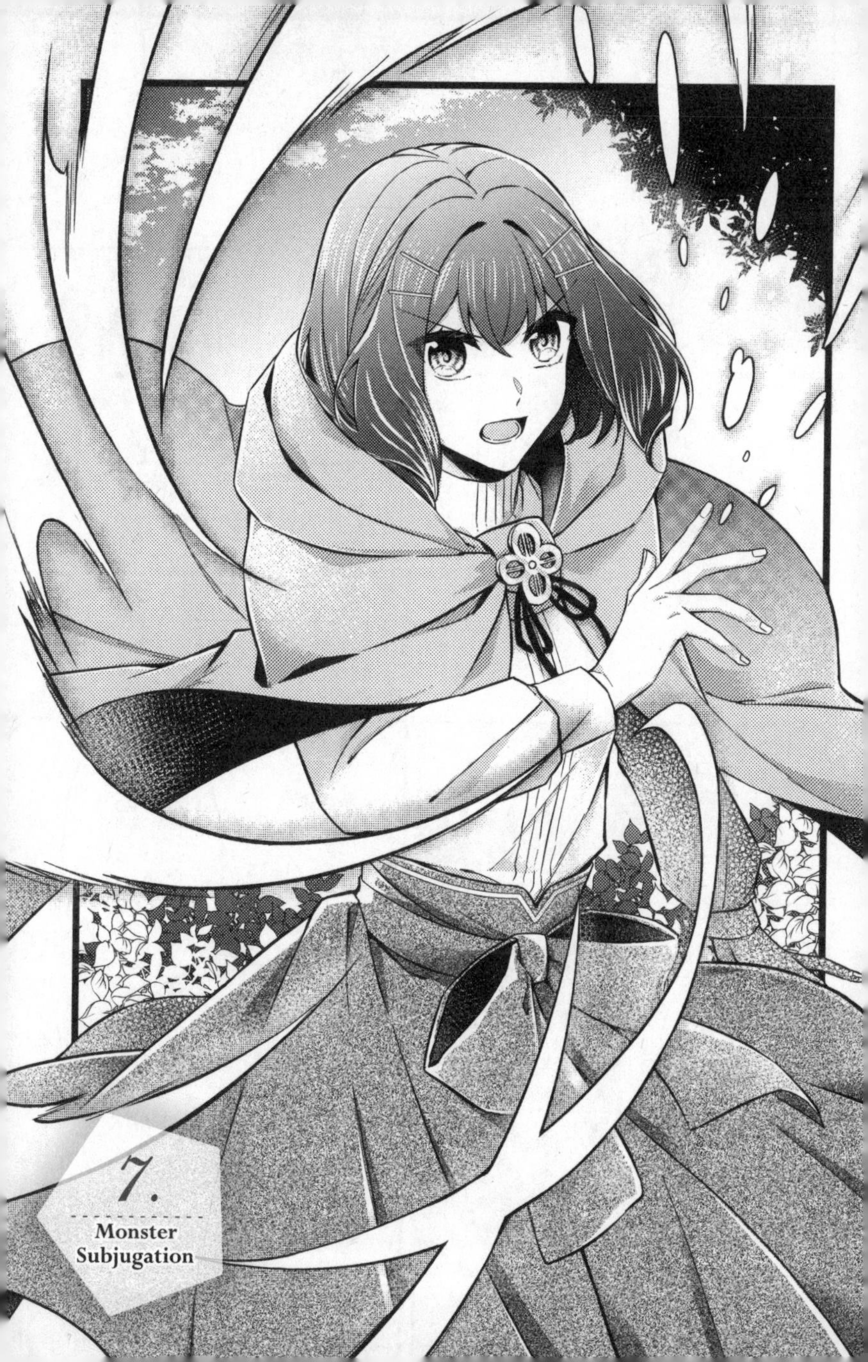
7.
Monster
Subjugation

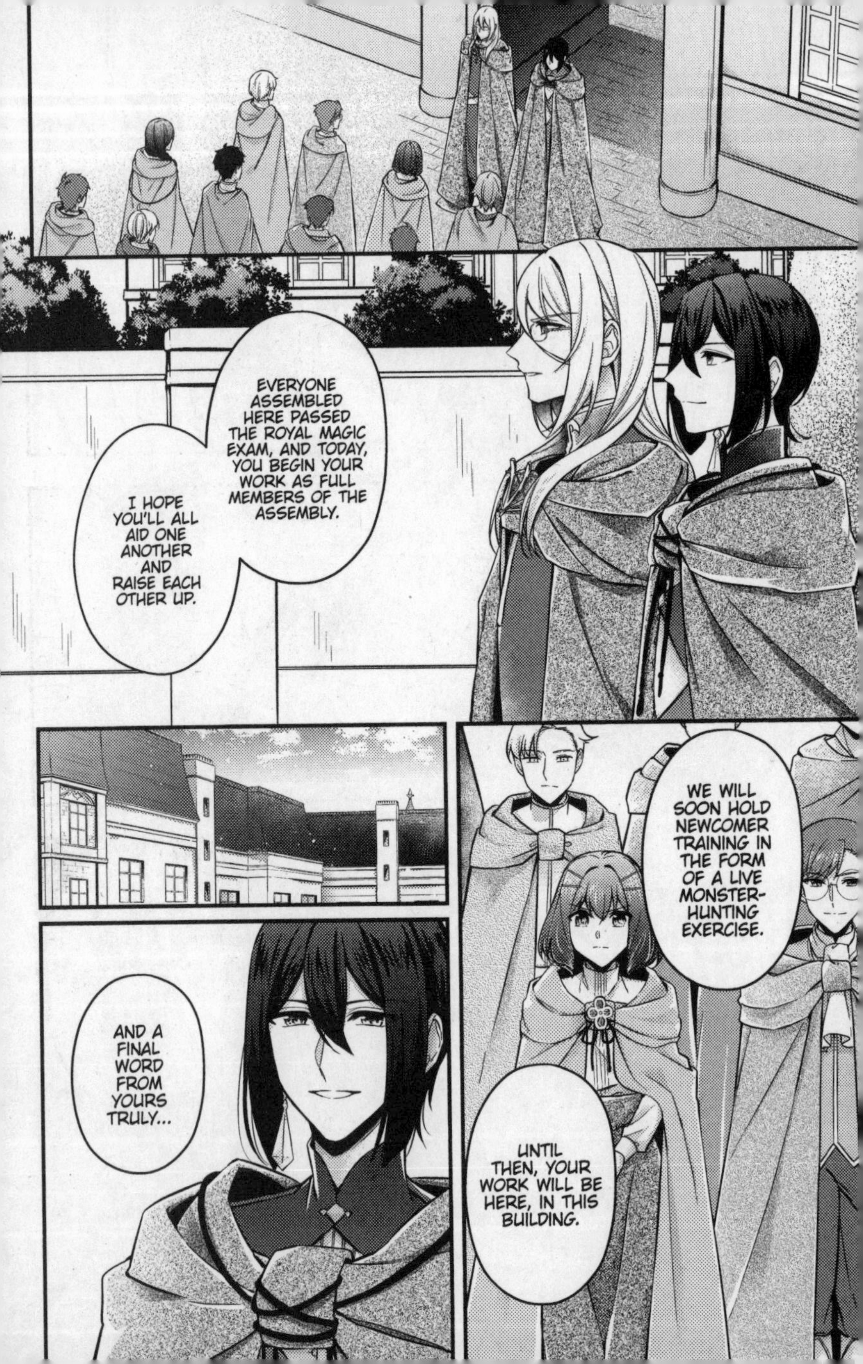
EVERYONE ASSEMBLED HERE PASSED THE ROYAL MAGIC EXAM, AND TODAY, YOU BEGIN YOUR WORK AS FULL MEMBERS OF THE ASSEMBLY.
I HOPE YOU'LL ALL AID ONE ANOTHER AND RAISE EACH OTHER UP.
WE WILL SOON HOLD NEWCOMER TRAINING IN THE FORM OF A LIVE MONSTER-HUNTING EXERCISE.
UNTIL THEN, YOUR WORK WILL BE HERE, IN THIS BUILDING.
AND A FINAL WORD FROM YOURS TRULY...

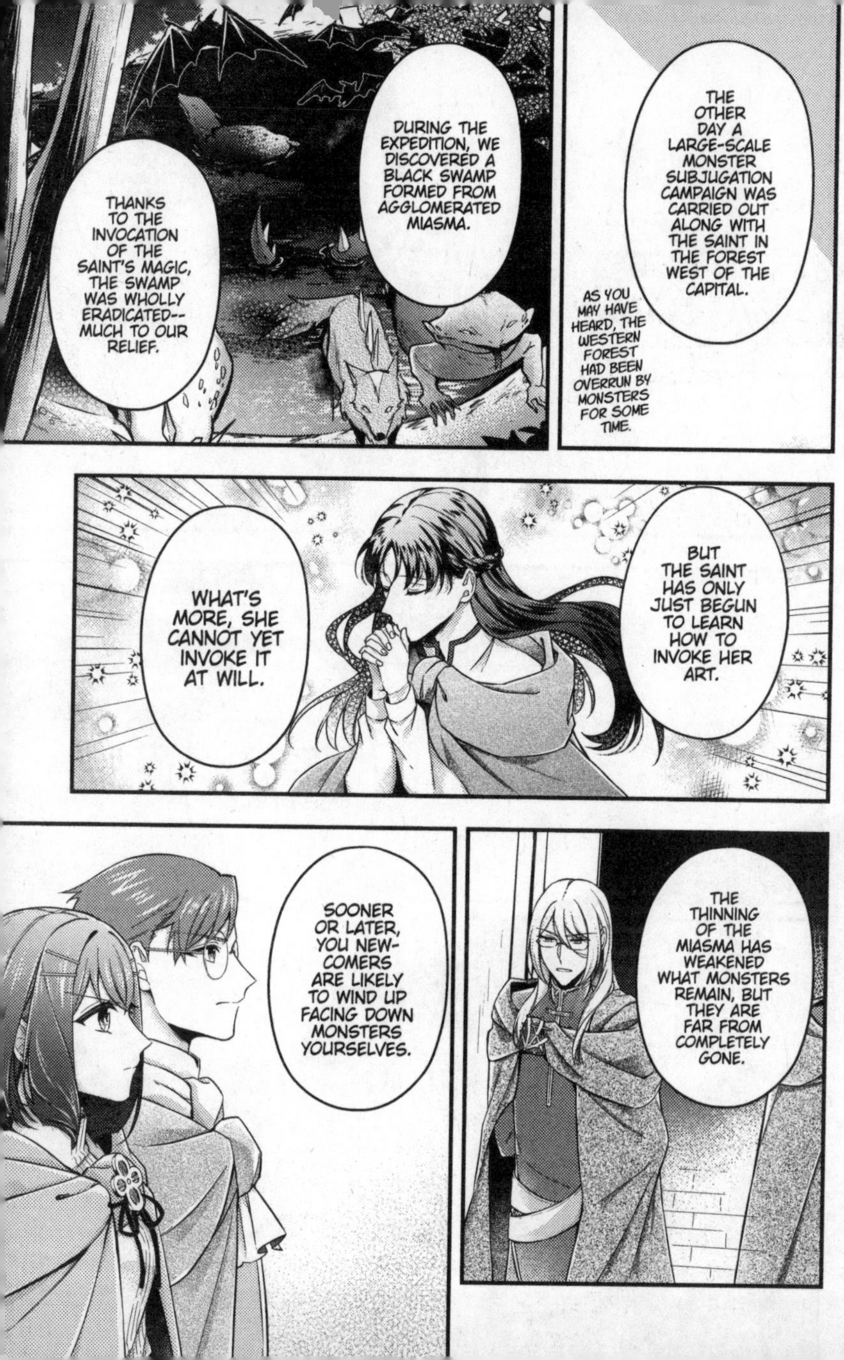
THE OTHER DAY A LARGE-SCALE MONSTER SUBJUGATION CAMPAIGN WAS CARRIED OUT ALONG WITH THE SAINT IN THE FOREST WEST OF THE CAPITAL.
AS YOU MAY HAVE HEARD, THE WESTERN FOREST HAD BEEN OVERRUN BY MONSTERS FOR SOME TIME.
DURING THE EXPEDITION, WE DISCOVERED A BLACK SWAMP FORMED FROM AGGLOMERATED MIASMA.
THANKS TO THE INVOCATION OF THE SAINT'S MAGIC, THE SWAMP WAS WHOLLY ERADICATED--MUCH TO OUR RELIEF.
BUT THE SAINT HAS ONLY JUST BEGUN TO LEARN HOW TO INVOKE HER ART.
WHAT'S MORE, SHE CANNOT YET INVOKE IT AT WILL.
THE THINNING OF THE MIASMA HAS WEAKENED WHAT MONSTERS REMAIN, BUT THEY ARE FAR FROM COMPLETELY GONE.
SOONER OR LATER, YOU NEW-COMERS ARE LIKELY TO WIND UP FACING DOWN MONSTERS YOURSELVES.

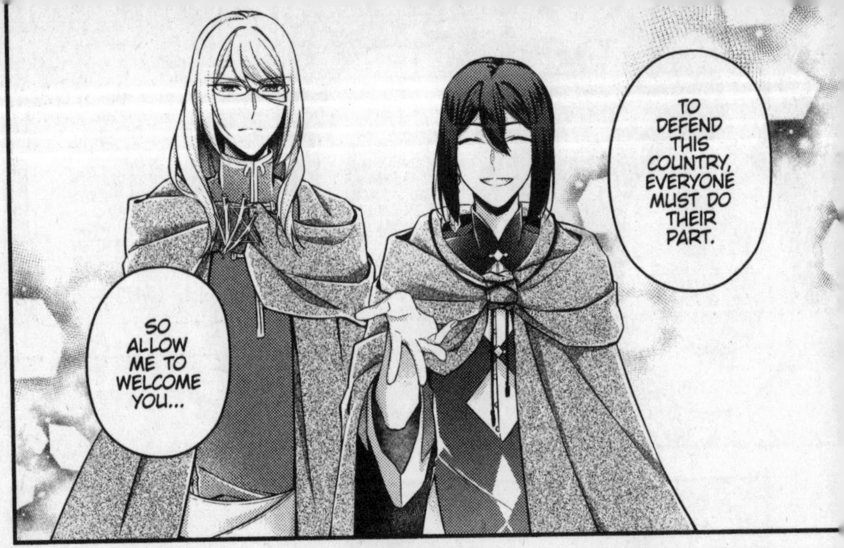
TO DEFEND THIS COUNTRY, EVERYONE MUST DO THEIR PART.
SO ALLOW ME TO WELCOME YOU...
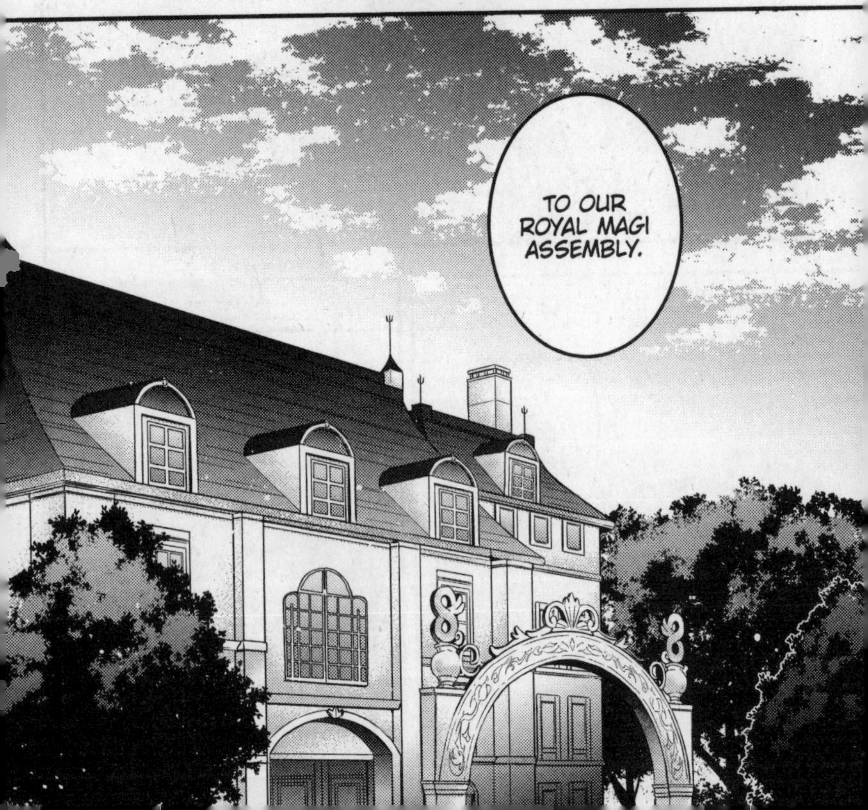
TO OUR ROYAL MAGI ASSEMBLY.

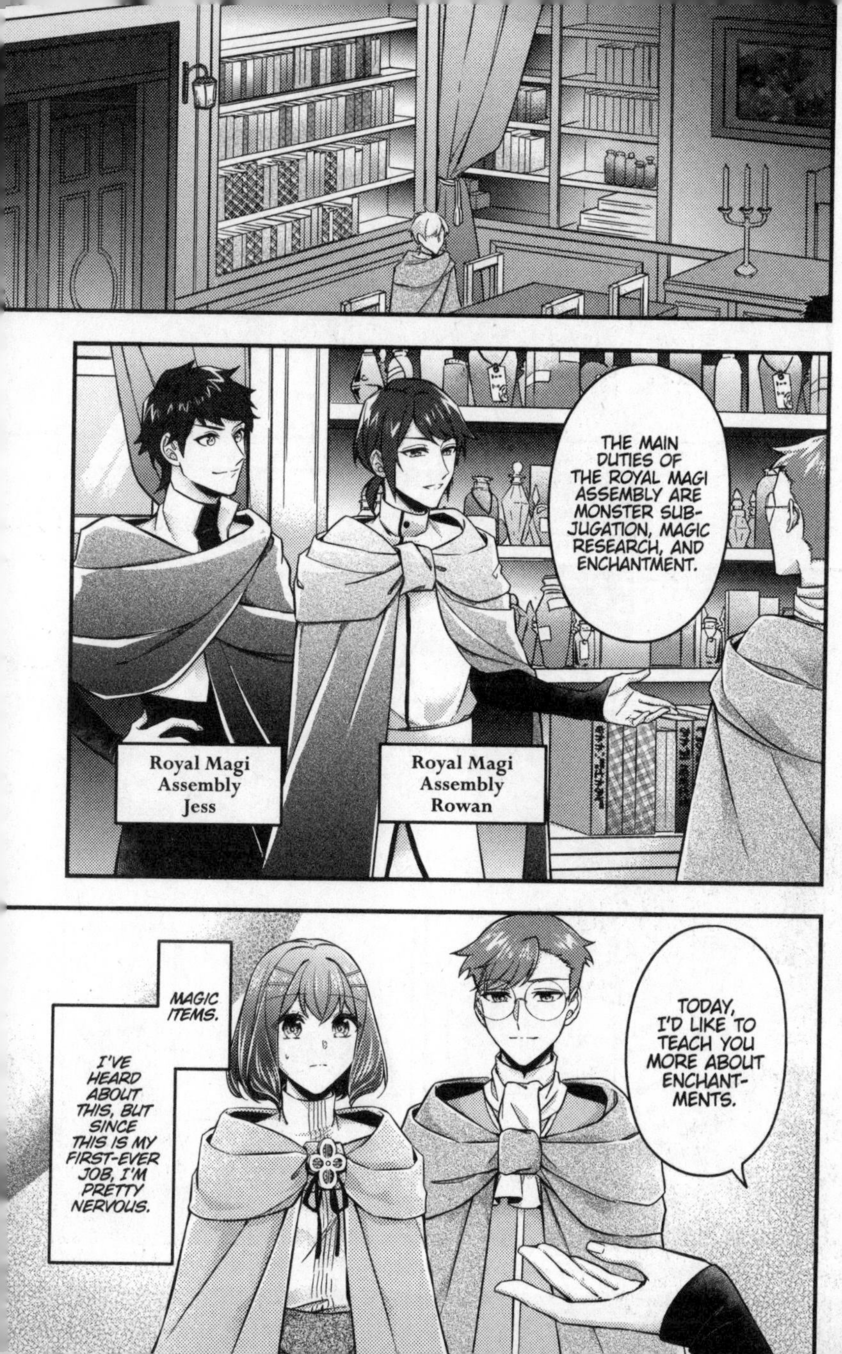
THE MAIN DUTIES OF THE ROYAL MAGI ASSEMBLY ARE MONSTER SUB-JUGATION, MAGIC RESEARCH, AND ENCHANTMENT.
Royal Magi Assembly Rowan
Royal Magi Assembly Jess
TODAY, I'D LIKE TO TEACH YOU MORE ABOUT ENCHANT-MENTS.
MAGIC ITEMS.
I'VE HEARD ABOUT THIS, BUT SINCE THIS IS MY FIRST-EVER JOB, I'M PRETTY NERVOUS.

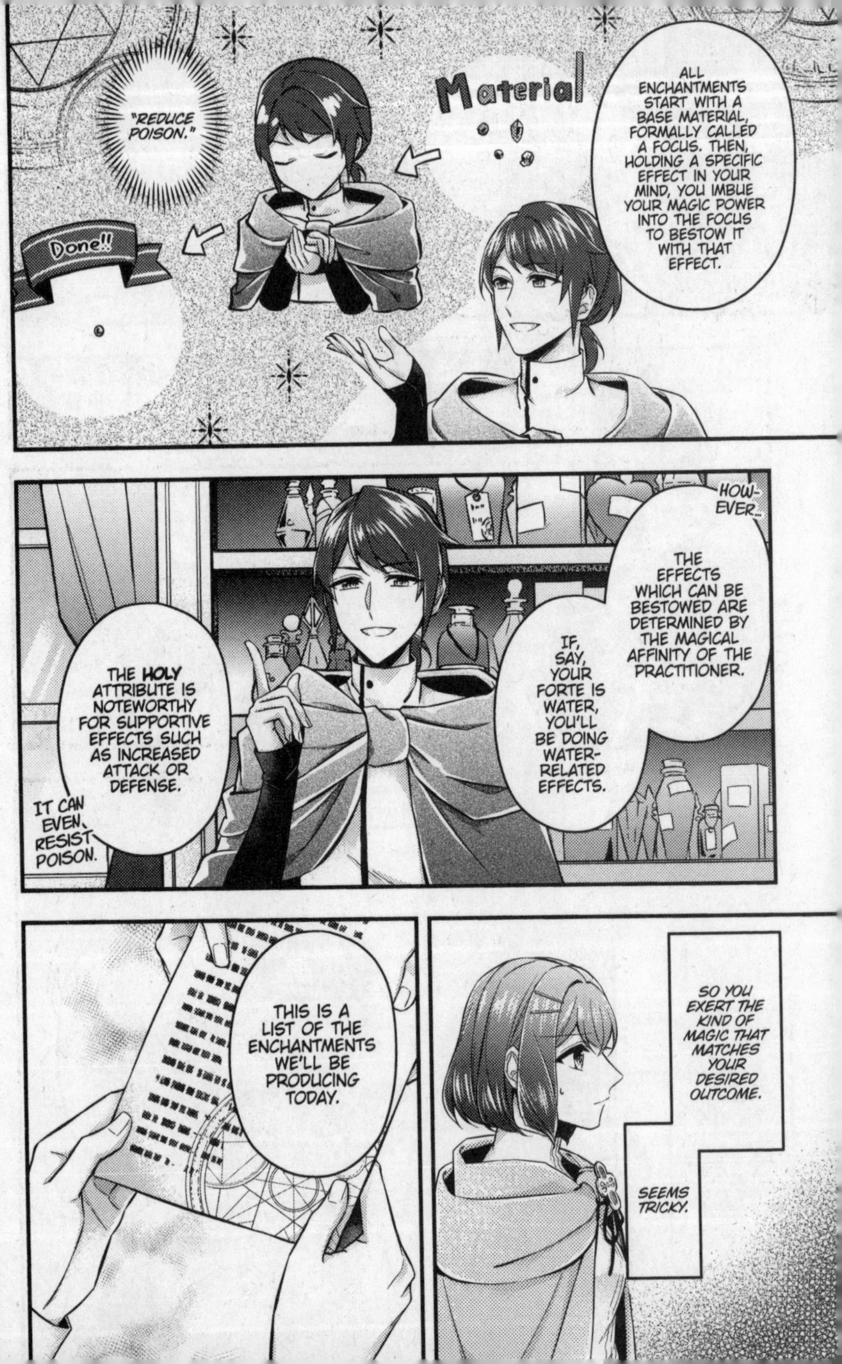
ALL ENCHANTMENTS START WITH A BASE MATERIAL, FORMALLY CALLED A FOCUS. THEN, HOLDING A SPECIFIC EFFECT IN YOUR MIND, YOU IMBUE YOUR MAGIC POWER INTO THE FOCUS TO BESTOW IT WITH THAT EFFECT.
Material
"REDUCE POISON."
Done!!
HOW-EVER...
THE EFFECTS WHICH CAN BE BESTOWED ARE DETERMINED BY THE MAGICAL AFFINITY OF THE PRACTITIONER.
IF, SAY, YOUR FORTE IS WATER, YOU'LL BE DOING WATER-RELATED EFFECTS.
THE **HOLY** ATTRIBUTE IS NOTEWORTHY FOR SUPPORTIVE EFFECTS SUCH AS INCREASED ATTACK OR DEFENSE.
IT CAN EVEN RESIST POISON.
SO YOU EXERT THE KIND OF MAGIC THAT MATCHES YOUR DESIRED OUTCOME.
SEEMS TRICKY.
THIS IS A LIST OF THE ENCHANTMENTS WE'LL BE PRODUCING TODAY.

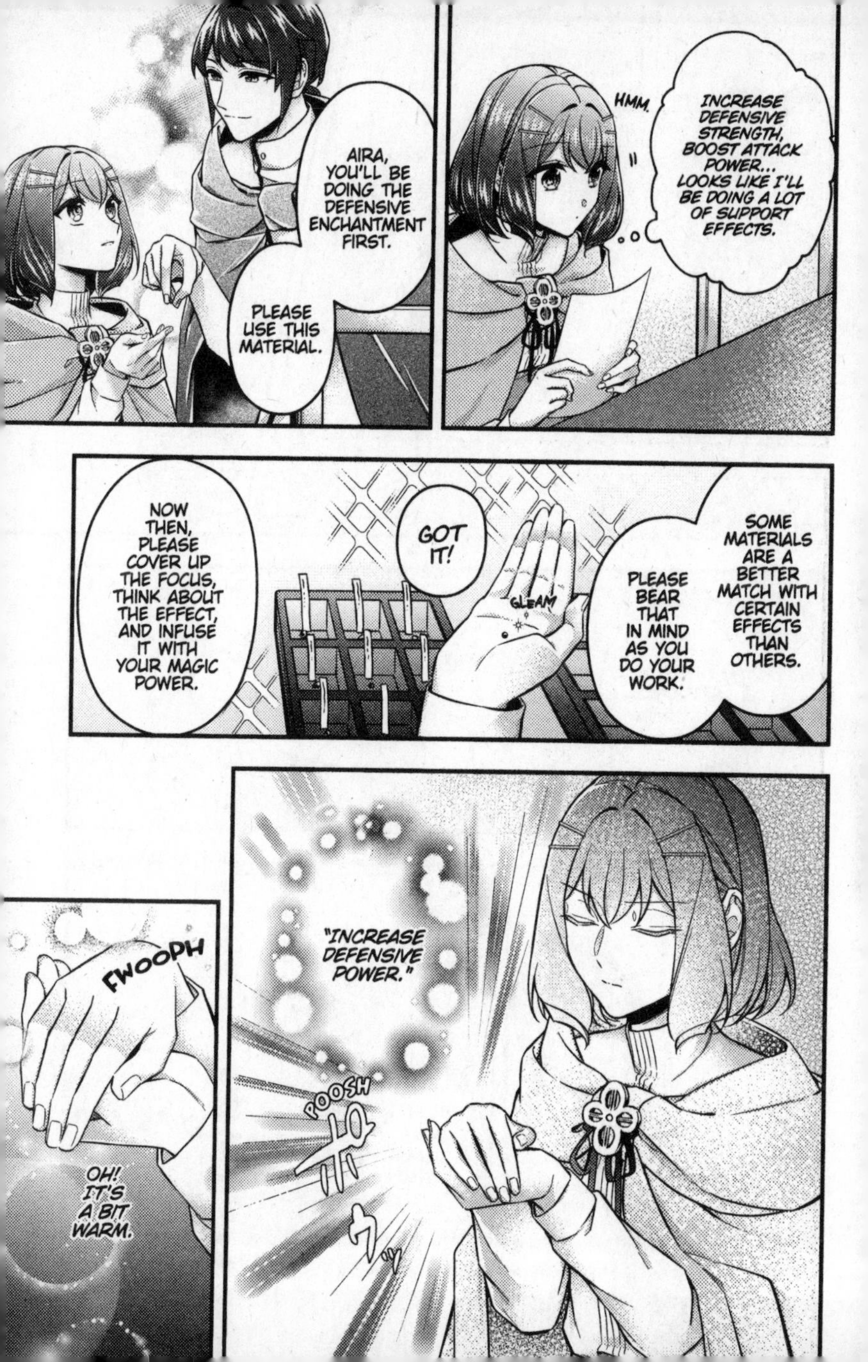
HMM.
INCREASE DEFENSIVE STRENGTH, BOOST ATTACK POWER... LOOKS LIKE I'LL BE DOING A LOT OF SUPPORT EFFECTS.
AIRA, YOU'LL BE DOING THE DEFENSIVE ENCHANTMENT FIRST.
PLEASE USE THIS MATERIAL.
SOME MATERIALS ARE A BETTER MATCH WITH CERTAIN EFFECTS THAN OTHERS.
PLEASE BEAR THAT IN MIND AS YOU DO YOUR WORK.
GOT IT!
GLEAM
NOW THEN, PLEASE COVER UP THE FOCUS, THINK ABOUT THE EFFECT, AND INFUSE IT WITH YOUR MAGIC POWER.
"INCREASE DEFENSIVE POWER."
POOSH
FWOOPH
OH! IT'S A BIT WARM.

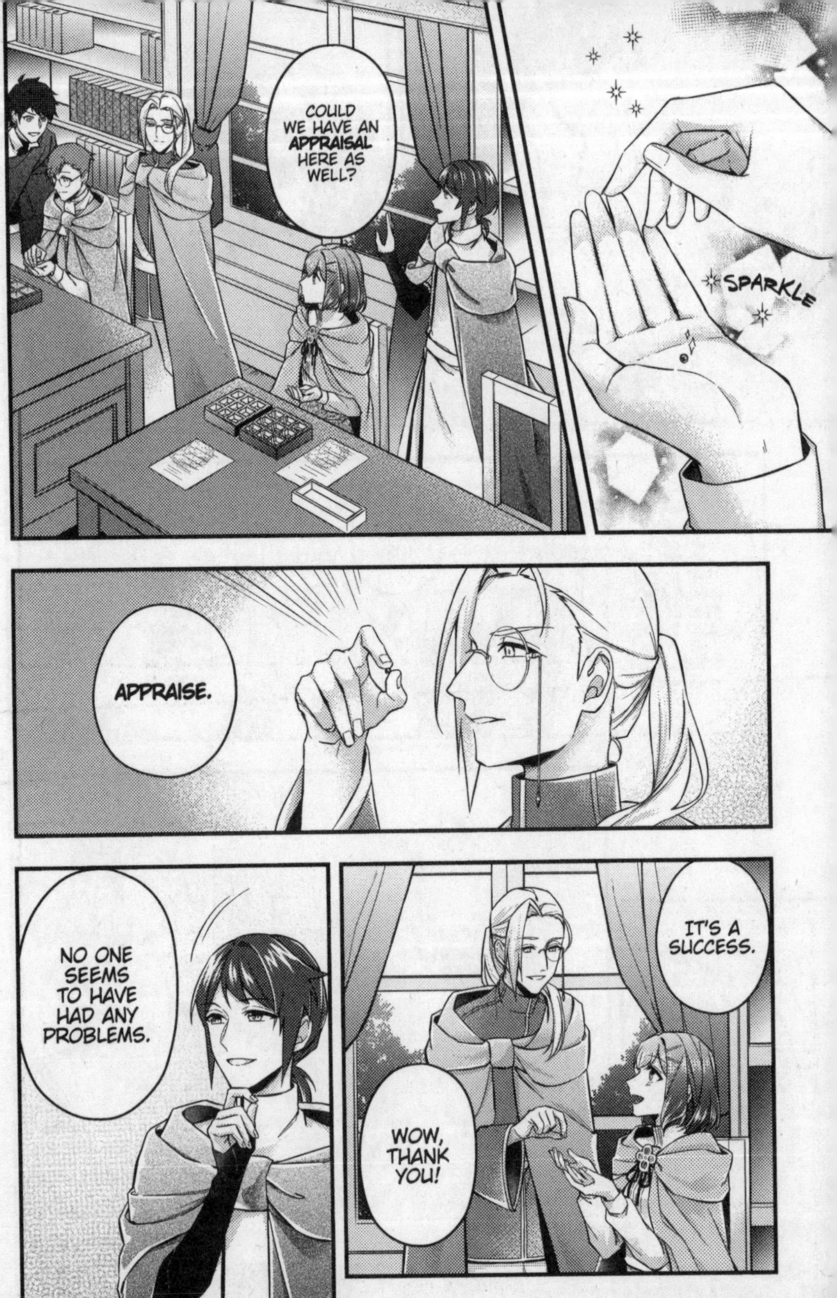
SPARKLE
COULD WE HAVE AN APPRAISAL HERE AS WELL?
APPRAISE.
IT'S A SUCCESS.
WOW, THANK YOU!
NO ONE SEEMS TO HAVE HAD ANY PROBLEMS.

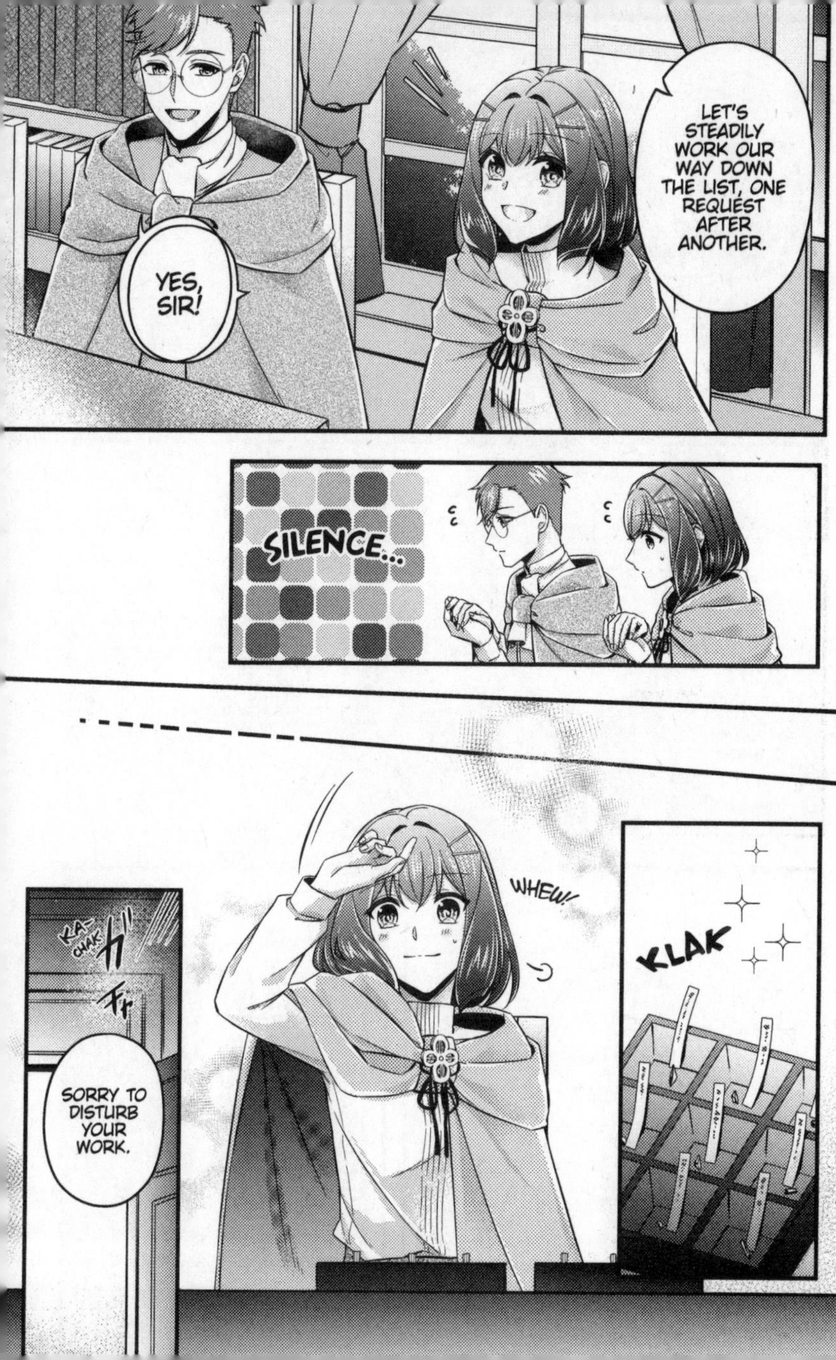
LET'S STEADILY WORK OUR WAY DOWN THE LIST, ONE REQUEST AFTER ANOTHER.
YES, SIR!
SILENCE...
KLAK
WHEW!
KA-CHAK
SORRY TO DISTURB YOUR WORK.

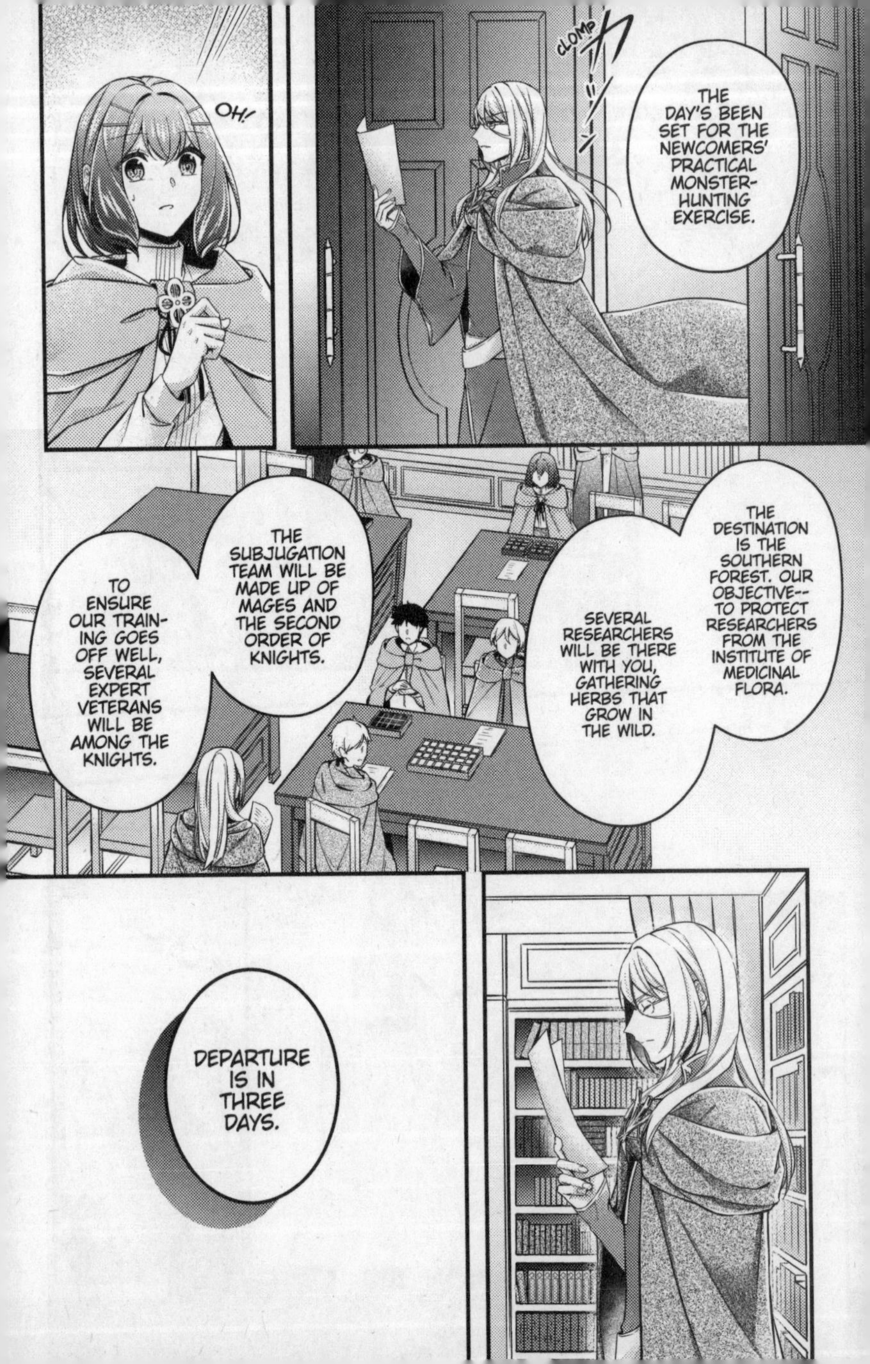
CLOMP
THE DAY'S BEEN SET FOR THE NEWCOMERS' PRACTICAL MONSTER-HUNTING EXERCISE.
OH!
THE DESTINATION IS THE SOUTHERN FOREST. OUR OBJECTIVE-- TO PROTECT RESEARCHERS FROM THE INSTITUTE OF MEDICINAL FLORA.
SEVERAL RESEARCHERS WILL BE THERE WITH YOU, GATHERING HERBS THAT GROW IN THE WILD.
THE SUBJUGATION TEAM WILL BE MADE UP OF MAGES AND THE SECOND ORDER OF KNIGHTS.
TO ENSURE OUR TRAIN-ING GOES OFF WELL, SEVERAL EXPERT VETERANS WILL BE AMONG THE KNIGHTS.
DEPARTURE IS IN THREE DAYS.

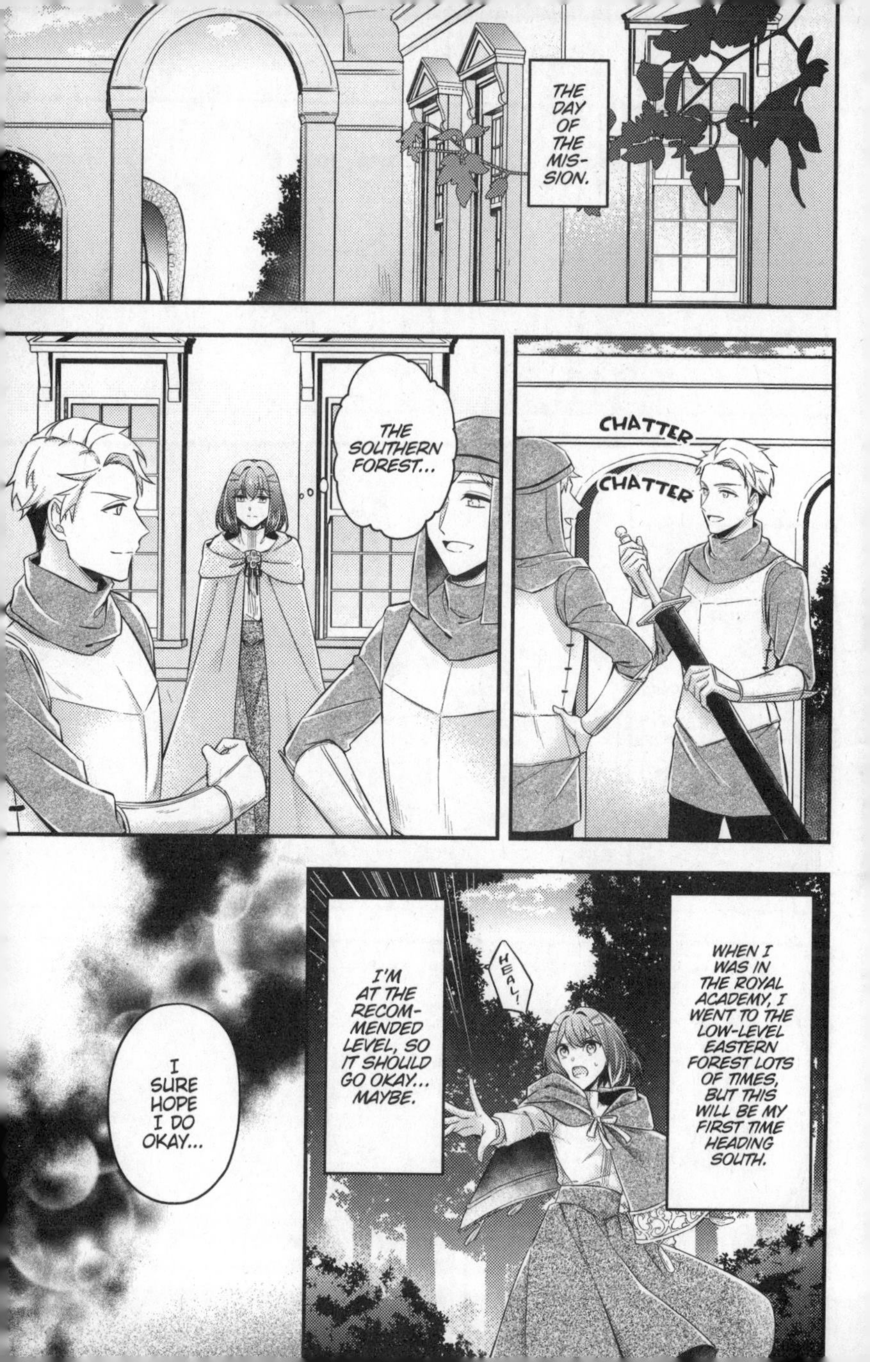
THE DAY OF THE MISSION.
CHATTER
CHATTER
THE SOUTHERN FOREST...
WHEN I WAS IN THE ROYAL ACADEMY, I WENT TO THE LOW-LEVEL EASTERN FOREST LOTS OF TIMES, BUT THIS WILL BE MY FIRST TIME HEADING SOUTH.
HEAL!
I'M AT THE RECOMMENDED LEVEL, SO IT SHOULD GO OKAY... MAYBE.
I SURE HOPE I DO OKAY...

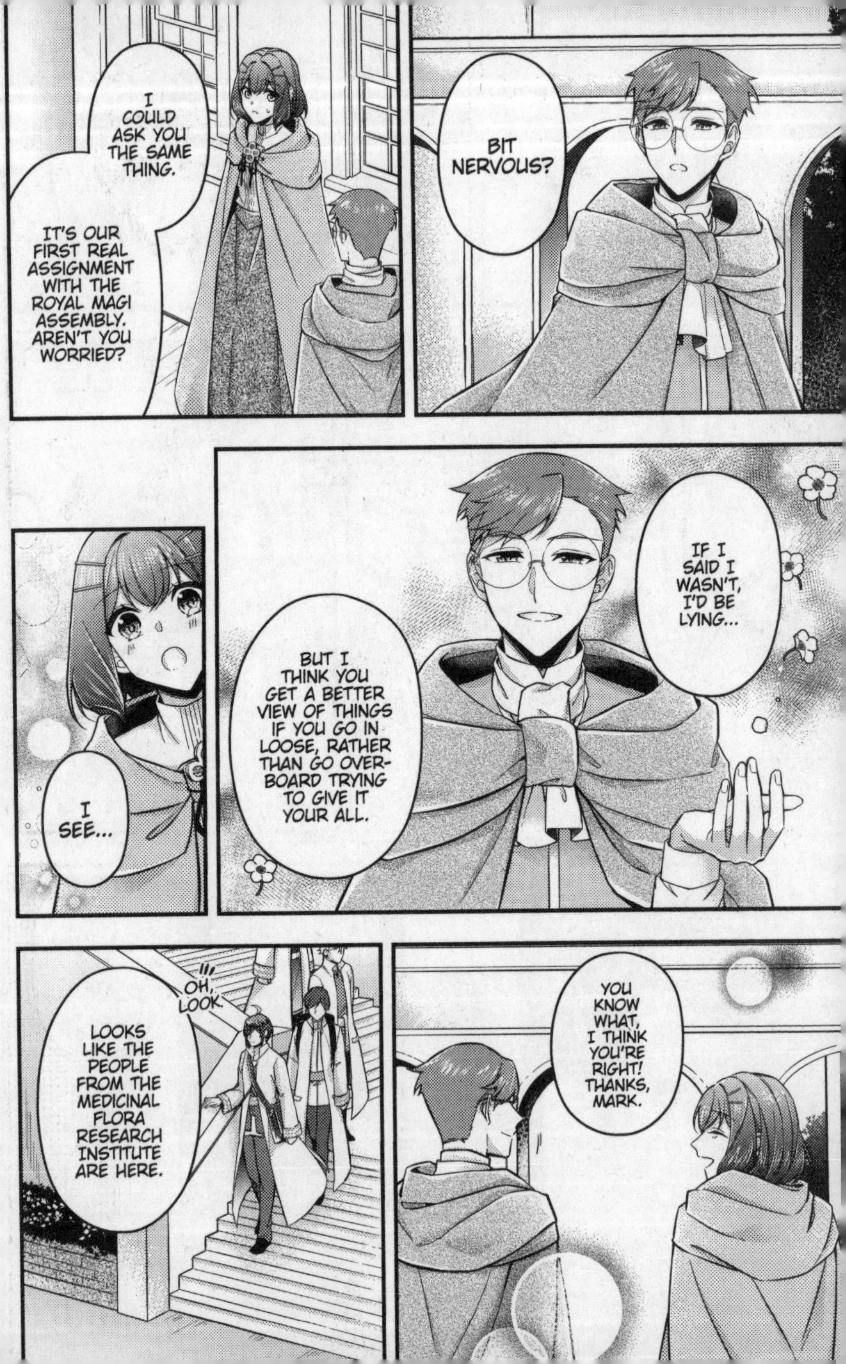
BIT NERVOUS?
I COULD ASK YOU THE SAME THING.
IT'S OUR FIRST REAL ASSIGNMENT WITH THE ROYAL MAGI ASSEMBLY. AREN'T YOU WORRIED?
IF I SAID I WASN'T, I'D BE LYING...
BUT I THINK YOU GET A BETTER VIEW OF THINGS IF YOU GO IN LOOSE, RATHER THAN GO OVER-BOARD TRYING TO GIVE IT YOUR ALL.
I SEE...
YOU KNOW WHAT, I THINK YOU'RE RIGHT! THANKS, MARK.
OH, LOOK.
LOOKS LIKE THE PEOPLE FROM THE MEDICINAL FLORA RESEARCH INSTITUTE ARE HERE.

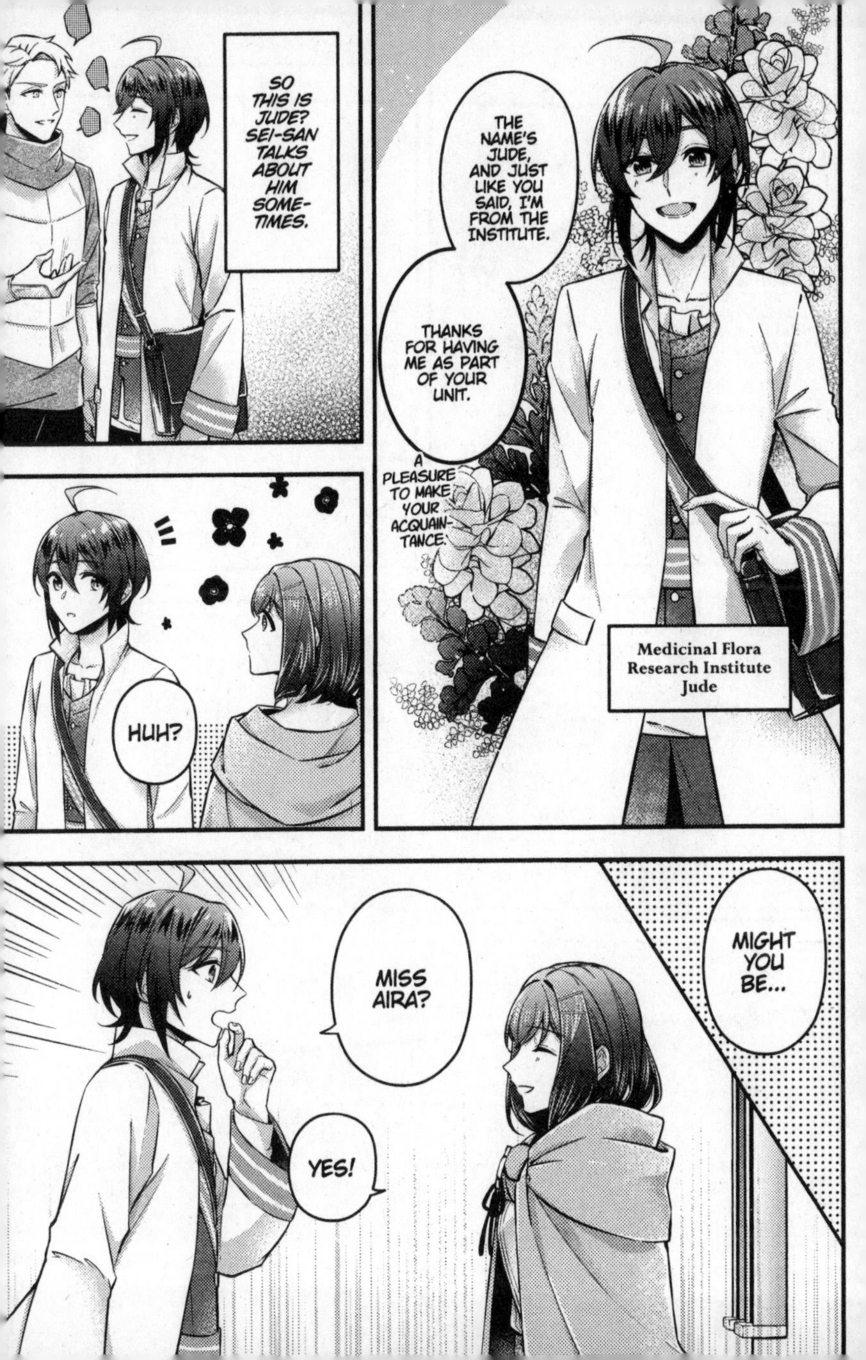
THE NAME'S JUDE, AND JUST LIKE YOU SAID, I'M FROM THE INSTITUTE.
THANKS FOR HAVING ME AS PART OF YOUR UNIT.
A PLEASURE TO MAKE YOUR ACQUAINTANCE.
Medicinal Flora Research Institute Jude
SO THIS IS JUDE? SEI-SAN TALKS ABOUT HIM SOMETIMES.
HUH?
MIGHT YOU BE...
MISS AIRA?
YES!

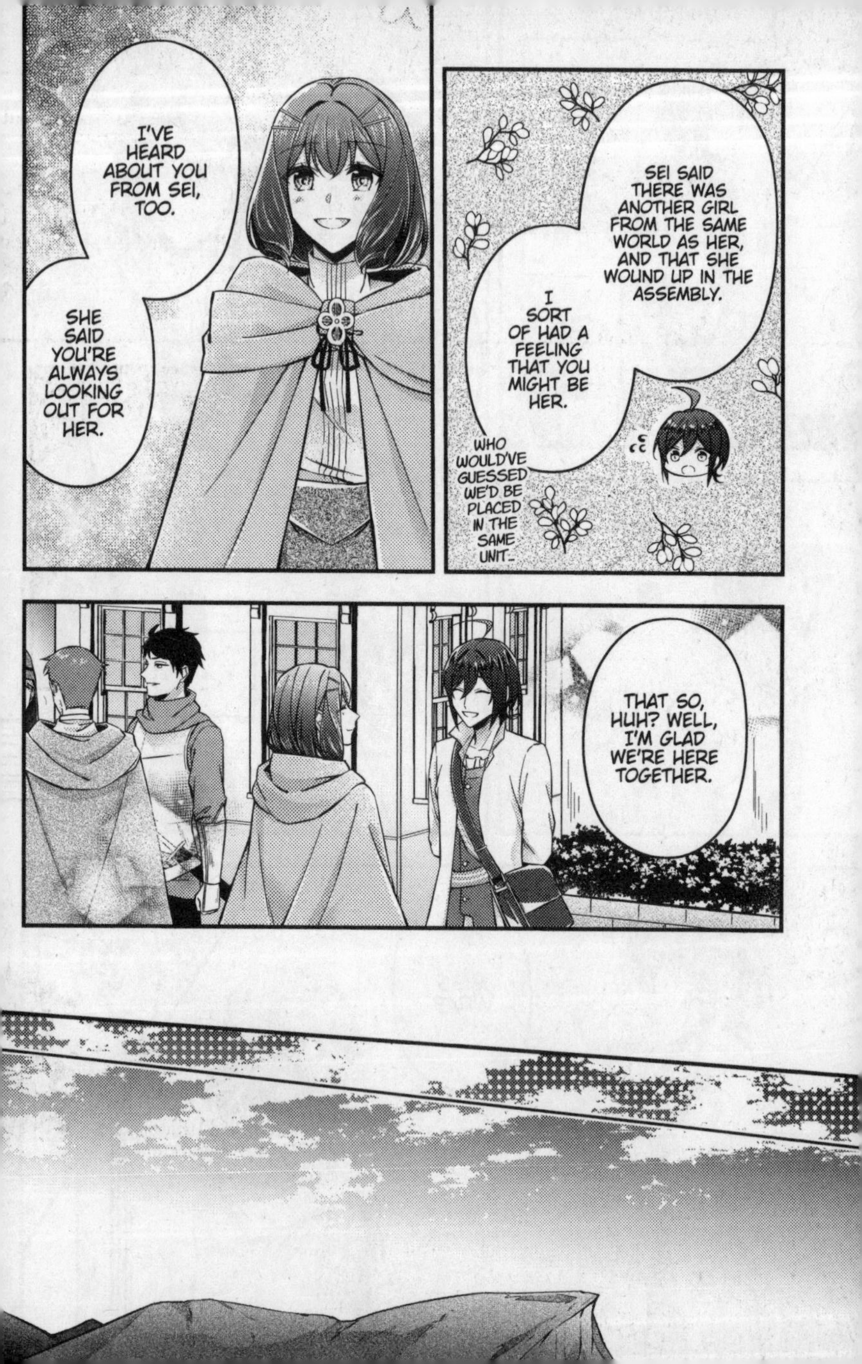
SEI SAID THERE WAS ANOTHER GIRL FROM THE SAME WORLD AS HER, AND THAT SHE WOUND UP IN THE ASSEMBLY.
I SORT OF HAD A FEELING THAT YOU MIGHT BE HER.
WHO WOULD'VE GUESSED WE'D BE PLACED IN THE SAME UNIT...
I'VE HEARD ABOUT YOU FROM SEI, TOO.
SHE SAID YOU'RE ALWAYS LOOKING OUT FOR HER.
THAT SO, HUH? WELL, I'M GLAD WE'RE HERE TOGETHER.

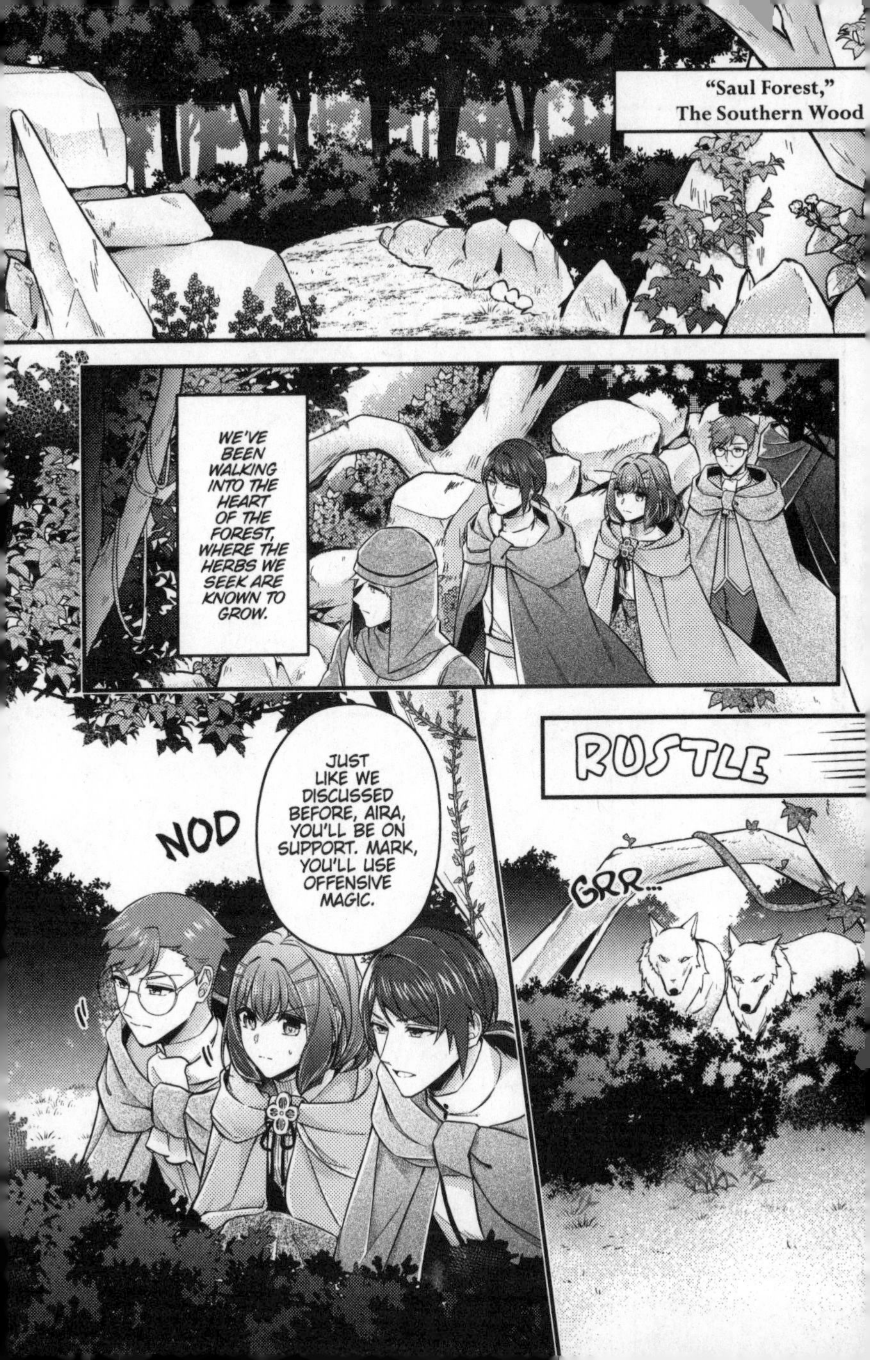
"Saul Forest," The Southern Wood
WE'VE BEEN WALKING INTO THE HEART OF THE FOREST, WHERE THE HERBS WE SEEK ARE KNOWN TO GROW.
RUSTLE
GRR...
JUST LIKE WE DISCUSSED BEFORE, AIRA, YOU'LL BE ON SUPPORT. MARK, YOU'LL USE OFFENSIVE MAGIC.
NOD

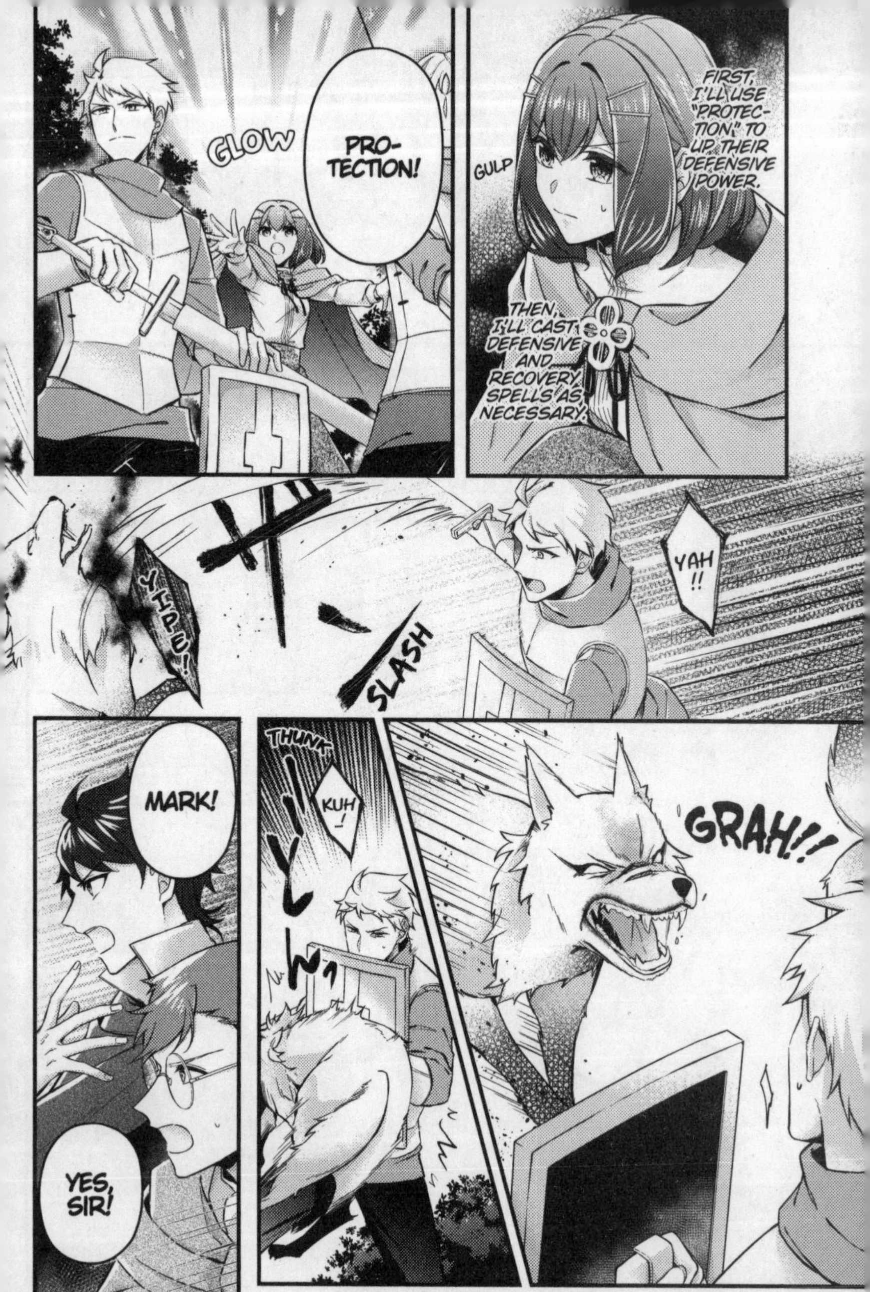
FIRST, I'LL USE "PROTECTION," TO UP THEIR DEFENSIVE POWER.
GULP
THEN, I'LL CAST DEFENSIVE AND RECOVERY SPELLS AS NECESSARY.
PRO-TECTION!
GLOW
YAH!!
SLASH
YIPE!
GRAH!!!
THUNK
KUH!
MARK!
YES, SIR!

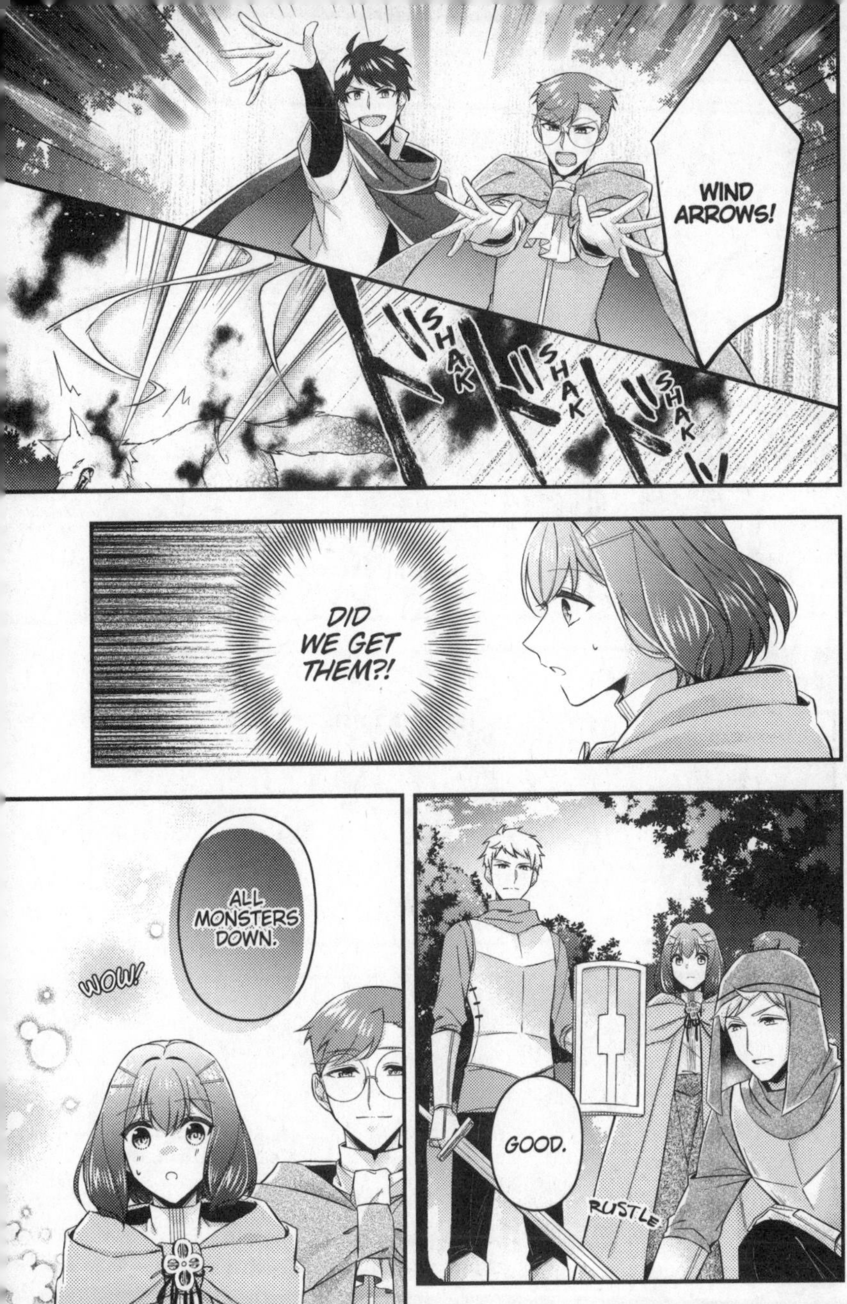
WIND ARROWS!
SHAK
SHAK
SHAK
DID WE GET THEM?!
GOOD.
RUSTLE
ALL MONSTERS DOWN.
WOW!

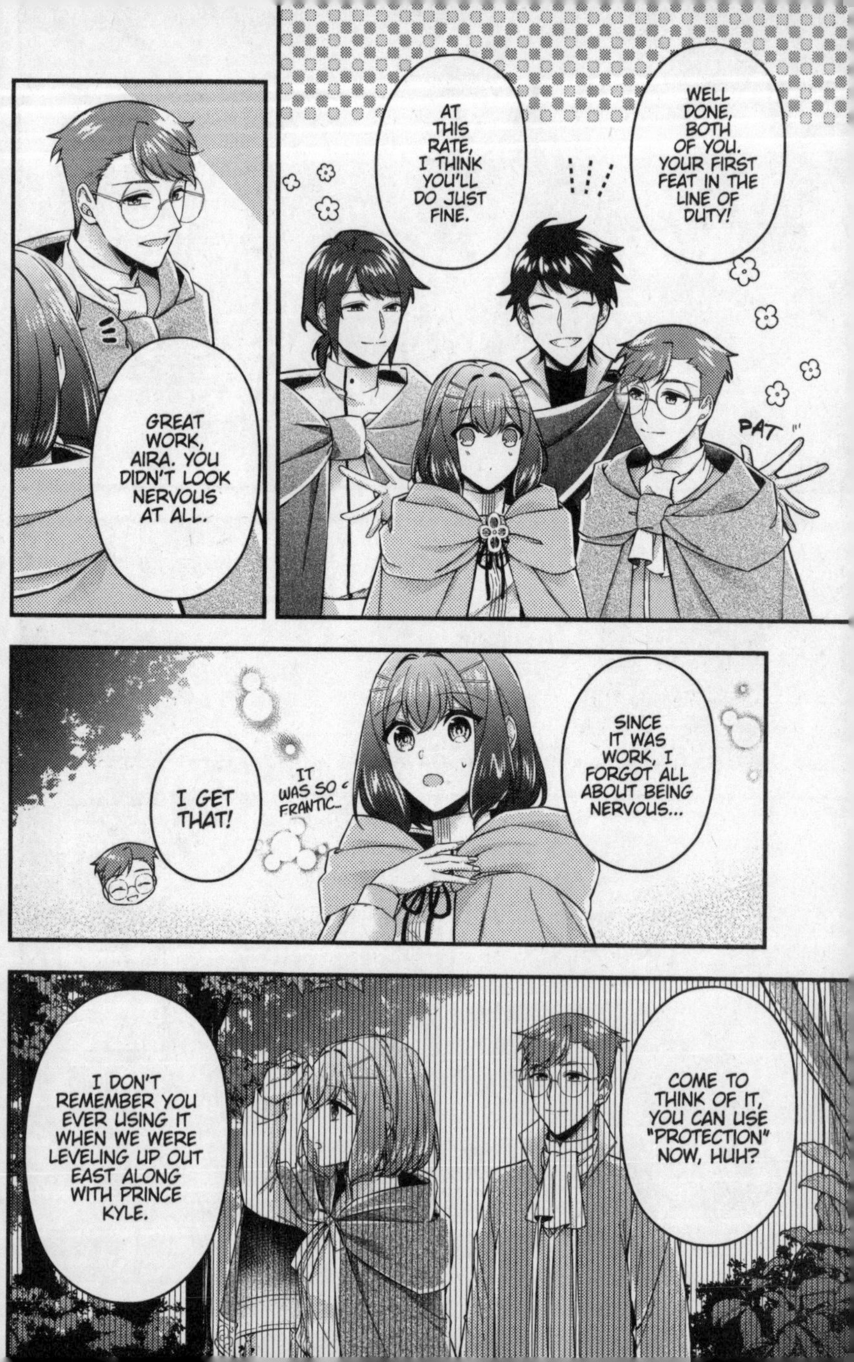
WELL DONE, BOTH OF YOU. YOUR FIRST FEAT IN THE LINE OF DUTY!
AT THIS RATE, I THINK YOU'LL DO JUST FINE.
PAT
GREAT WORK, AIRA. YOU DIDN'T LOOK NERVOUS AT ALL.
SINCE IT WAS WORK, I FORGOT ALL ABOUT BEING NERVOUS...
IT WAS SO FRANTIC...
I GET THAT!
COME TO THINK OF IT, YOU CAN USE "PROTECTION" NOW, HUH?
I DON'T REMEMBER YOU EVER USING IT WHEN WE WERE LEVELING UP OUT EAST ALONG WITH PRINCE KYLE.

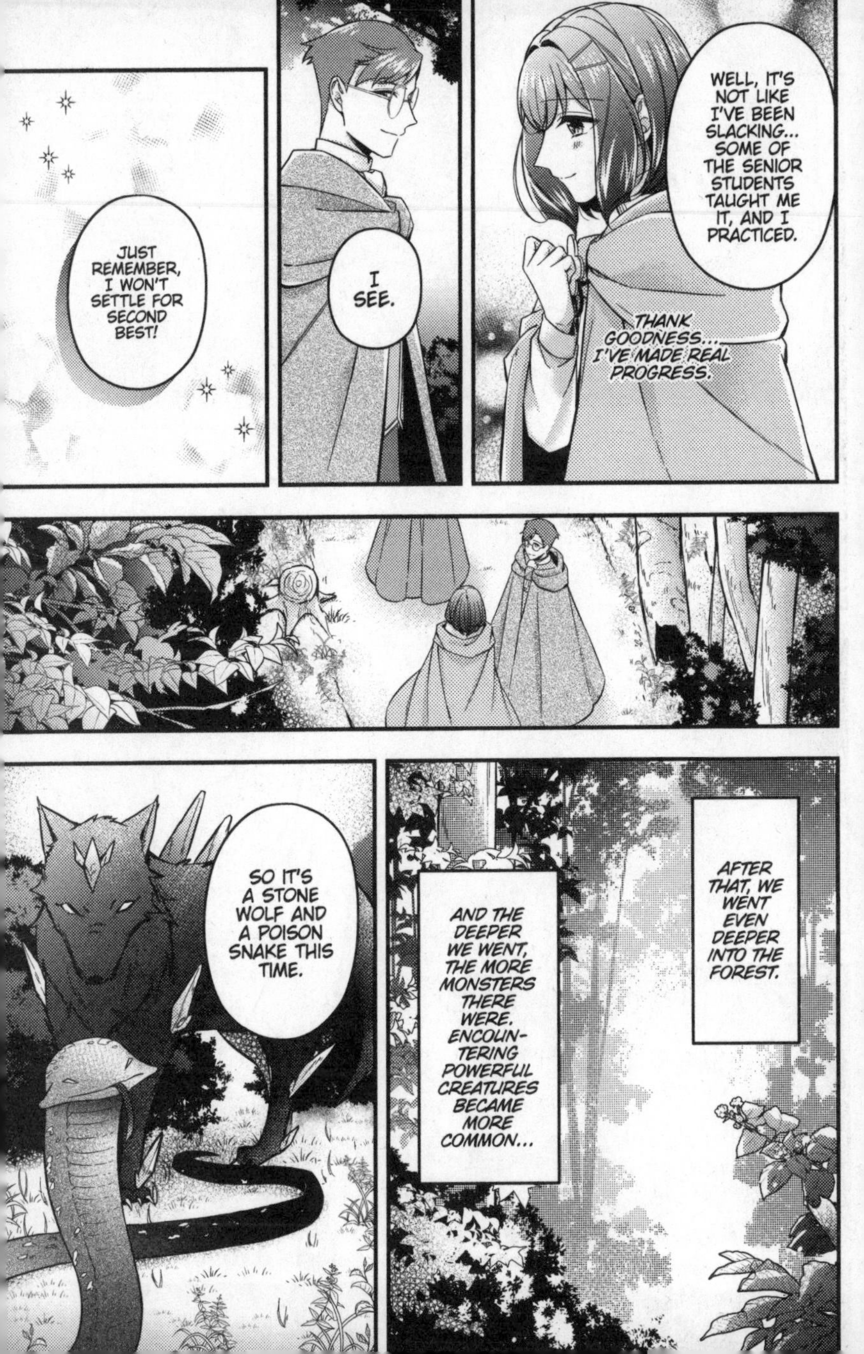
WELL, IT'S NOT LIKE I'VE BEEN SLACKING... SOME OF THE SENIOR STUDENTS TAUGHT ME IT, AND I PRACTICED.
THANK GOODNESS... I'VE MADE REAL PROGRESS.
I SEE.
JUST REMEMBER, I WON'T SETTLE FOR SECOND BEST!
AFTER THAT, WE WENT EVEN DEEPER INTO THE FOREST.
AND THE DEEPER WE WENT, THE MORE MONSTERS THERE WERE. ENCOUN-TERING POWERFUL CREATURES BECAME MORE COMMON...
SO IT'S A STONE WOLF AND A POISON SNAKE THIS TIME.

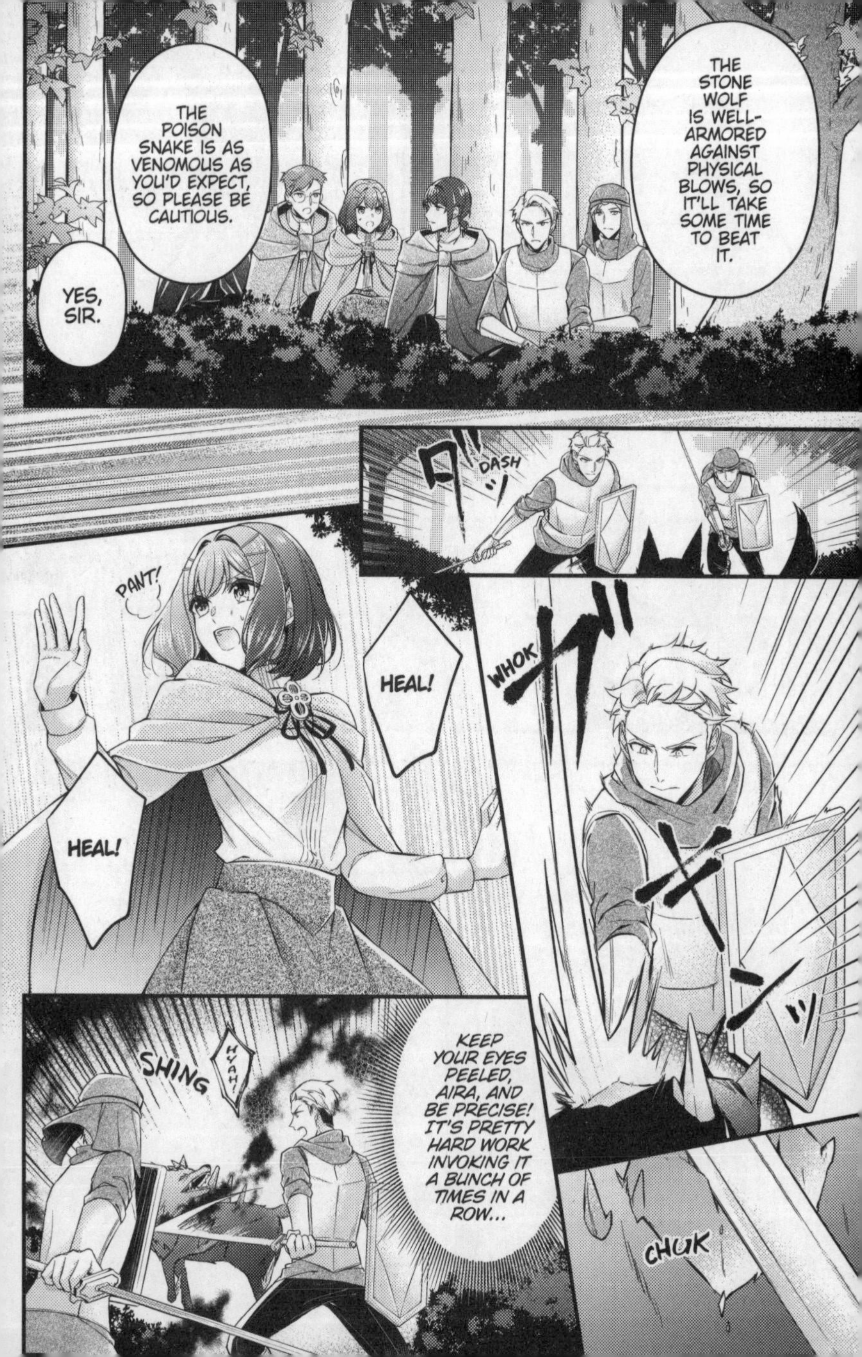
THE STONE WOLF IS WELL-ARMORED AGAINST PHYSICAL BLOWS, SO IT'LL TAKE SOME TIME TO BEAT IT.
THE POISON SNAKE IS AS VENOMOUS AS YOU'D EXPECT, SO PLEASE BE CAUTIOUS.
YES, SIR.
DASH
WHOK
CHUK
PANT!
HEAL!
HEAL!
KEEP YOUR EYES PEELED, AIRA, AND BE PRECISE! IT'S PRETTY HARD WORK INVOKING IT A BUNCH OF TIMES IN A ROW...
HYAH!
SHING

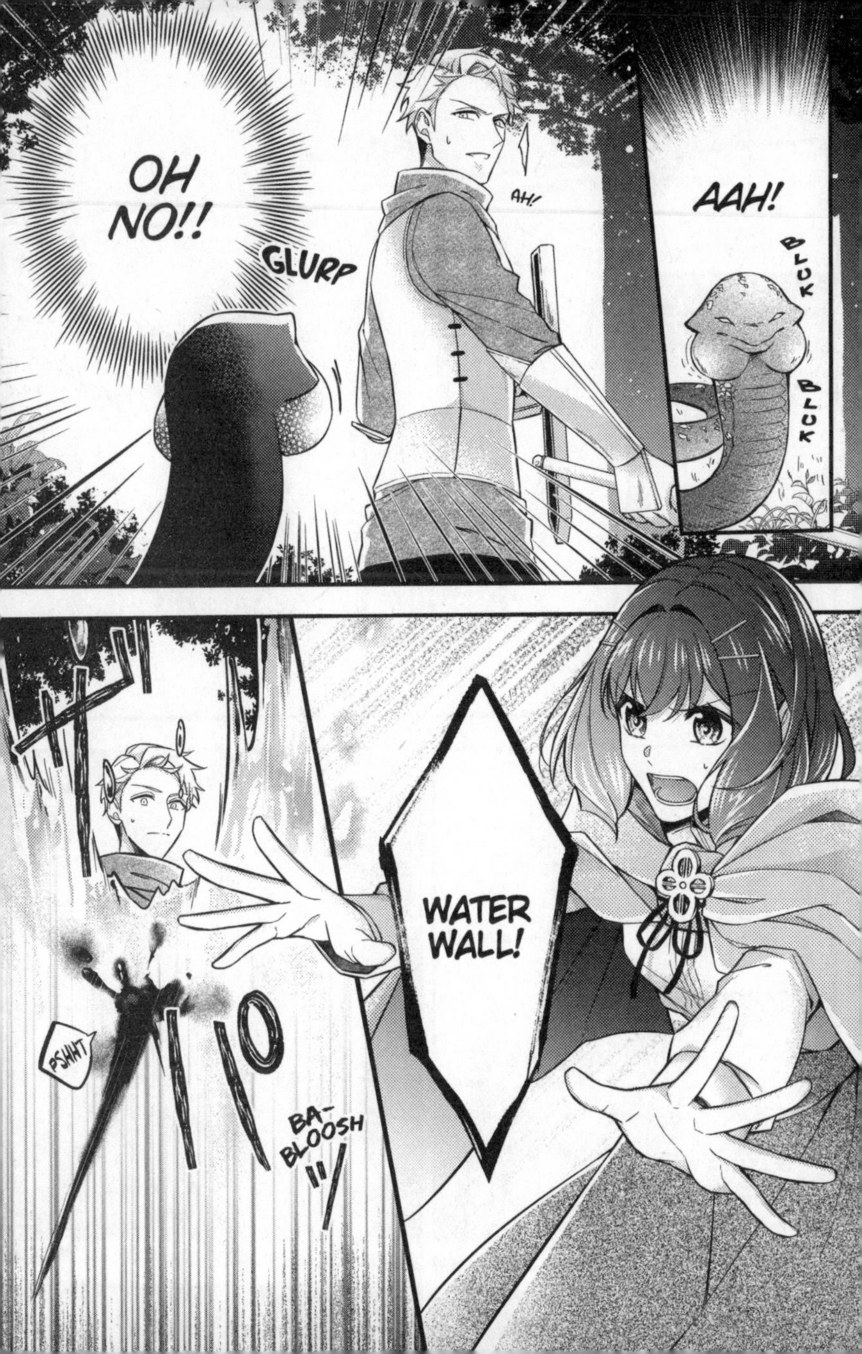
AAH!
BLUK
BLUK
AH!
OH NO!!
GLURP
WATER WALL!
BA-BLOOSH
PSHHT

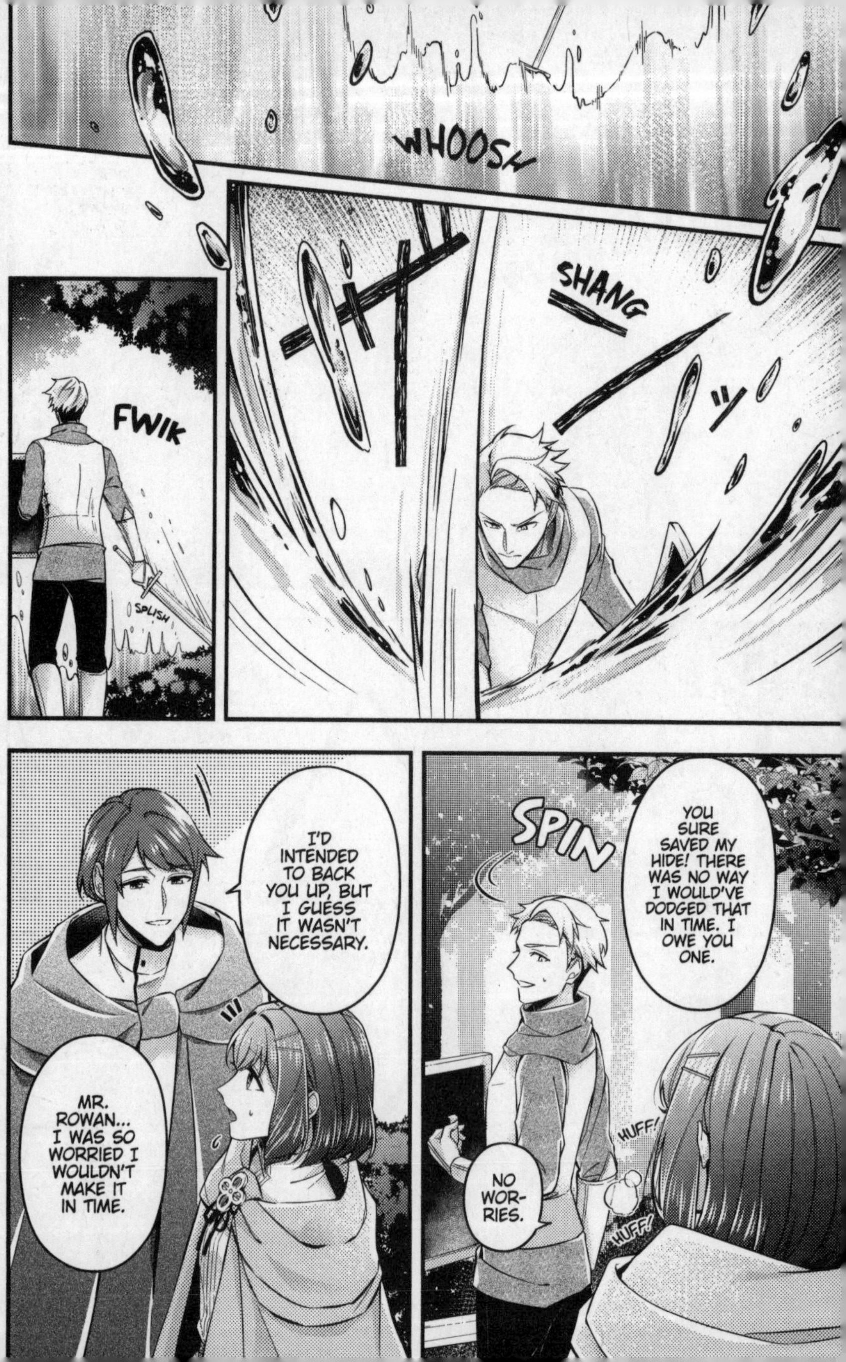
WHOOSH
SHANG
FWIK
SPLISH
SPIN
YOU SURE SAVED MY HIDE! THERE WAS NO WAY I WOULD'VE DODGED THAT IN TIME. I OWE YOU ONE.
NO WORRIES.
HUFF!
HUFF!
I'D INTENDED TO BACK YOU UP, BUT I GUESS IT WASN'T NECESSARY.
MR. ROWAN... I WAS SO WORRIED I WOULDN'T MAKE IT IN TIME.

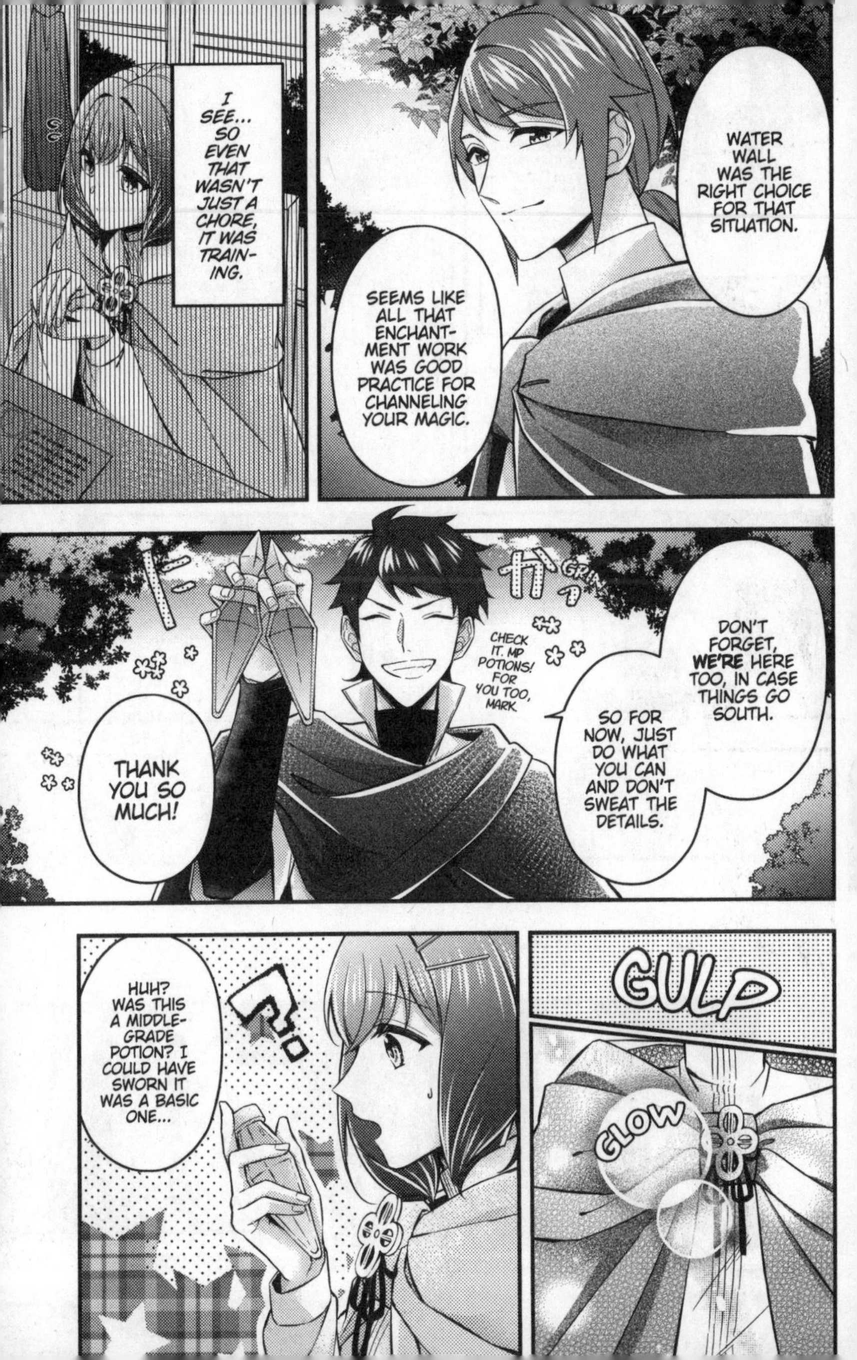
WATER WALL WAS THE RIGHT CHOICE FOR THAT SITUATION.
SEEMS LIKE ALL THAT ENCHANTMENT WORK WAS GOOD PRACTICE FOR CHANNELING YOUR MAGIC.
I SEE... SO EVEN THAT WASN'T JUST A CHORE, IT WAS TRAINING.
DON'T FORGET, **WE'RE** HERE TOO, IN CASE THINGS GO SOUTH.
SO FOR NOW, JUST DO WHAT YOU CAN AND DON'T SWEAT THE DETAILS.
CHECK IT. MP POTIONS! FOR YOU TOO, MARK.
THANK YOU SO MUCH!
GULP
GLOW
HUH? WAS THIS A MIDDLE-GRADE POTION? I COULD HAVE SWORN IT WAS A BASIC ONE...

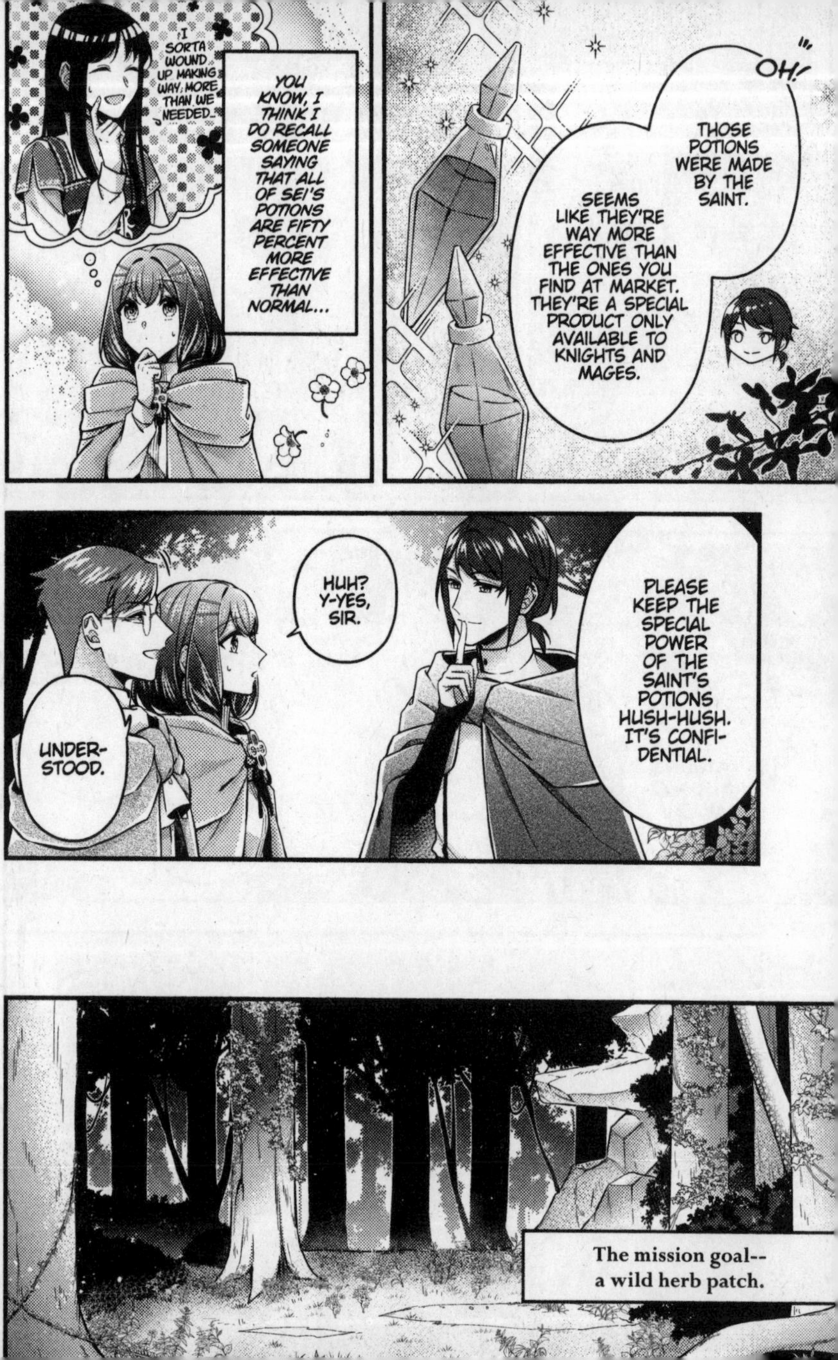
"OH!"
THOSE POTIONS WERE MADE BY THE SAINT.
SEEMS LIKE THEY'RE WAY MORE EFFECTIVE THAN THE ONES YOU FIND AT MARKET. THEY'RE A SPECIAL PRODUCT ONLY AVAILABLE TO KNIGHTS AND MAGES.
YOU KNOW, I THINK I DO RECALL SOMEONE SAYING THAT ALL OF SEI'S POTIONS ARE FIFTY PERCENT MORE EFFECTIVE THAN NORMAL...
I SORTA WOUND UP MAKING WAY, MORE THAN WE NEEDED...
PLEASE KEEP THE SPECIAL POWER OF THE SAINT'S POTIONS HUSH-HUSH. IT'S CONFI-DENTIAL.
HUH? Y-YES, SIR.
UNDER-STOOD.
The mission goal-- a wild herb patch.

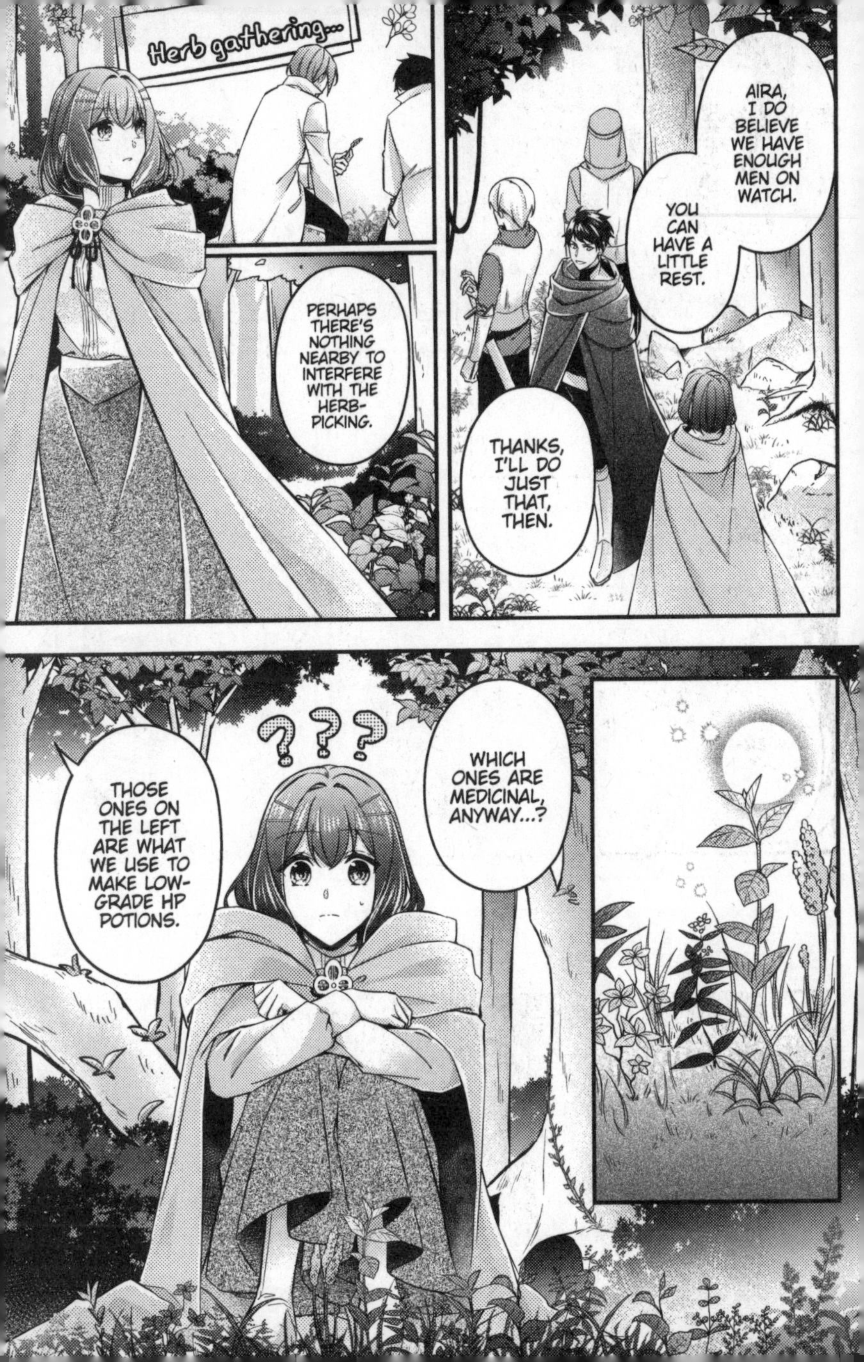
AIRA, I DO BELIEVE WE HAVE ENOUGH MEN ON WATCH.
YOU CAN HAVE A LITTLE REST.
THANKS, I'LL DO JUST THAT, THEN.
Herb gathering...
PERHAPS THERE'S NOTHING NEARBY TO INTERFERE WITH THE HERB-PICKING.
WHICH ONES ARE MEDICINAL, ANYWAY...?
???
THOSE ONES ON THE LEFT ARE WHAT WE USE TO MAKE LOW-GRADE HP POTIONS.

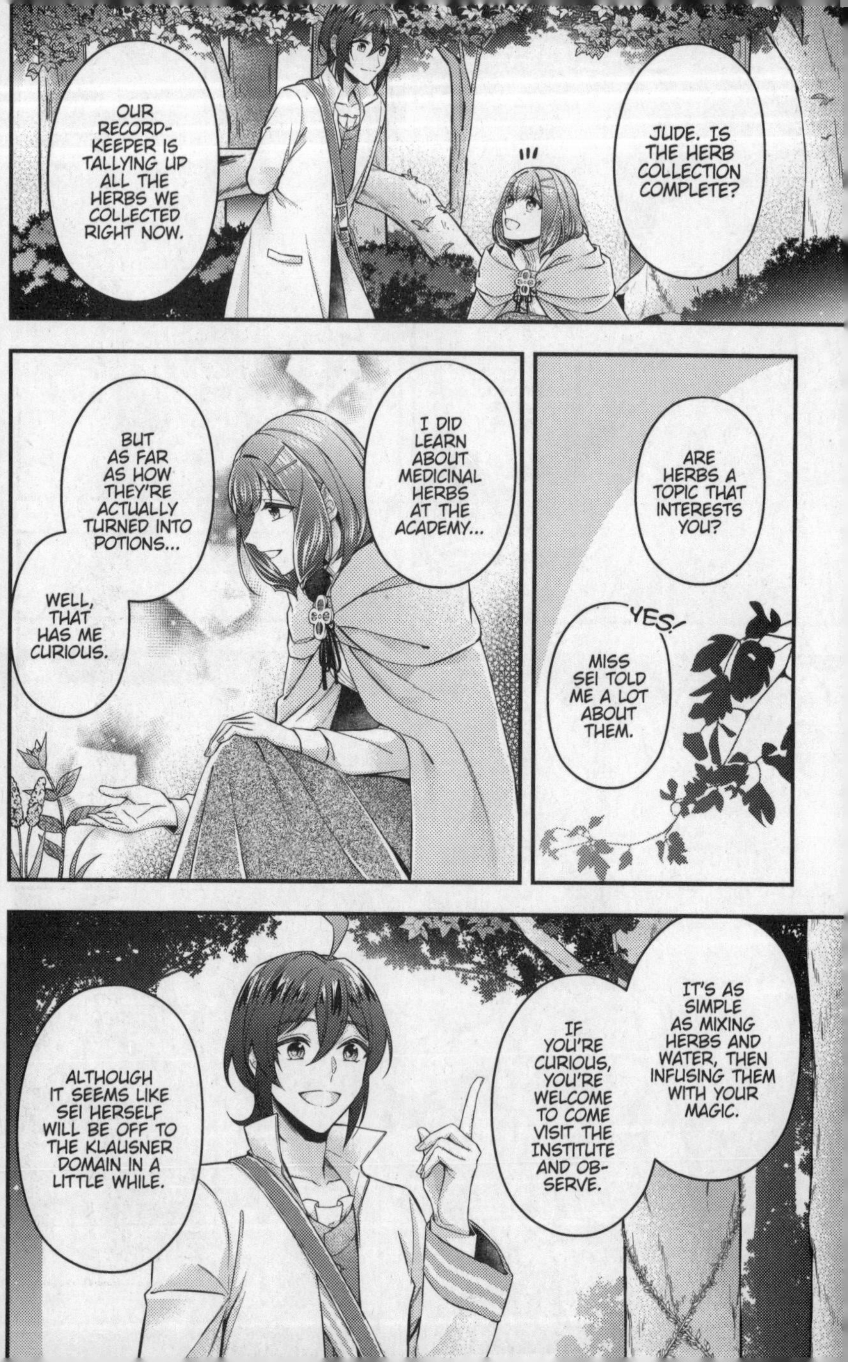
JUDE. IS THE HERB COLLECTION COMPLETE?
OUR RECORD-KEEPER IS TALLYING UP ALL THE HERBS WE COLLECTED RIGHT NOW.
ARE HERBS A TOPIC THAT INTERESTS YOU?
YES!
MISS SEI TOLD ME A LOT ABOUT THEM.
I DID LEARN ABOUT MEDICINAL HERBS AT THE ACADEMY...
BUT AS FAR AS HOW THEY'RE ACTUALLY TURNED INTO POTIONS...
WELL, THAT HAS ME CURIOUS.
IT'S AS SIMPLE AS MIXING HERBS AND WATER, THEN INFUSING THEM WITH YOUR MAGIC.
IF YOU'RE CURIOUS, YOU'RE WELCOME TO COME VISIT THE INSTITUTE AND OB-SERVE.
ALTHOUGH IT SEEMS LIKE SEI HERSELF WILL BE OFF TO THE KLAUSNER DOMAIN IN A LITTLE WHILE.

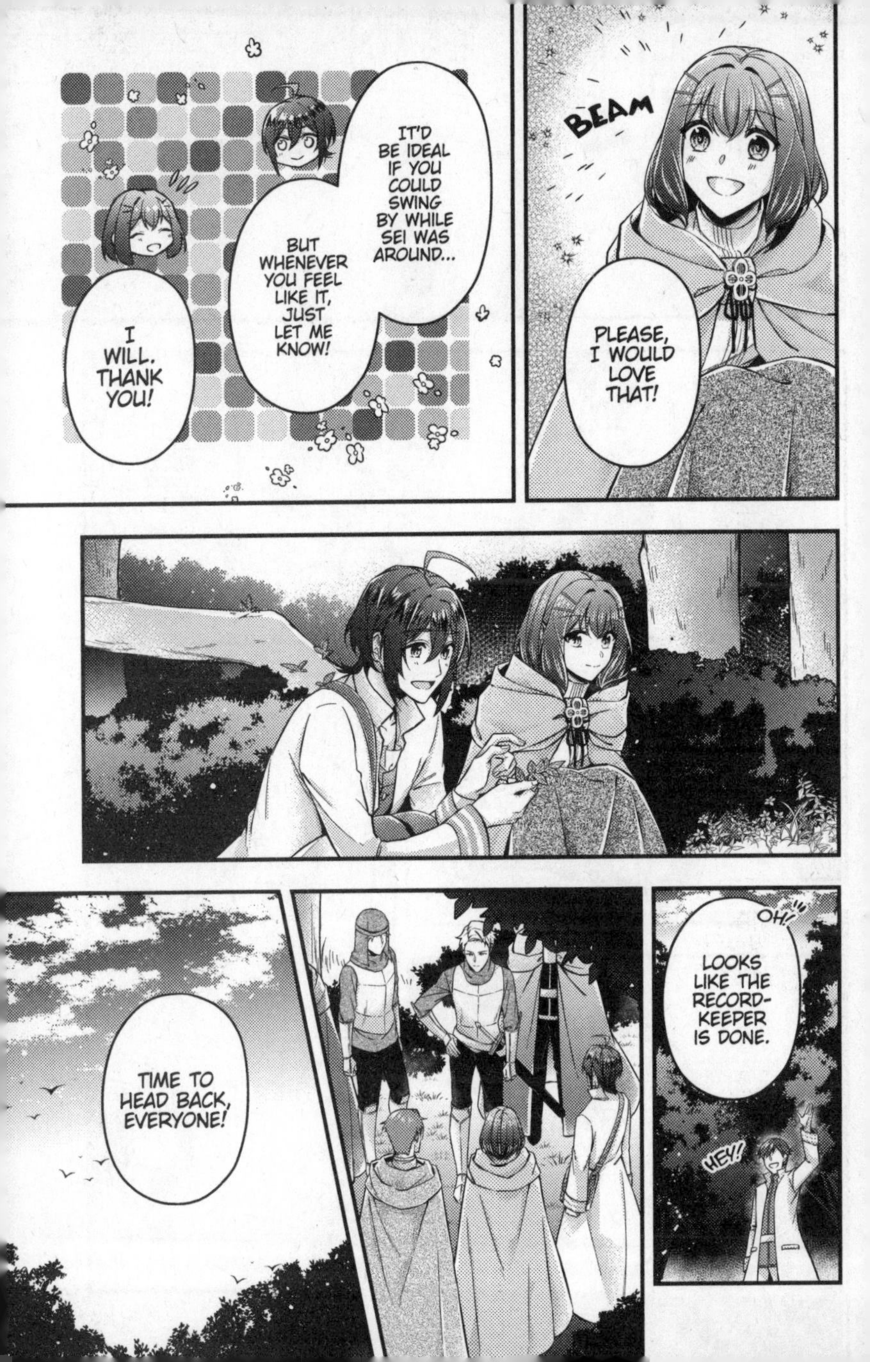
BEAM
PLEASE, I WOULD LOVE THAT!
IT'D BE IDEAL IF YOU COULD SWING BY WHILE SEI WAS AROUND...
BUT WHENEVER YOU FEEL LIKE IT, JUST LET ME KNOW!
I WILL. THANK YOU!
OH!
LOOKS LIKE THE RECORD-KEEPER IS DONE.
HEY!
TIME TO HEAD BACK, EVERYONE!

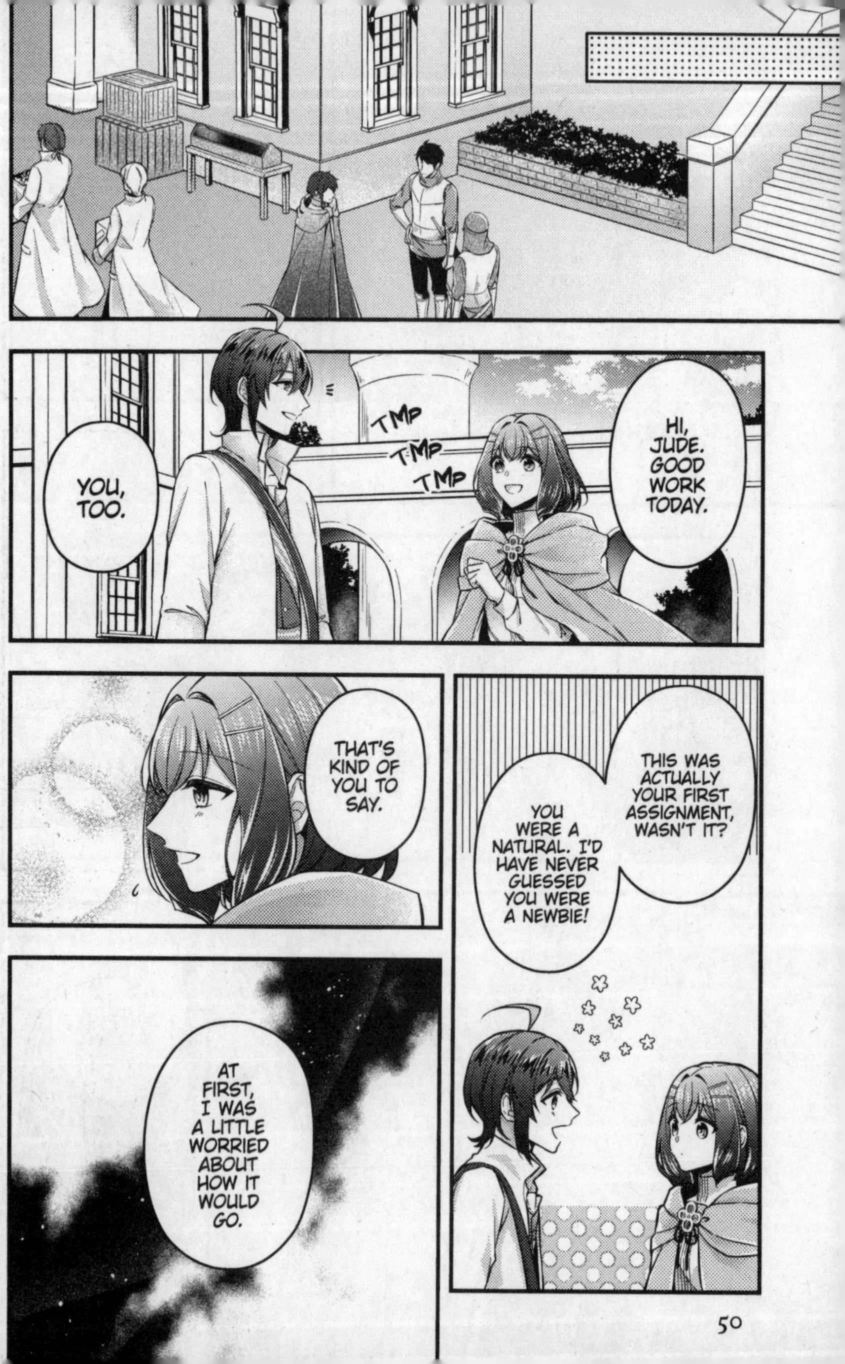
HI, JUDE. GOOD WORK TODAY.
TMP TMP TMP
YOU, TOO.
THIS WAS ACTUALLY YOUR FIRST ASSIGNMENT, WASN'T IT?
YOU WERE A NATURAL. I'D HAVE NEVER GUESSED YOU WERE A NEWBIE!
THAT'S KIND OF YOU TO SAY.
AT FIRST, I WAS A LITTLE WORRIED ABOUT HOW IT WOULD GO.

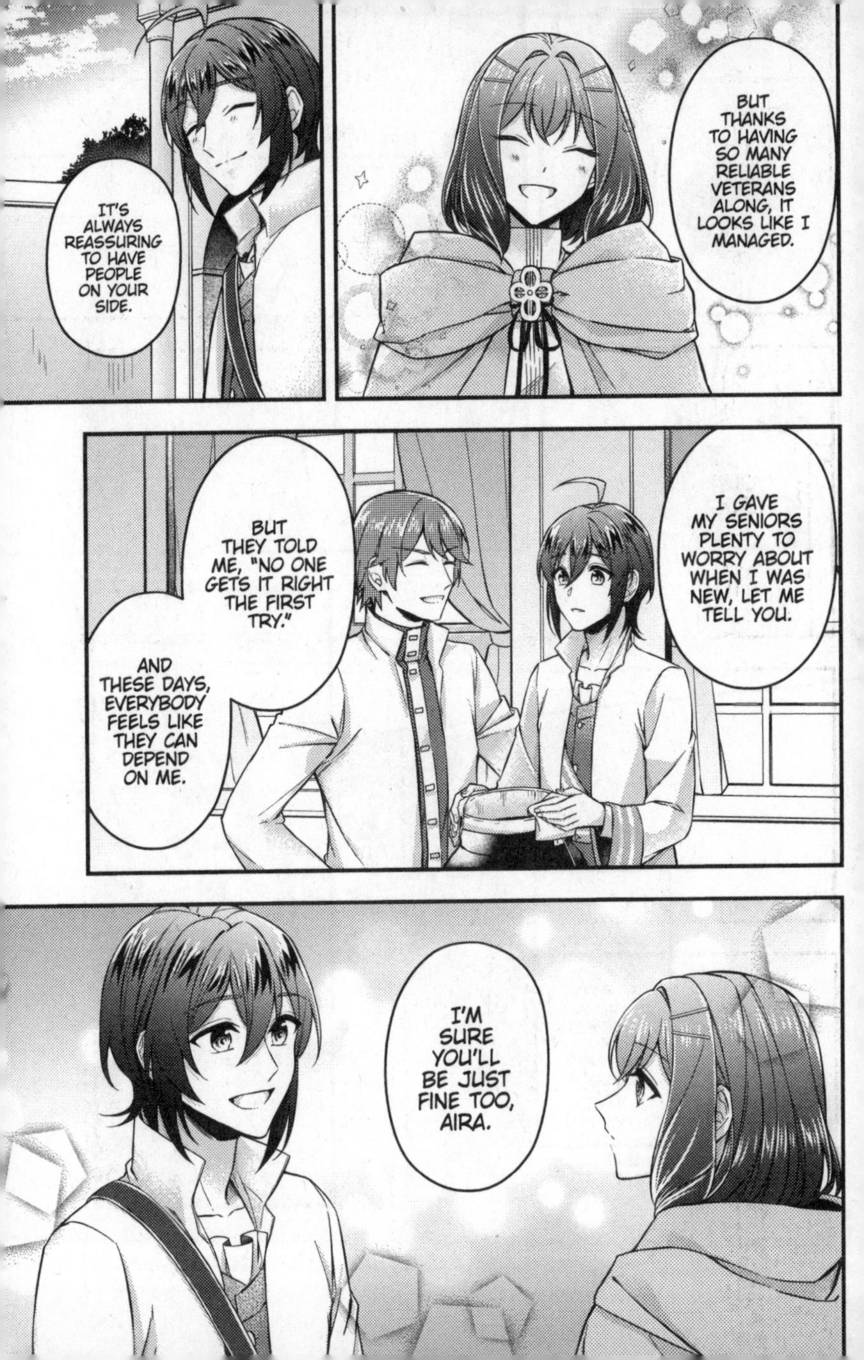
BUT THANKS TO HAVING SO MANY RELIABLE VETERANS ALONG, IT LOOKS LIKE I MANAGED.
IT'S ALWAYS REASSURING TO HAVE PEOPLE ON YOUR SIDE.
I GAVE MY SENIORS PLENTY TO WORRY ABOUT WHEN I WAS NEW, LET ME TELL YOU.
BUT THEY TOLD ME, "NO ONE GETS IT RIGHT THE FIRST TRY."
AND THESE DAYS, EVERYBODY FEELS LIKE THEY CAN DEPEND ON ME.
I'M SURE YOU'LL BE JUST FINE TOO, AIRA.

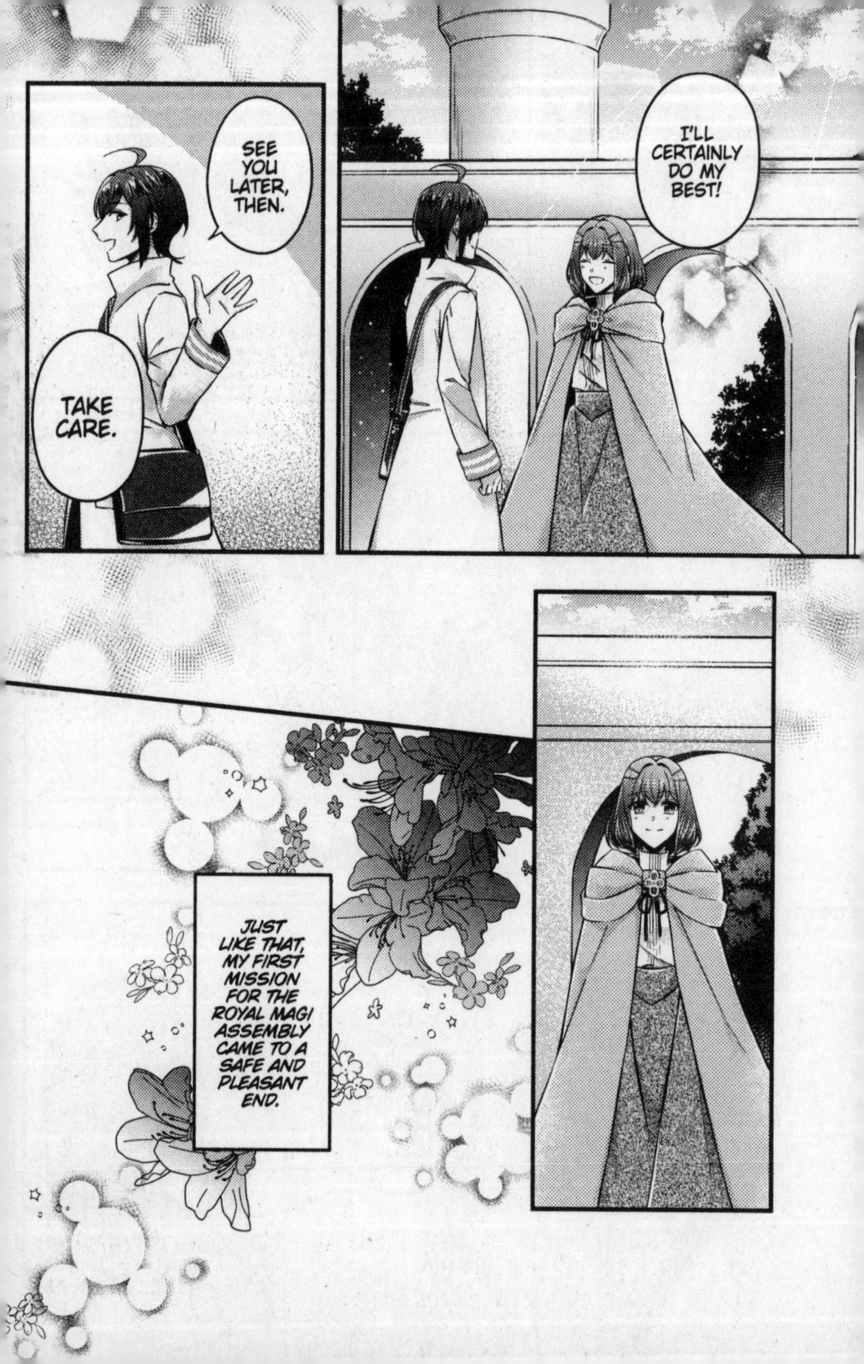
SEE YOU LATER, THEN.
TAKE CARE.
I'LL CERTAINLY DO MY BEST!
JUST LIKE THAT, MY FIRST MISSION FOR THE ROYAL MAGI ASSEMBLY CAME TO A SAFE AND PLEASANT END.

The Saint's **Saint's**
Magic Power is
Omnipotent
The Other Saint

The Saint's
Magic Power is
Omnipotent
The Other Saint

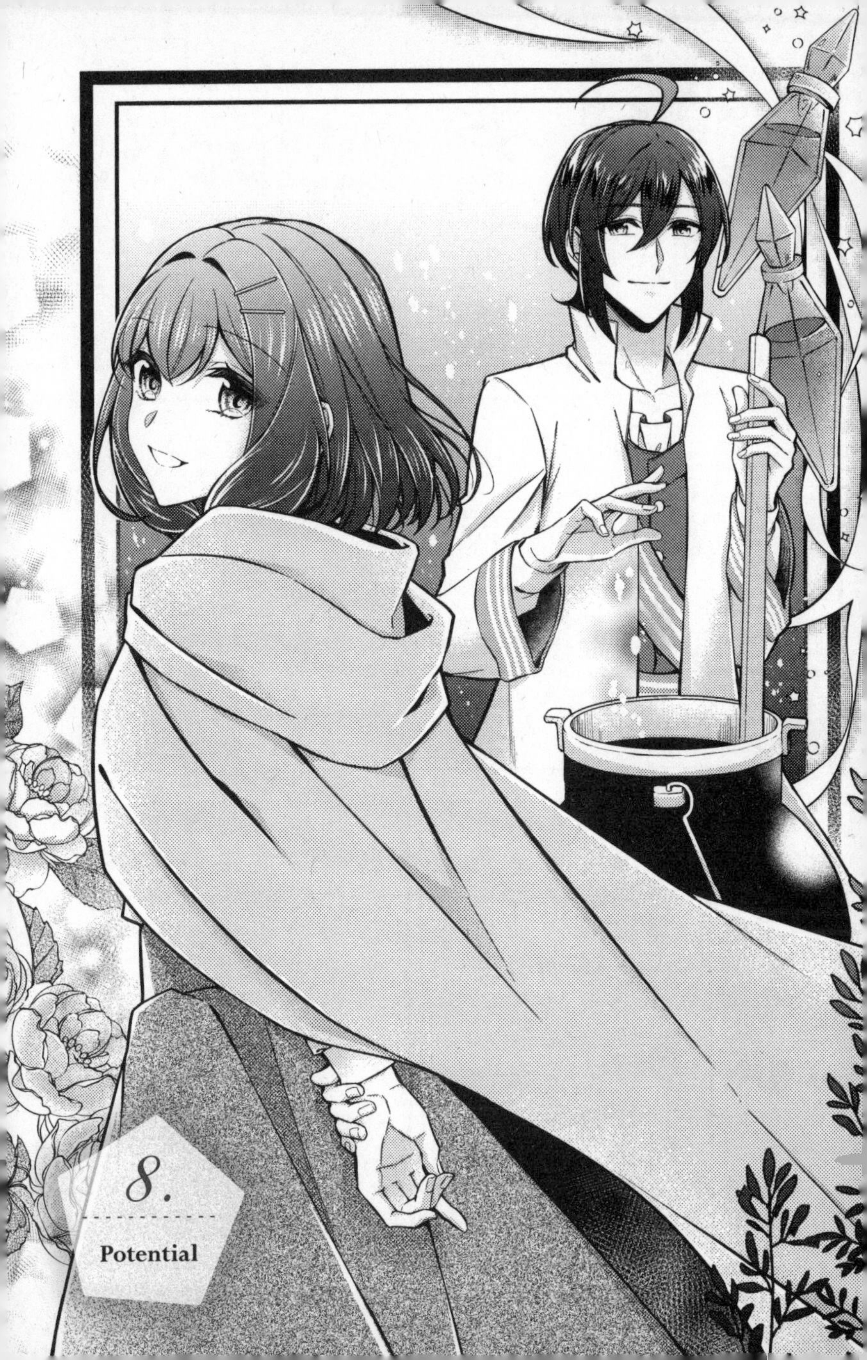
8.
Potential

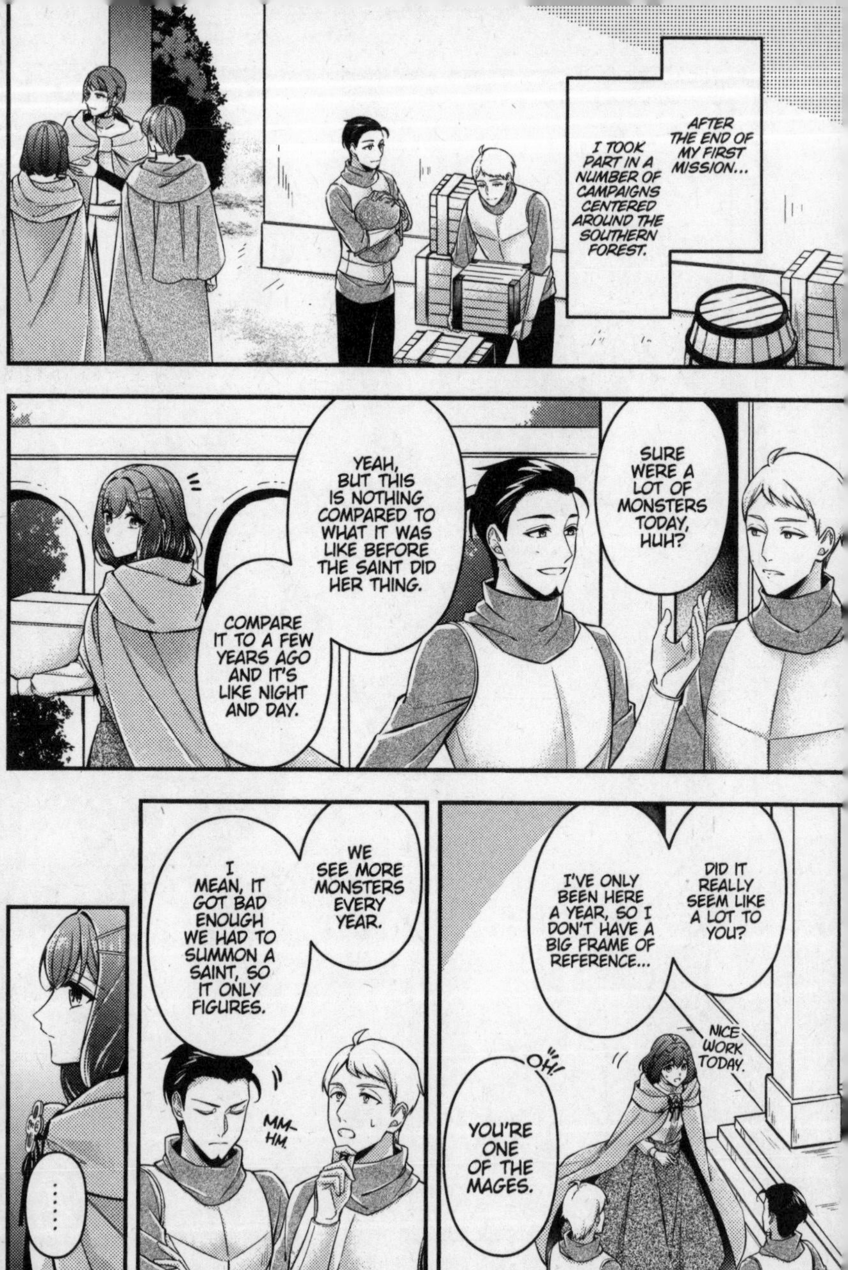
AFTER THE END OF MY FIRST MISSION...
I TOOK PART IN A NUMBER OF CAMPAIGNS CENTERED AROUND THE SOUTHERN FOREST.
SURE WERE A LOT OF MONSTERS TODAY, HUH?
YEAH, BUT THIS IS NOTHING COMPARED TO WHAT IT WAS LIKE BEFORE THE SAINT DID HER THING.
COMPARE IT TO A FEW YEARS AGO AND IT'S LIKE NIGHT AND DAY.
DID IT REALLY SEEM LIKE A LOT TO YOU?
I'VE ONLY BEEN HERE A YEAR, SO I DON'T HAVE A BIG FRAME OF REFERENCE...
NICE WORK TODAY.
OH!
YOU'RE ONE OF THE MAGES.
WE SEE MORE MONSTERS EVERY YEAR.
I MEAN, IT GOT BAD ENOUGH WE HAD TO SUMMON A SAINT, SO IT ONLY FIGURES.
MM-HM.
......

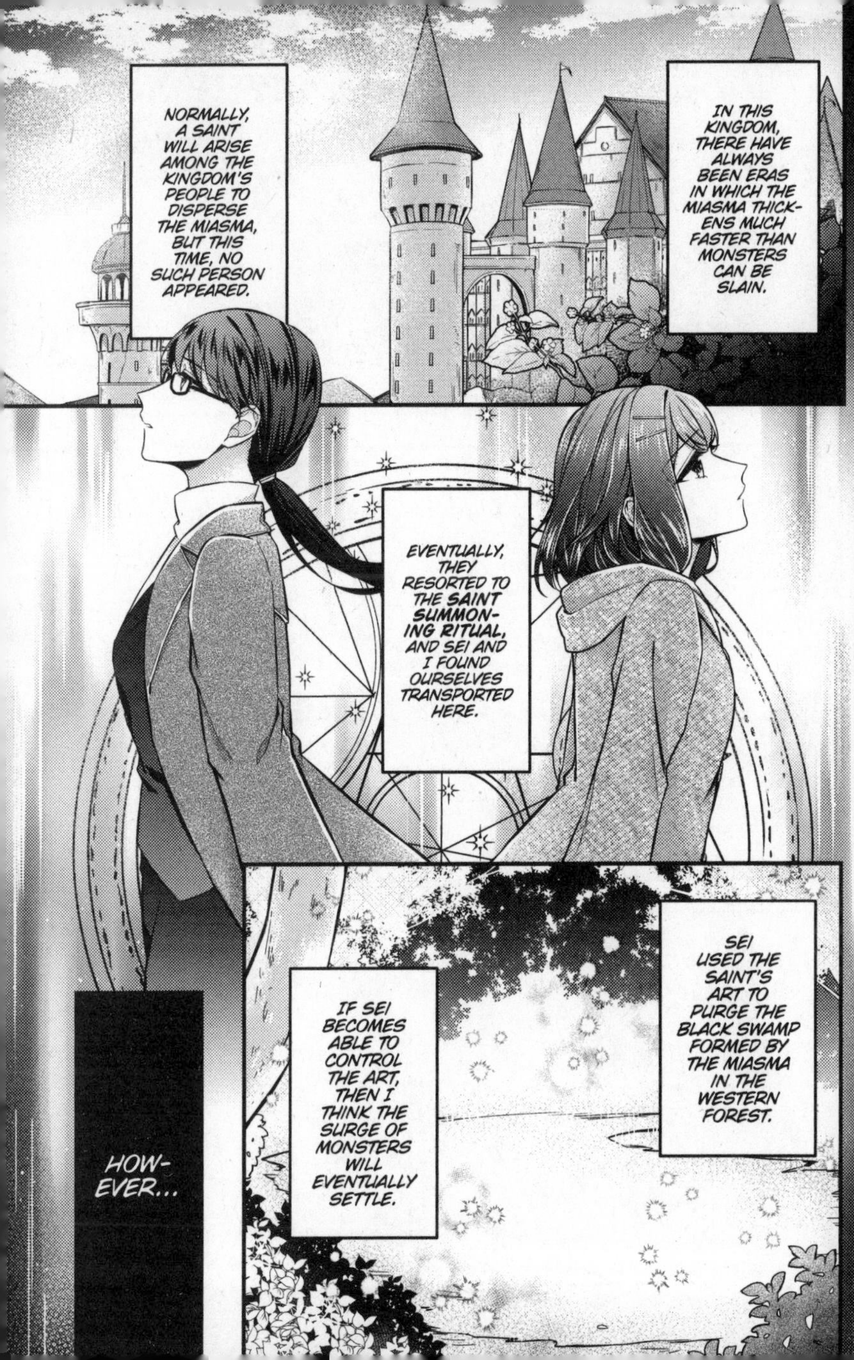
IN THIS KINGDOM, THERE HAVE ALWAYS BEEN ERAS IN WHICH THE MIASMA THICK-ENS MUCH FASTER THAN MONSTERS CAN BE SLAIN.
NORMALLY, A SAINT WILL ARISE AMONG THE KINGDOM'S PEOPLE TO DISPERSE THE MIASMA, BUT THIS TIME, NO SUCH PERSON APPEARED.
EVENTUALLY, THEY RESORTED TO THE SAINT SUMMON-ING RITUAL, AND SEI AND I FOUND OURSELVES TRANSPORTED HERE.
SEI USED THE SAINT'S ART TO PURGE THE BLACK SWAMP FORMED BY THE MIASMA IN THE WESTERN FOREST.
IF SEI BECOMES ABLE TO CONTROL THE ART, THEN I THINK THE SURGE OF MONSTERS WILL EVENTUALLY SETTLE.
HOW-EVER...

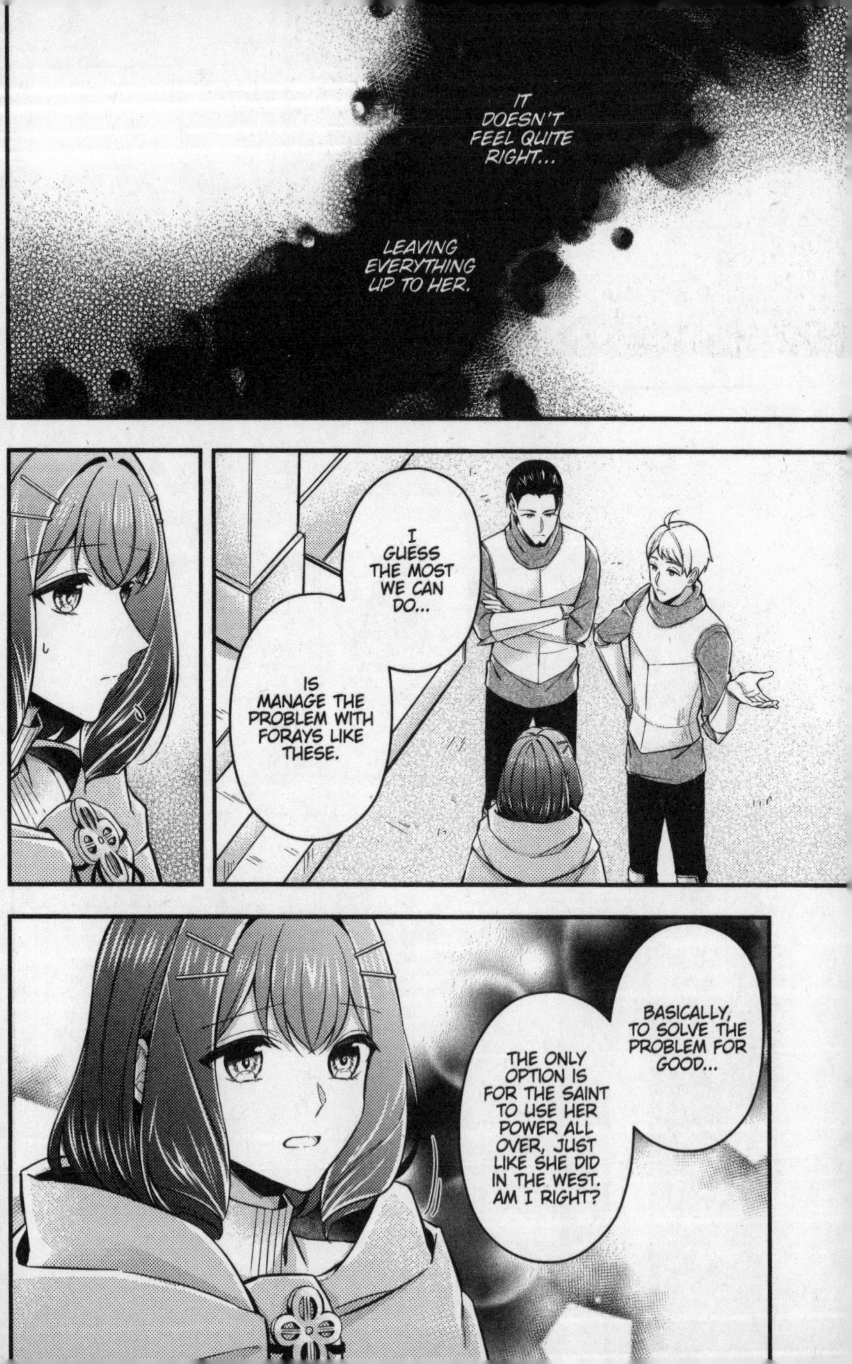
IT DOESN'T FEEL QUITE RIGHT...
LEAVING EVERYTHING UP TO HER.
I GUESS THE MOST WE CAN DO...
IS MANAGE THE PROBLEM WITH FORAYS LIKE THESE.
BASICALLY, TO SOLVE THE PROBLEM FOR GOOD...
THE ONLY OPTION IS FOR THE SAINT TO USE HER POWER ALL OVER, JUST LIKE SHE DID IN THE WEST. AM I RIGHT?

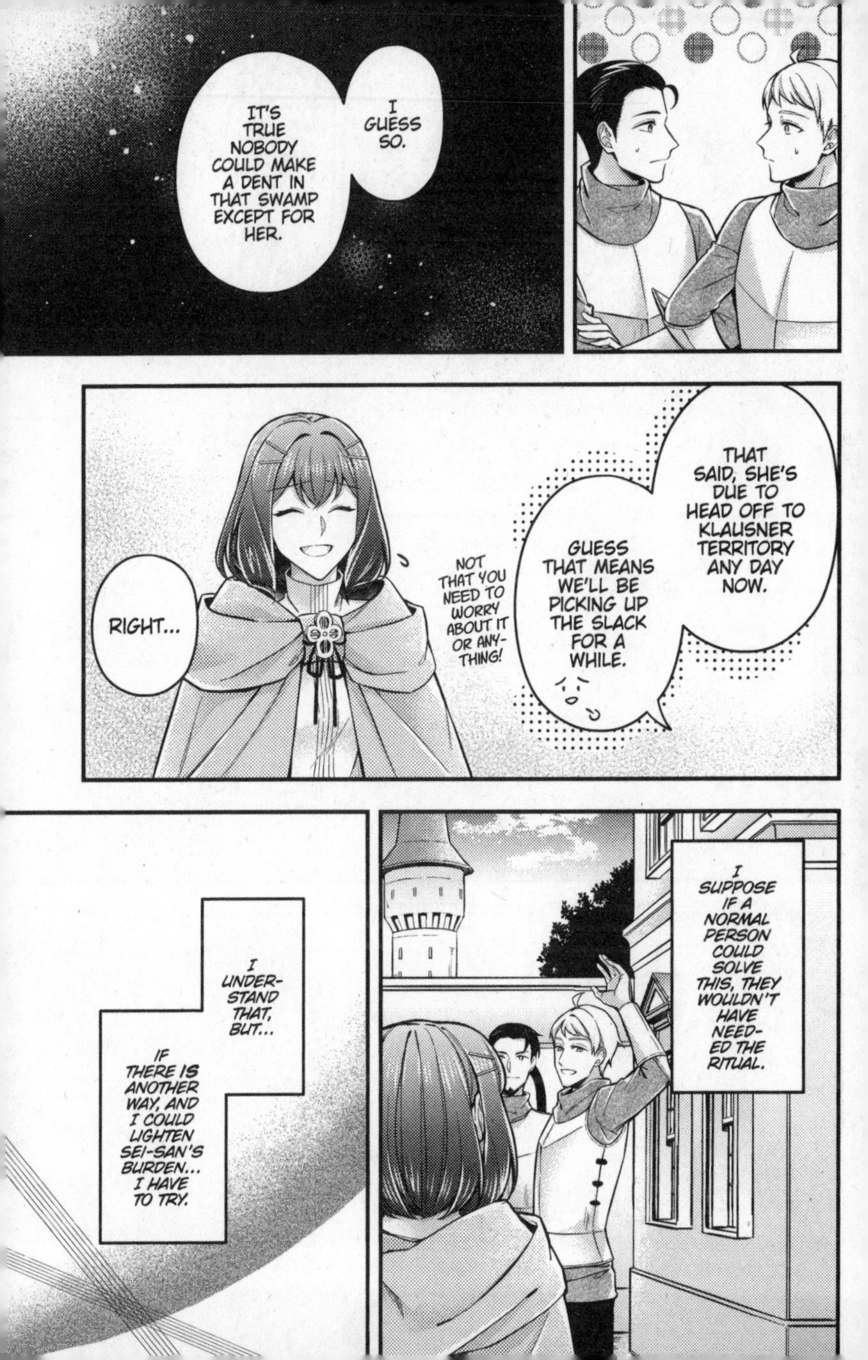
I GUESS SO.
IT'S TRUE NOBODY COULD MAKE A DENT IN THAT SWAMP EXCEPT FOR HER.
THAT SAID, SHE'S DUE TO HEAD OFF TO KLAUSNER TERRITORY ANY DAY NOW.
GUESS THAT MEANS WE'LL BE PICKING UP THE SLACK FOR A WHILE.
NOT THAT YOU NEED TO WORRY ABOUT IT OR ANY-THING!
RIGHT...
I SUPPOSE IF A NORMAL PERSON COULD SOLVE THIS, THEY WOULDN'T HAVE NEED-ED THE RITUAL.
I UNDER-STAND THAT, BUT...
IF THERE IS ANOTHER WAY, AND I COULD LIGHTEN SEI-SAN'S BURDEN... I HAVE TO TRY.

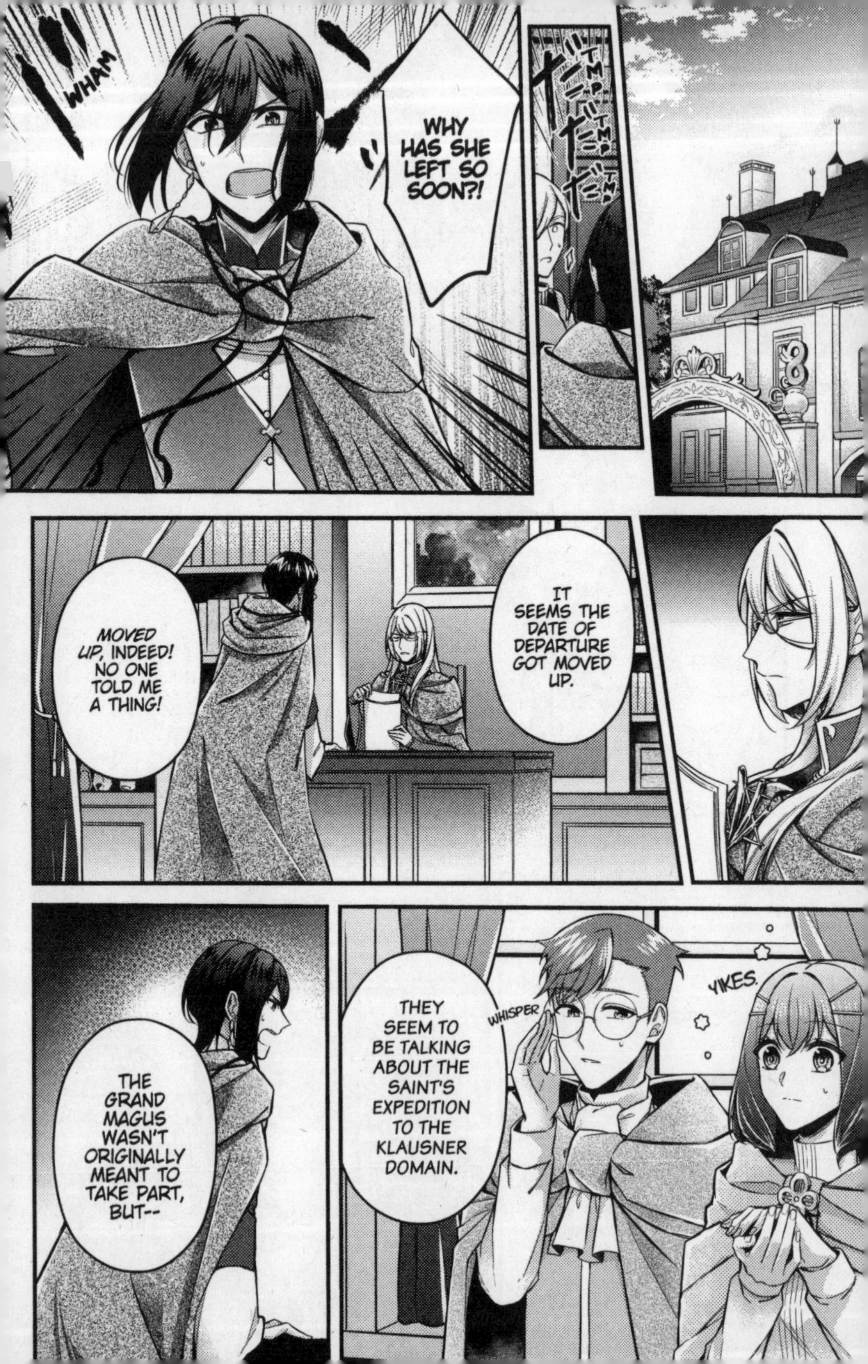
TMP TMP TMP
WHAM
WHY HAS SHE LEFT SO SOON?!
IT SEEMS THE DATE OF DEPARTURE GOT MOVED UP.
MOVED UP, INDEED! NO ONE TOLD ME A THING!
YIKES.
WHISPER
THEY SEEM TO BE TALKING ABOUT THE SAINT'S EXPEDITION TO THE KLAUSNER DOMAIN.
THE GRAND MAGUS WASN'T ORIGINALLY MEANT TO TAKE PART, BUT--

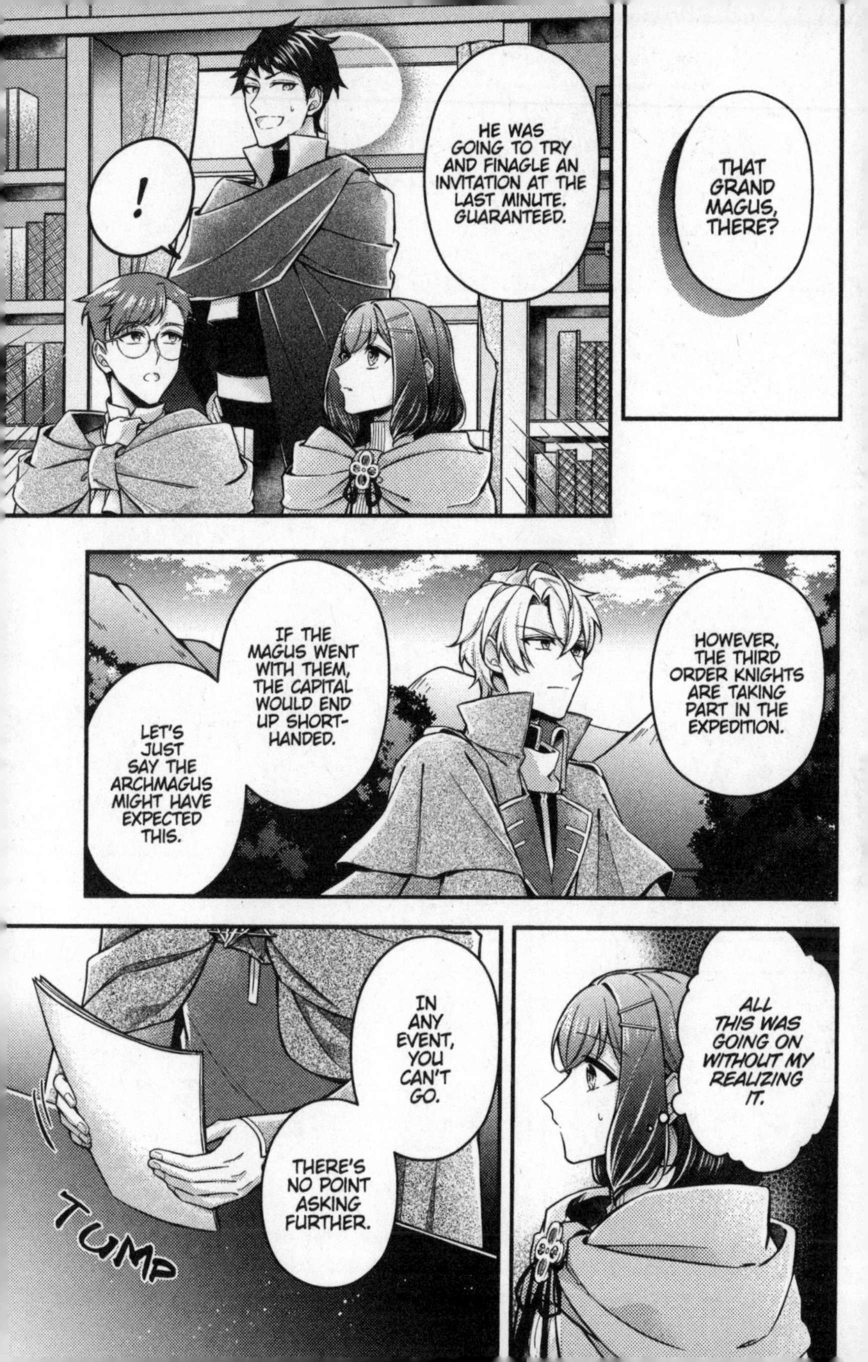
THAT GRAND MAGUS, THERE?
HE WAS GOING TO TRY AND FINAGLE AN INVITATION AT THE LAST MINUTE. GUARANTEED.
!
HOWEVER, THE THIRD ORDER KNIGHTS ARE TAKING PART IN THE EXPEDITION.
IF THE MAGUS WENT WITH THEM, THE CAPITAL WOULD END UP SHORT-HANDED.
LET'S JUST SAY THE ARCHMAGUS MIGHT HAVE EXPECTED THIS.
ALL THIS WAS GOING ON WITHOUT MY REALIZING IT.
IN ANY EVENT, YOU CAN'T GO.
THERE'S NO POINT ASKING FURTHER.
TUMP

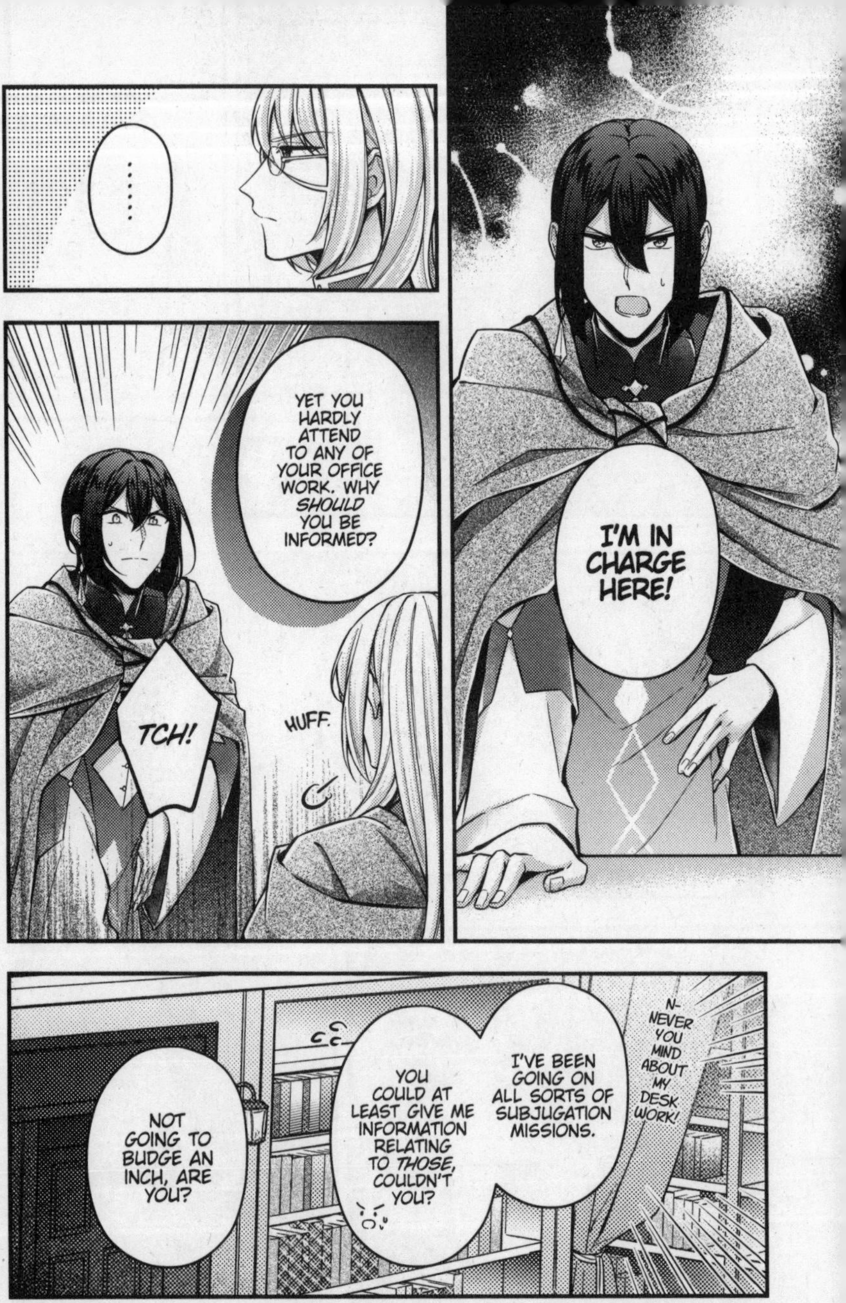
I'M IN CHARGE HERE!
……
YET YOU HARDLY ATTEND TO ANY OF YOUR OFFICE WORK. WHY *SHOULD* YOU BE INFORMED?
HUFF.
TCH!
N-NEVER YOU MIND ABOUT MY DESK WORK!
I'VE BEEN GOING ON ALL SORTS OF SUBJUGATION MISSIONS.
YOU COULD AT LEAST GIVE ME INFORMATION RELATING TO *THOSE*, COULDN'T YOU?
NOT GOING TO BUDGE AN INCH, ARE YOU?

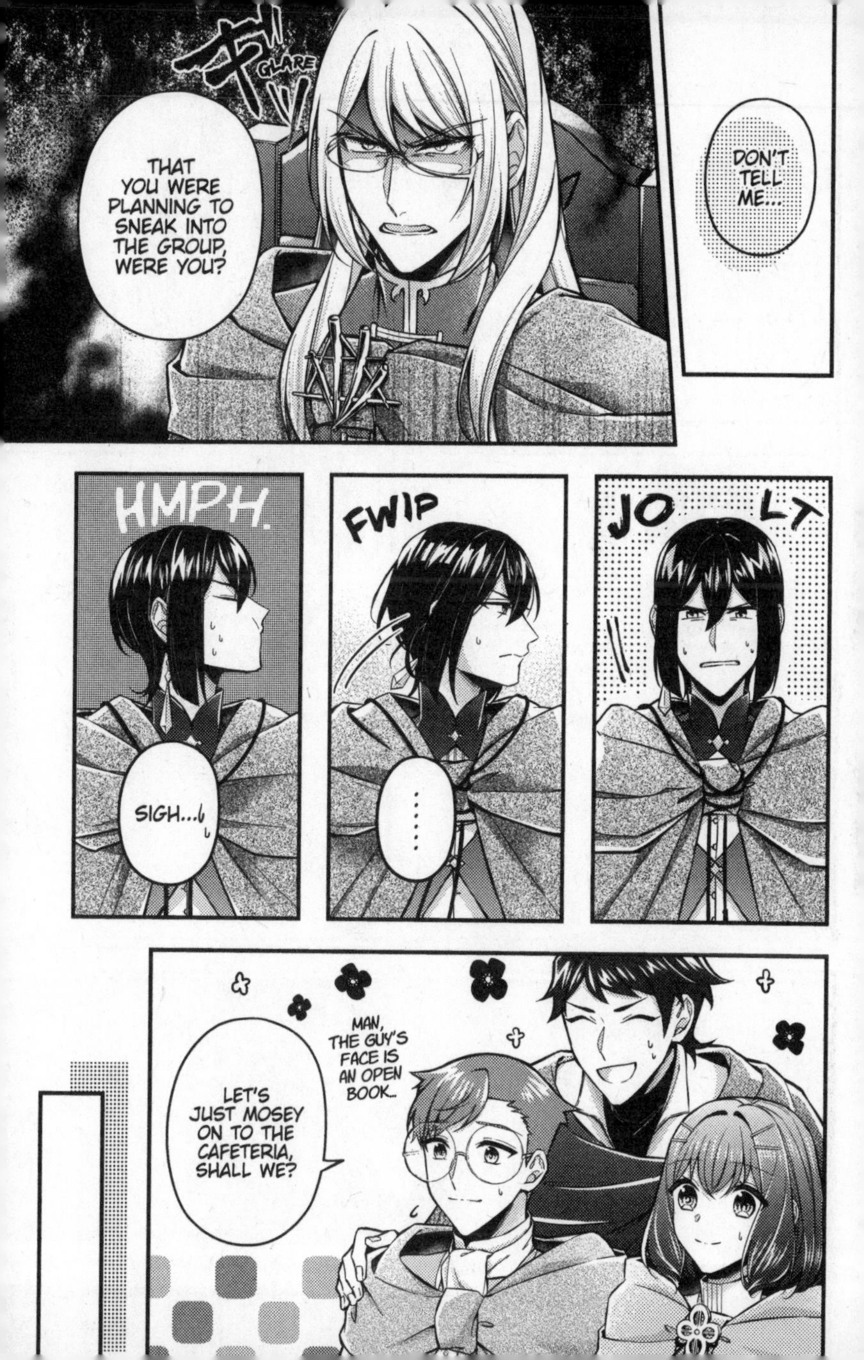

DON'T TELL ME...
GLARE
THAT YOU WERE PLANNING TO SNEAK INTO THE GROUP, WERE YOU?
JOLT
FWIP
......
HMPH.
SIGH...
MAN, THE GUY'S FACE IS AN OPEN BOOK...
LET'S JUST MOSEY ON TO THE CAFETERIA, SHALL WE?

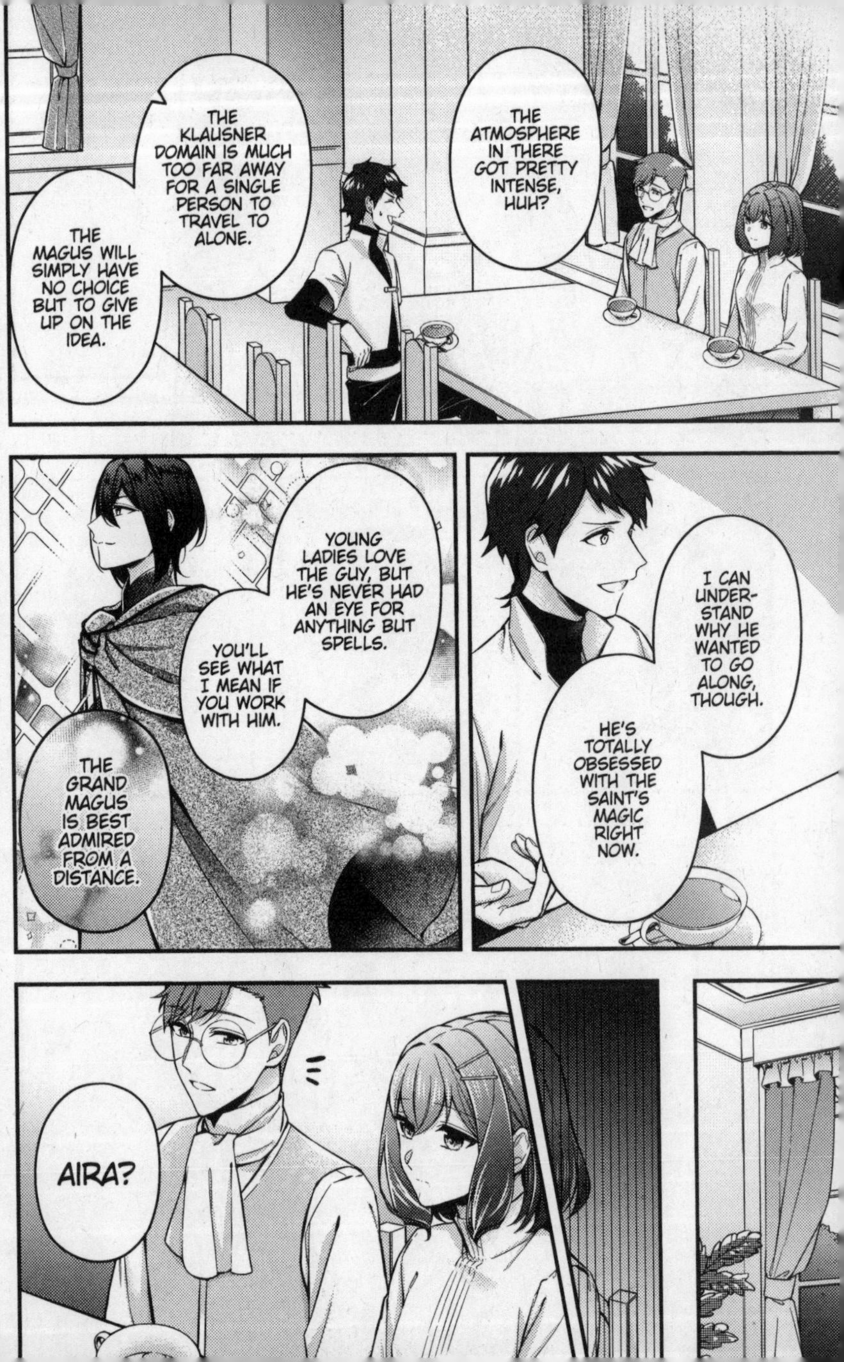
THE ATMOSPHERE IN THERE GOT PRETTY INTENSE, HUH?
THE KLAUSNER DOMAIN IS MUCH TOO FAR AWAY FOR A SINGLE PERSON TO TRAVEL TO ALONE.
THE MAGUS WILL SIMPLY HAVE NO CHOICE BUT TO GIVE UP ON THE IDEA.
I CAN UNDER-STAND WHY HE WANTED TO GO ALONG, THOUGH.
HE'S TOTALLY OBSESSED WITH THE SAINT'S MAGIC RIGHT NOW.
YOUNG LADIES LOVE THE GUY, BUT HE'S NEVER HAD AN EYE FOR ANYTHING BUT SPELLS.
YOU'LL SEE WHAT I MEAN IF YOU WORK WITH HIM.
THE GRAND MAGUS IS BEST ADMIRED FROM A DISTANCE.
AIRA?

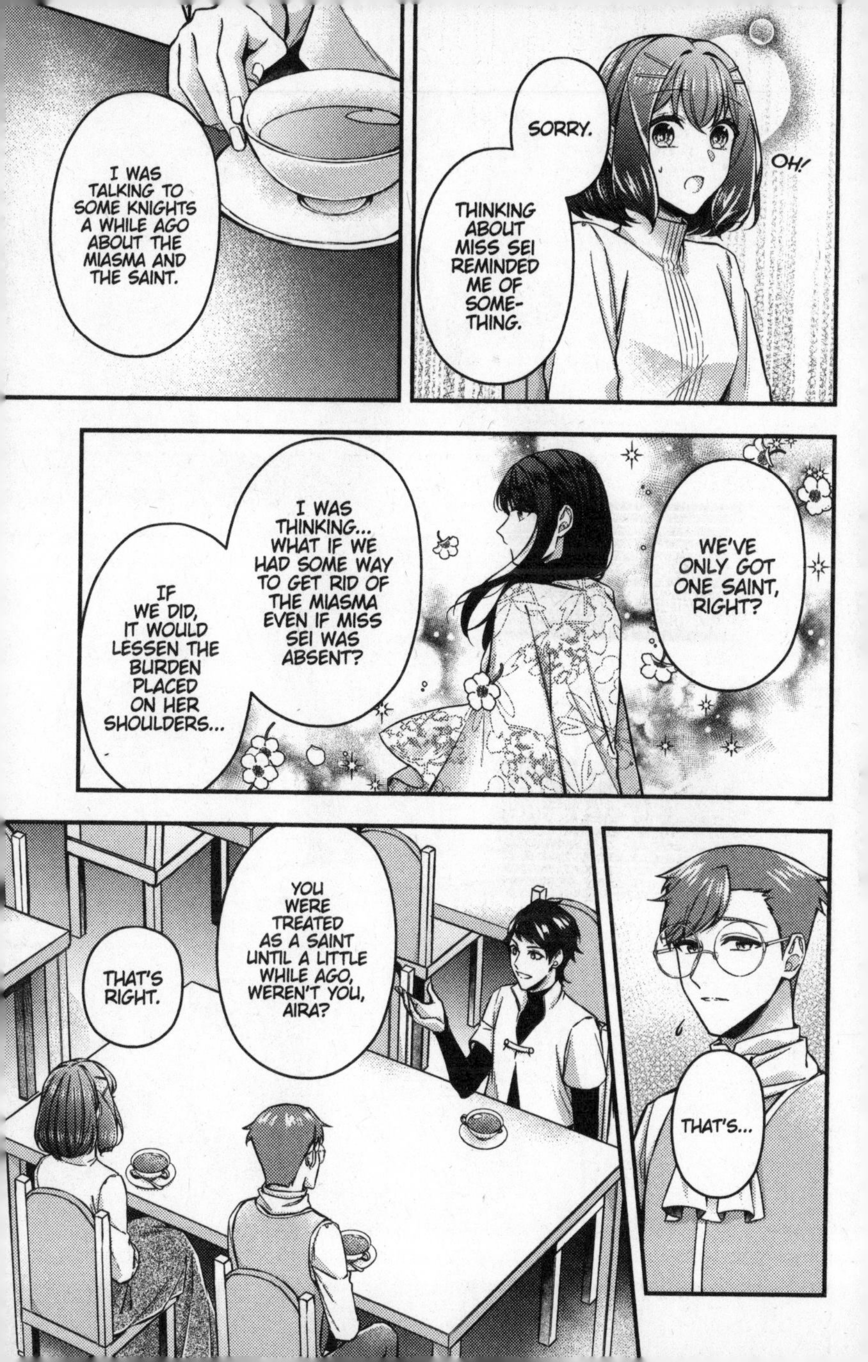
OH!
SORRY.
THINKING ABOUT MISS SEI REMINDED ME OF SOME-THING.
I WAS TALKING TO SOME KNIGHTS A WHILE AGO ABOUT THE MIASMA AND THE SAINT.
WE'VE ONLY GOT ONE SAINT, RIGHT?
I WAS THINKING... WHAT IF WE HAD SOME WAY TO GET RID OF THE MIASMA EVEN IF MISS SEI WAS ABSENT?
IF WE DID, IT WOULD LESSEN THE BURDEN PLACED ON HER SHOULDERS...
THAT'S...
YOU WERE TREATED AS A SAINT UNTIL A LITTLE WHILE AGO, WEREN'T YOU, AIRA?
THAT'S RIGHT.

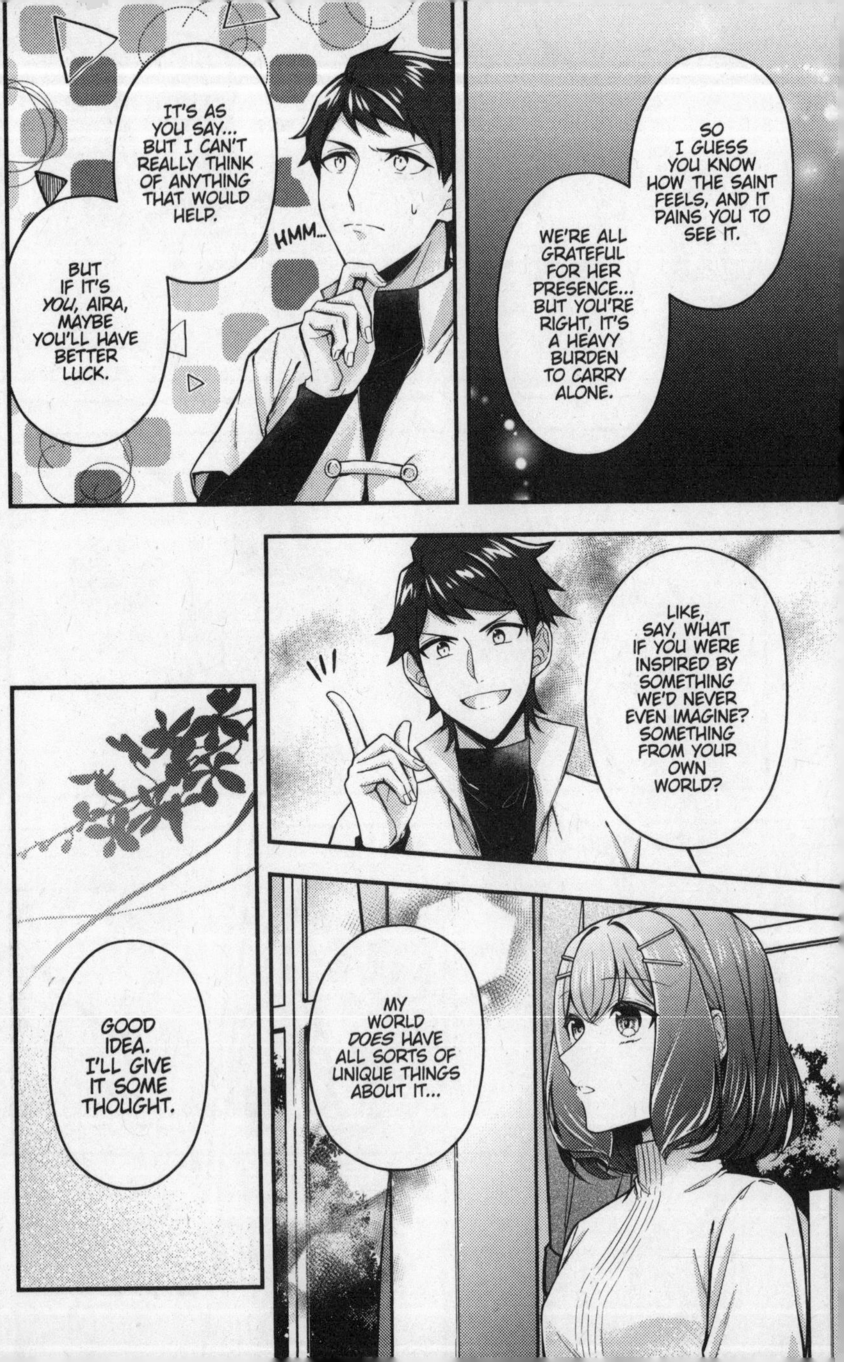
SO I GUESS YOU KNOW HOW THE SAINT FEELS, AND IT PAINS YOU TO SEE IT.
WE'RE ALL GRATEFUL FOR HER PRESENCE... BUT YOU'RE RIGHT, IT'S A HEAVY BURDEN TO CARRY ALONE.
IT'S AS YOU SAY... BUT I CAN'T REALLY THINK OF ANYTHING THAT WOULD HELP.
HMM...
BUT IF IT'S *YOU*, AIRA, MAYBE YOU'LL HAVE BETTER LUCK.
LIKE, SAY, WHAT IF YOU WERE INSPIRED BY SOMETHING WE'D NEVER EVEN IMAGINE? SOMETHING FROM YOUR OWN WORLD?
MY WORLD *DOES* HAVE ALL SORTS OF UNIQUE THINGS ABOUT IT...
GOOD IDEA. I'LL GIVE IT SOME THOUGHT.

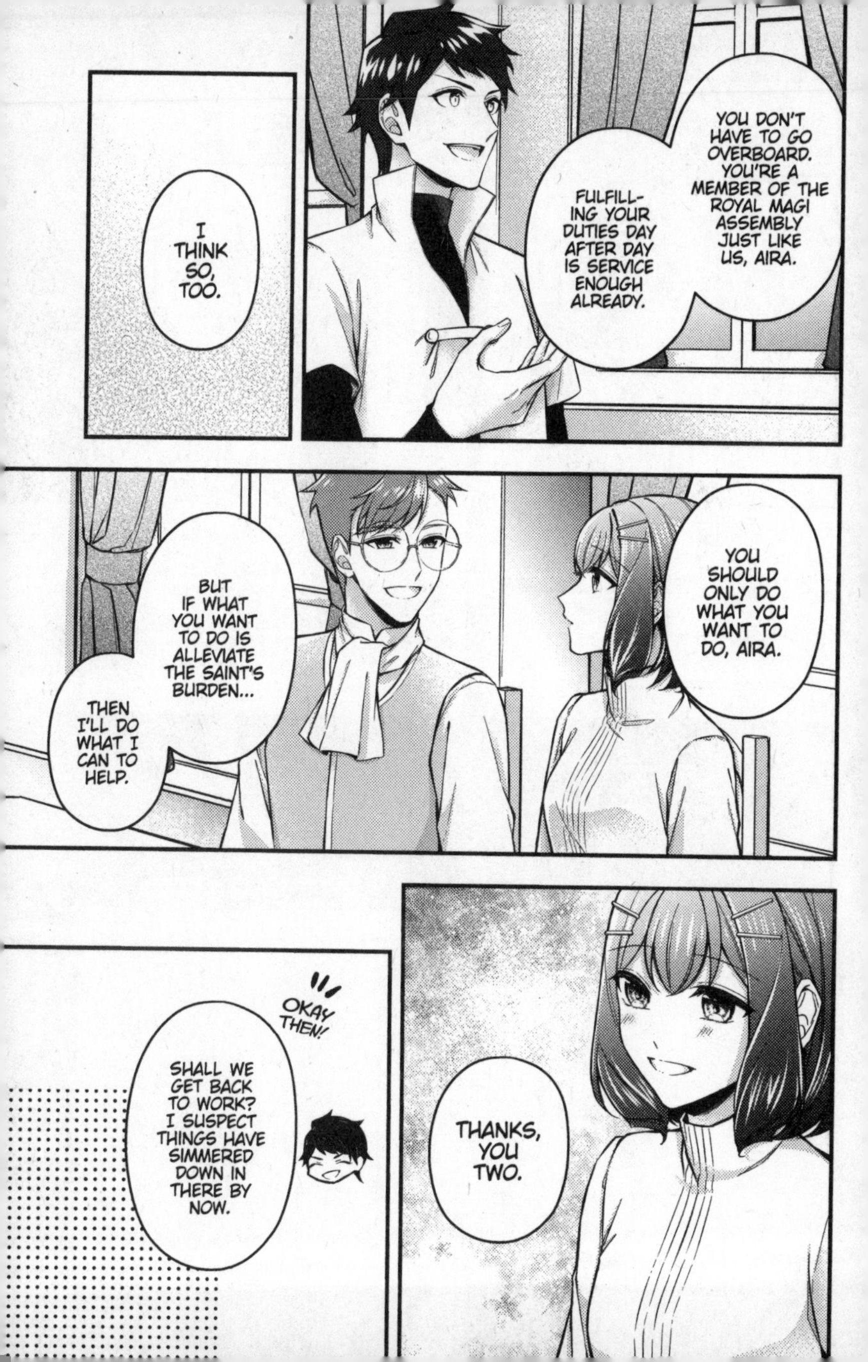
YOU DON'T HAVE TO GO OVERBOARD. YOU'RE A MEMBER OF THE ROYAL MAGI ASSEMBLY JUST LIKE US, AIRA.
FULFILL-ING YOUR DUTIES DAY AFTER DAY IS SERVICE ENOUGH ALREADY.
I THINK SO, TOO.
YOU SHOULD ONLY DO WHAT YOU WANT TO DO, AIRA.
BUT IF WHAT YOU WANT TO DO IS ALLEVIATE THE SAINT'S BURDEN...
THEN I'LL DO WHAT I CAN TO HELP.
THANKS, YOU TWO.
OKAY THEN!
SHALL WE GET BACK TO WORK? I SUSPECT THINGS HAVE SIMMERED DOWN IN THERE BY NOW.

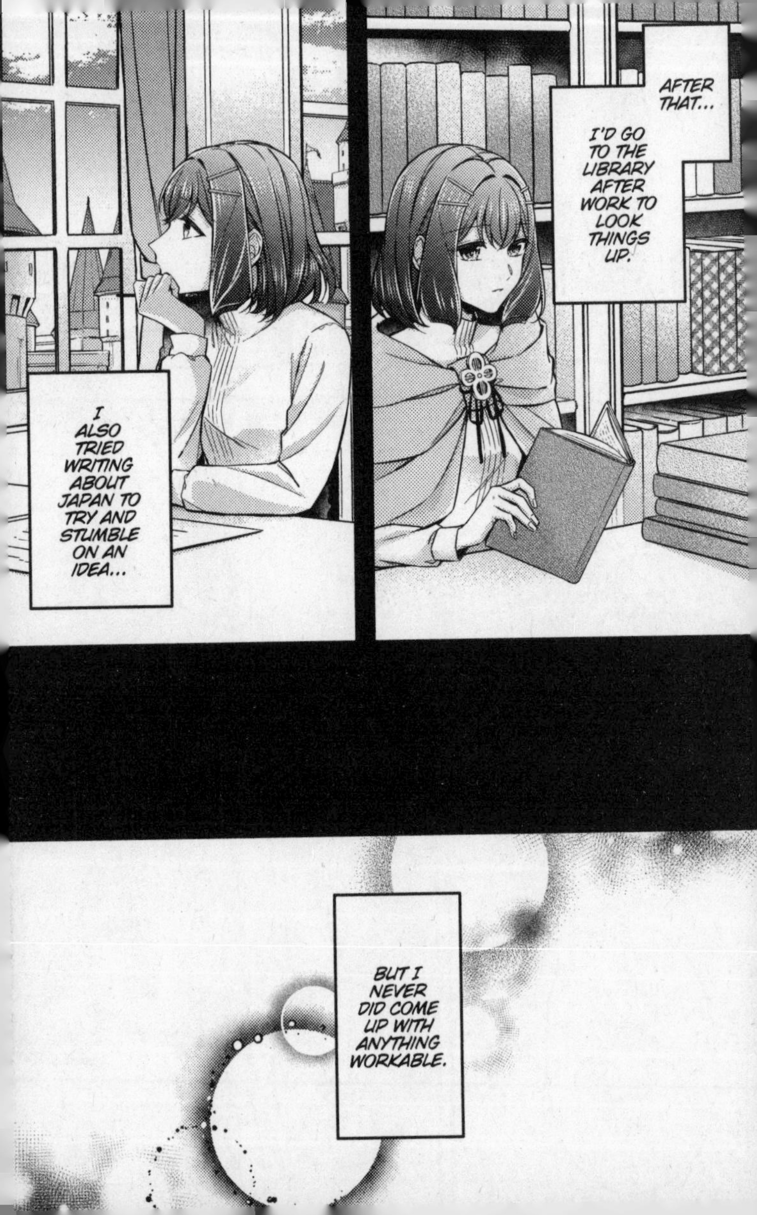
AFTER THAT...
I'D GO TO THE LIBRARY AFTER WORK TO LOOK THINGS UP.
I ALSO TRIED WRITING ABOUT JAPAN TO TRY AND STUMBLE ON AN IDEA...
BUT I NEVER DID COME UP WITH ANYTHING WORKABLE.

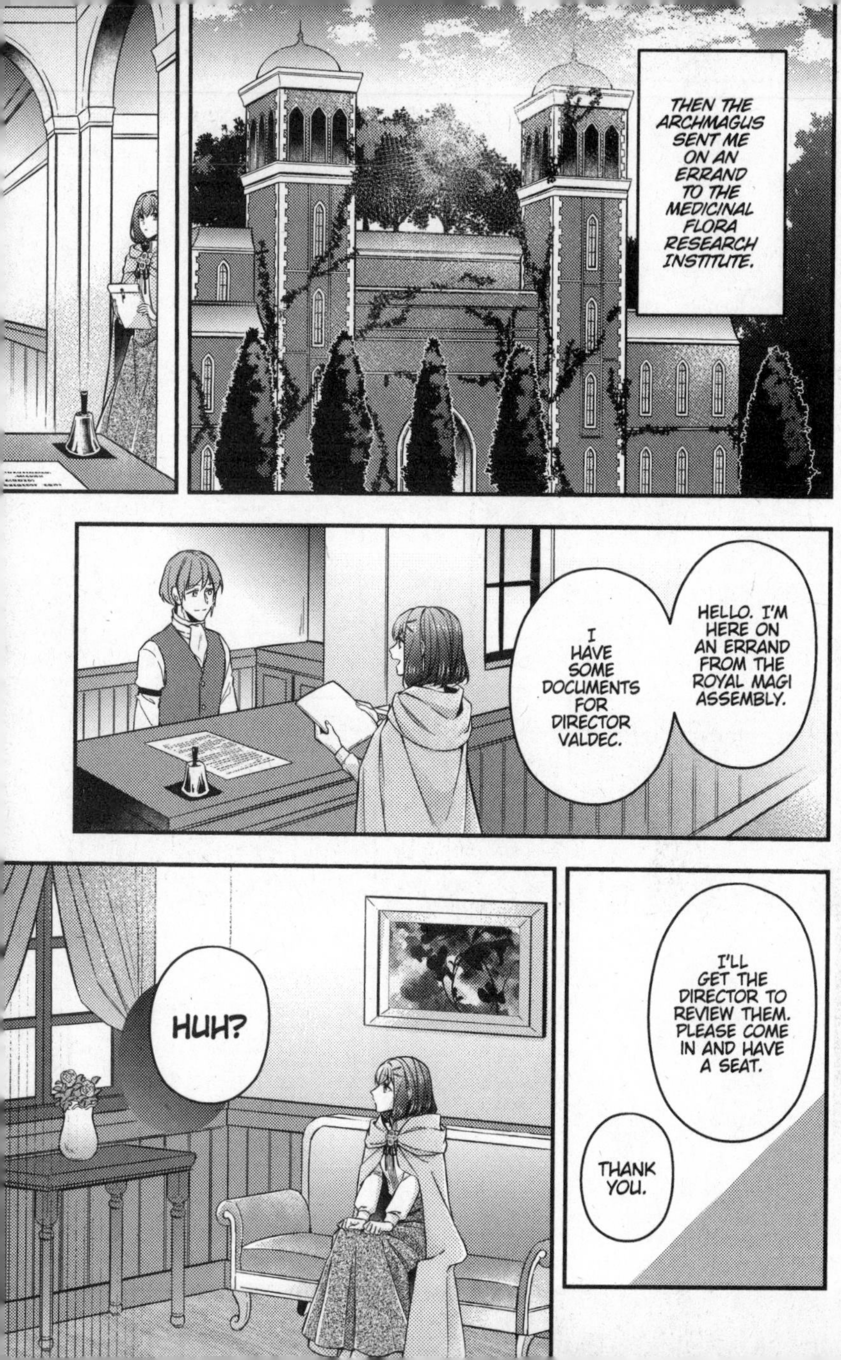
THEN THE ARCHMAGUS SENT ME ON AN ERRAND TO THE MEDICINAL FLORA RESEARCH INSTITUTE.
HELLO. I'M HERE ON AN ERRAND FROM THE ROYAL MAGI ASSEMBLY.
I HAVE SOME DOCUMENTS FOR DIRECTOR VALDEC.
I'LL GET THE DIRECTOR TO REVIEW THEM. PLEASE COME IN AND HAVE A SEAT.
THANK YOU.
HUH?

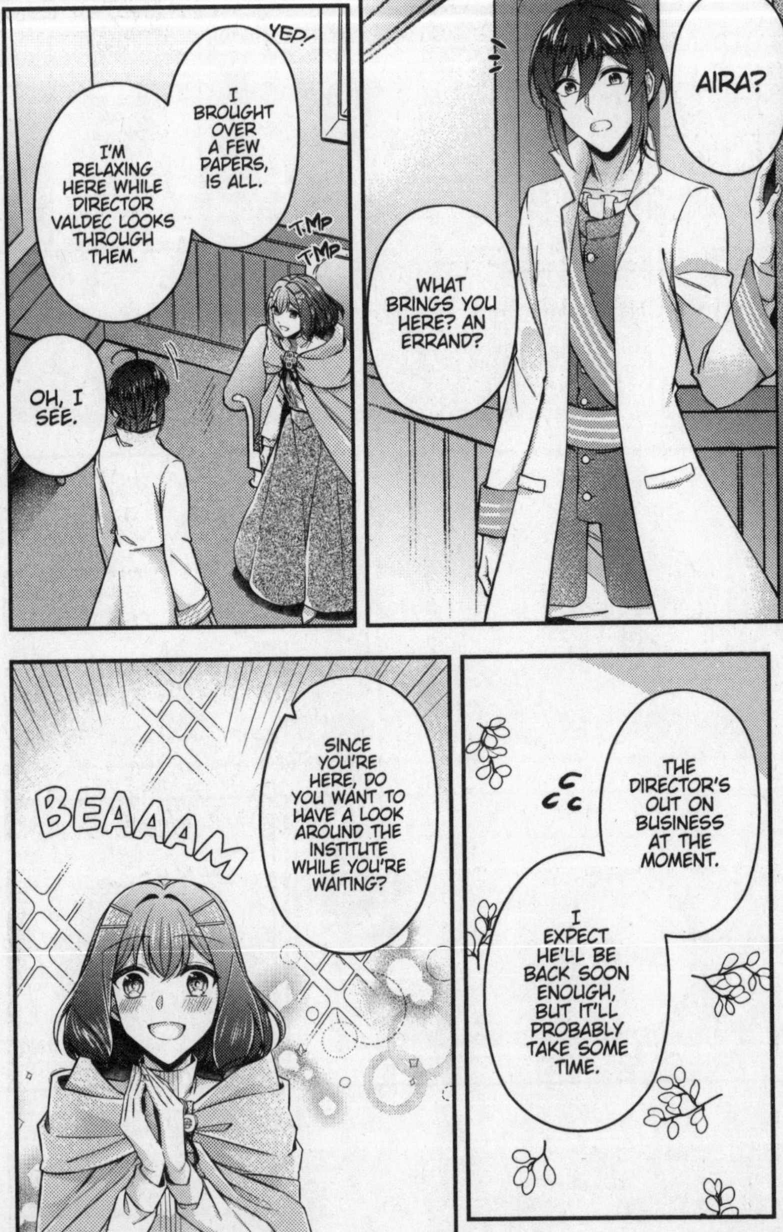
AIRA?
WHAT BRINGS YOU HERE? AN ERRAND?
YEP!
I BROUGHT OVER A FEW PAPERS, IS ALL.
I'M RELAXING HERE WHILE DIRECTOR VALDEC LOOKS THROUGH THEM.
TMP TMP
OH, I SEE.
THE DIRECTOR'S OUT ON BUSINESS AT THE MOMENT.
I EXPECT HE'LL BE BACK SOON ENOUGH, BUT IT'LL PROBABLY TAKE SOME TIME.
SINCE YOU'RE HERE, DO YOU WANT TO HAVE A LOOK AROUND THE INSTITUTE WHILE YOU'RE WAITING?
BEAAAM

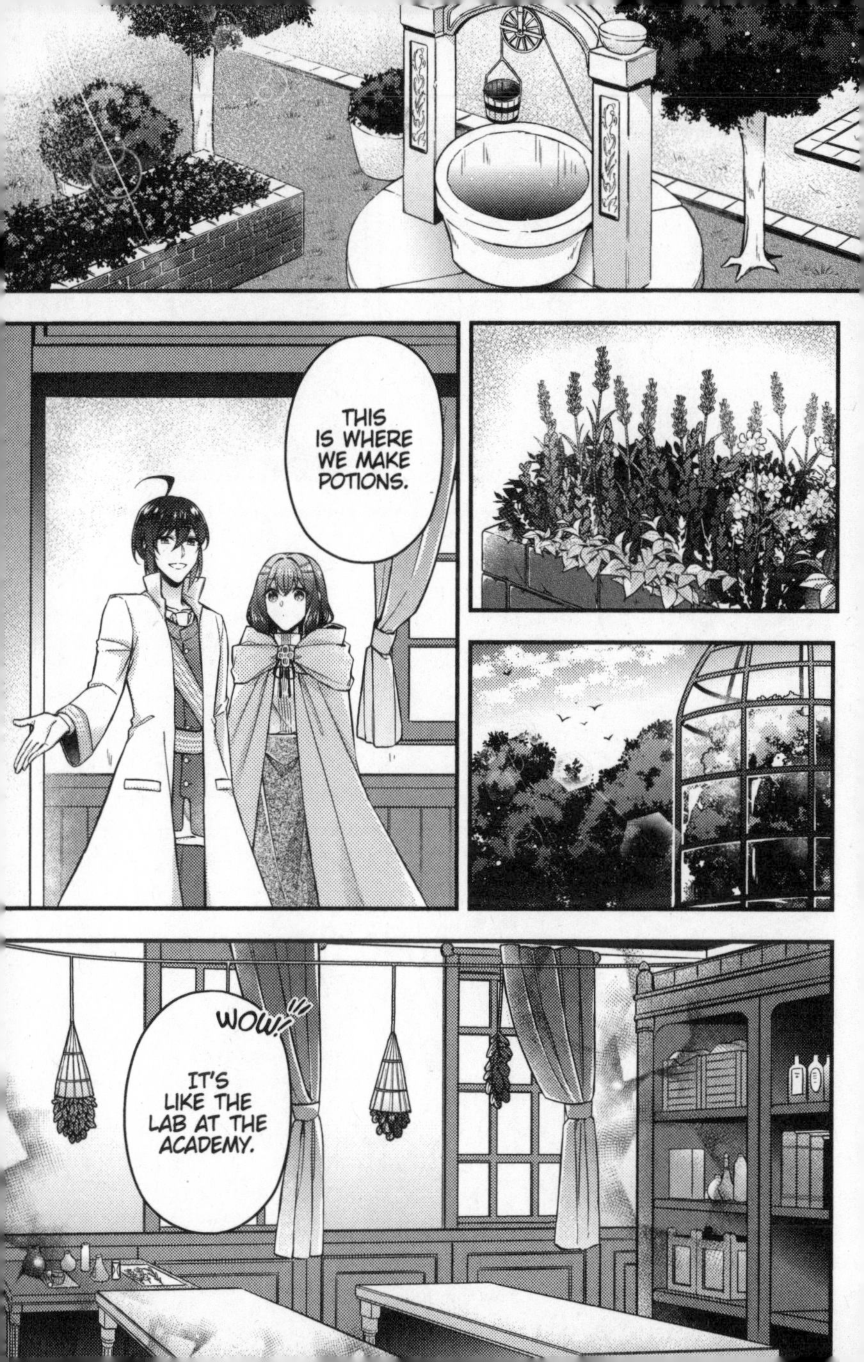
THIS IS WHERE WE MAKE POTIONS.
WOW!!
IT'S LIKE THE LAB AT THE ACADEMY.

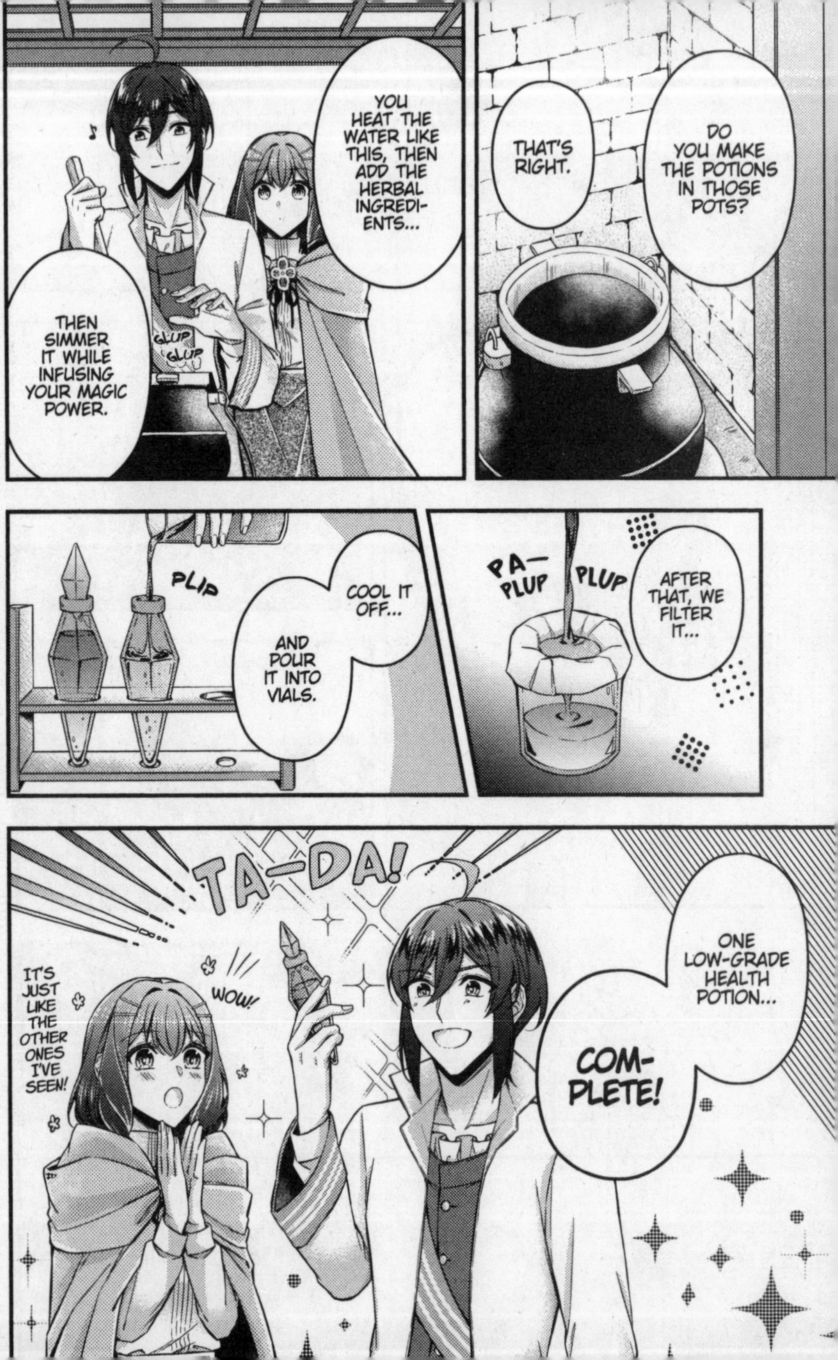
DO YOU MAKE THE POTIONS IN THOSE POTS?
THAT'S RIGHT.
YOU HEAT THE WATER LIKE THIS, THEN ADD THE HERBAL INGREDI-ENTS...
GLUP GLUP
THEN SIMMER IT WHILE INFUSING YOUR MAGIC POWER.
AFTER THAT, WE FILTER IT...
PLUP
PA-PLUP
COOL IT OFF...
AND POUR IT INTO VIALS.
PLIP
ONE LOW-GRADE HEALTH POTION...
COM-PLETE!
TA-DA!
WOW!
IT'S JUST LIKE THE OTHER ONES I'VE SEEN!

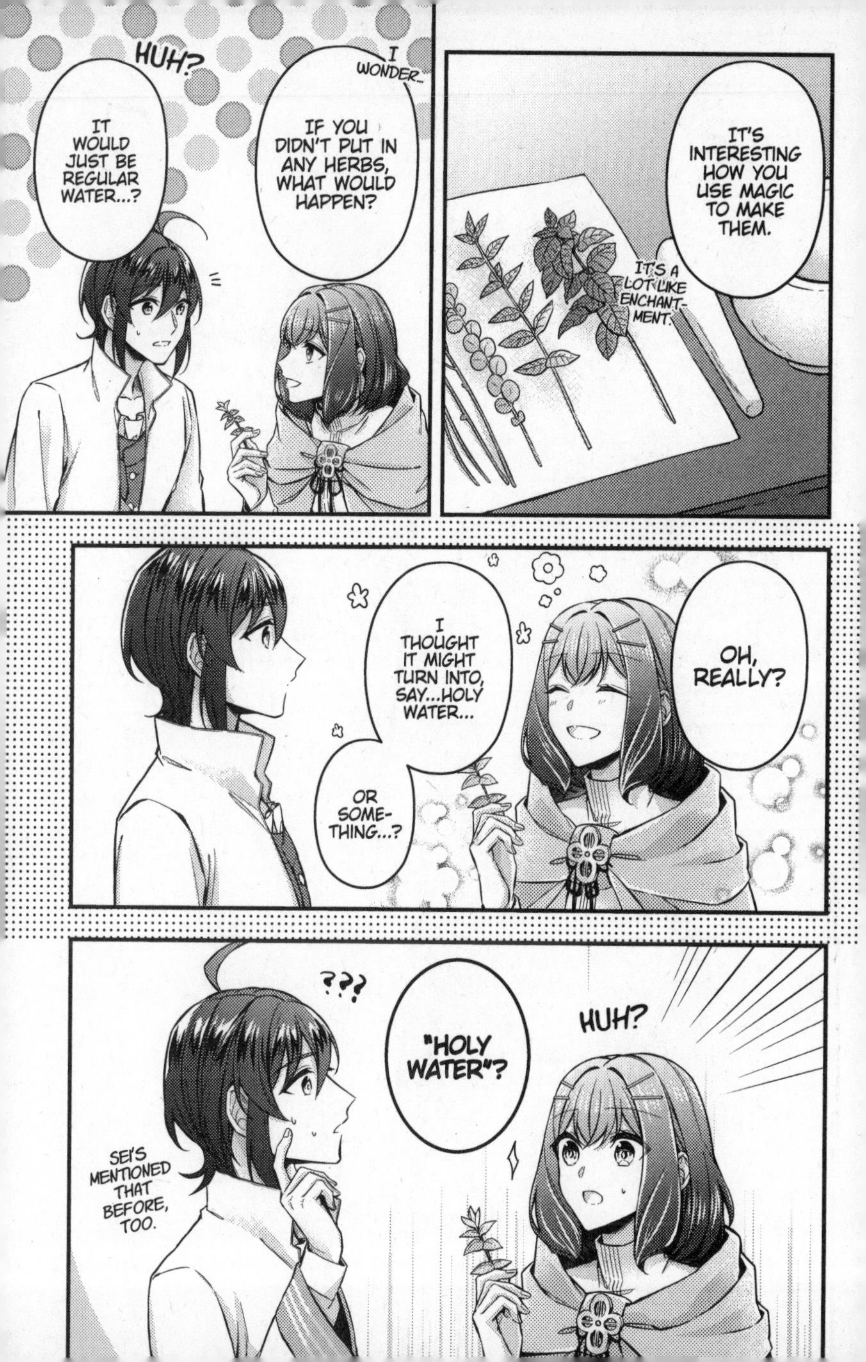
IT'S INTERESTING HOW YOU USE MAGIC TO MAKE THEM.
IT'S A LOT LIKE ENCHANTMENT.
I WONDER...
IF YOU DIDN'T PUT IN ANY HERBS, WHAT WOULD HAPPEN?
HUH?
IT WOULD JUST BE REGULAR WATER...?
OH, REALLY?
I THOUGHT IT MIGHT TURN INTO, SAY...HOLY WATER...
OR SOMETHING...?
HUH?
"HOLY WATER"?
???
SEI'S MENTIONED THAT BEFORE, TOO.

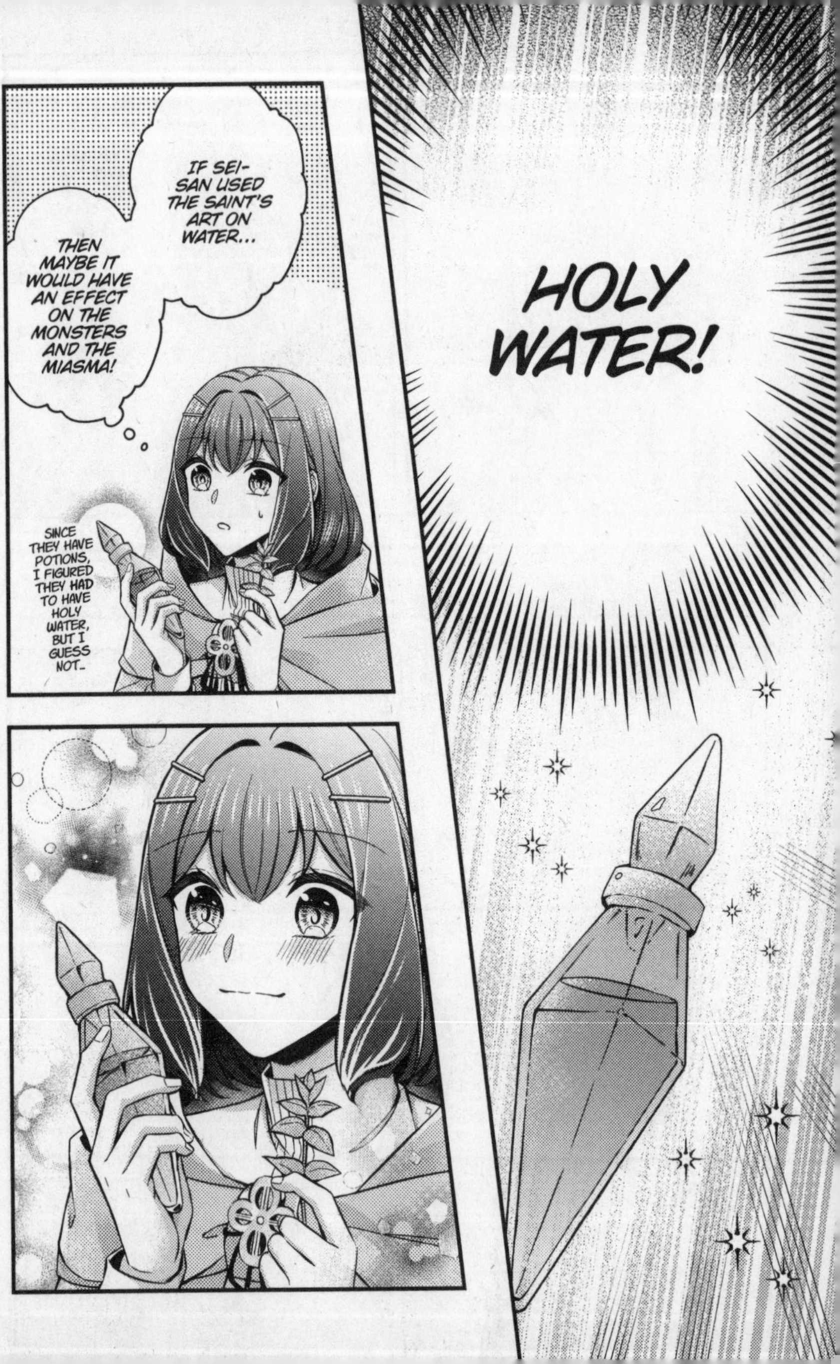

IF SEI-SAN USED THE SAINT'S ART ON WATER...
THEN MAYBE IT WOULD HAVE AN EFFECT ON THE MONSTERS AND THE MIASMA!
SINCE THEY HAVE POTIONS, I FIGURED THEY HAD TO HAVE HOLY WATER, BUT I GUESS NOT...
HOLY WATER!

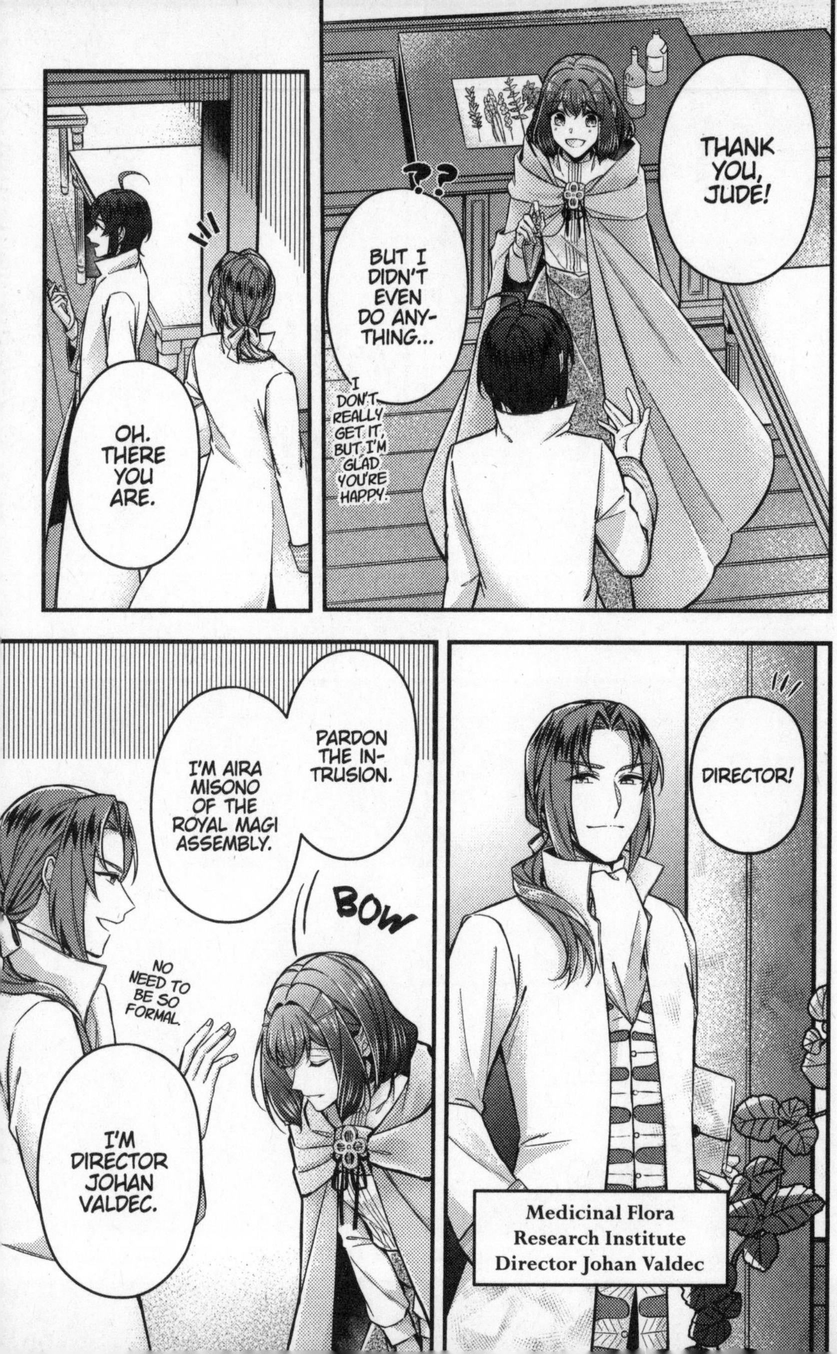
THANK YOU, JUDE!
??
BUT I DIDN'T EVEN DO ANYTHING...
I DON'T REALLY GET IT, BUT I'M GLAD YOU'RE HAPPY.
OH. THERE YOU ARE.
DIRECTOR!
Medicinal Flora Research Institute Director Johan Valdec
PARDON THE INTRUSION.
I'M AIRA MISONO OF THE ROYAL MAGI ASSEMBLY.
BOW
NO NEED TO BE SO FORMAL.
I'M DIRECTOR JOHAN VALDEC.

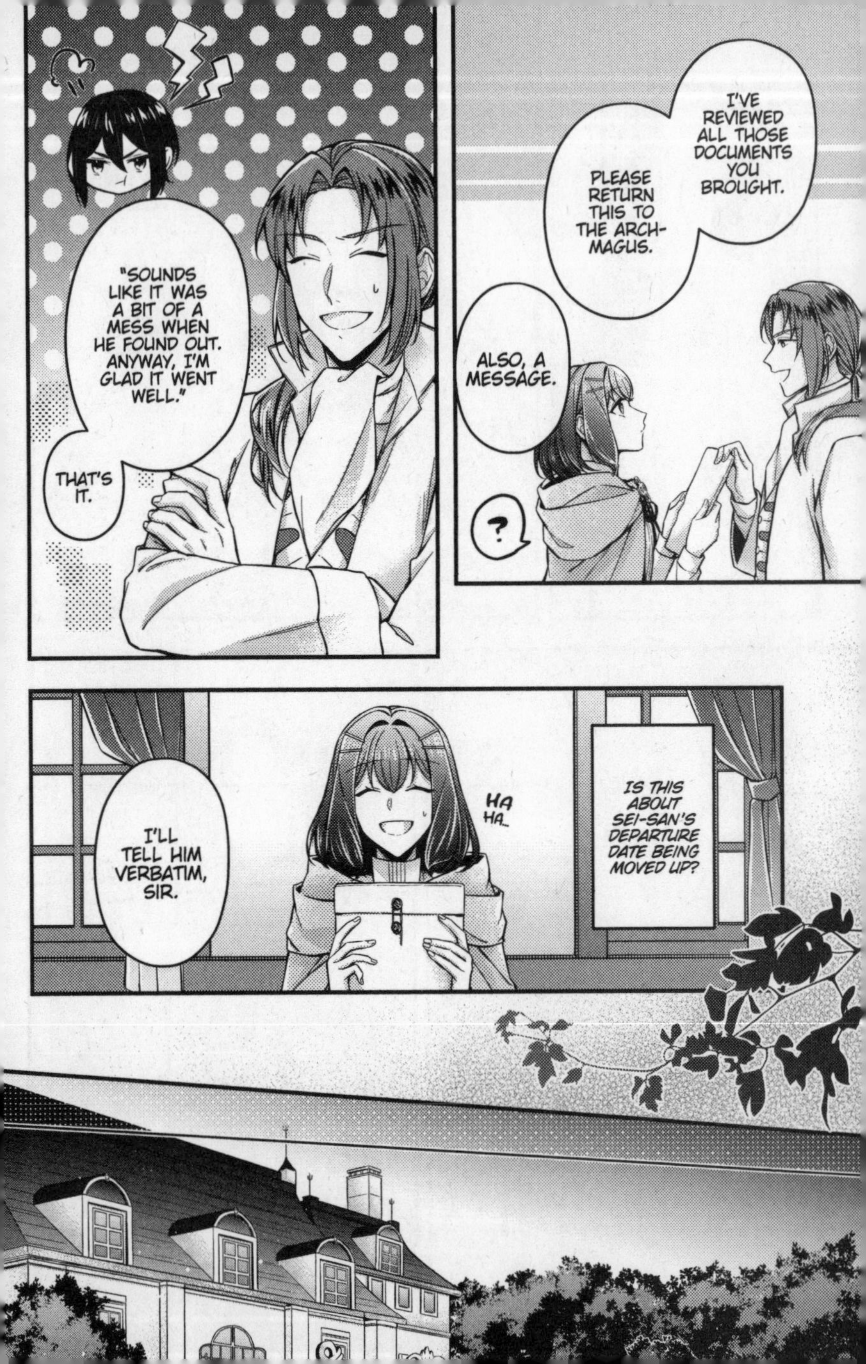
I'VE REVIEWED ALL THOSE DOCUMENTS YOU BROUGHT.
PLEASE RETURN THIS TO THE ARCH-MAGUS.
ALSO, A MESSAGE.
?
"SOUNDS LIKE IT WAS A BIT OF A MESS WHEN HE FOUND OUT. ANYWAY, I'M GLAD IT WENT WELL."
THAT'S IT.
IS THIS ABOUT SEI-SAN'S DEPARTURE DATE BEING MOVED UP?
HA HA...
I'LL TELL HIM VERBATIM, SIR.

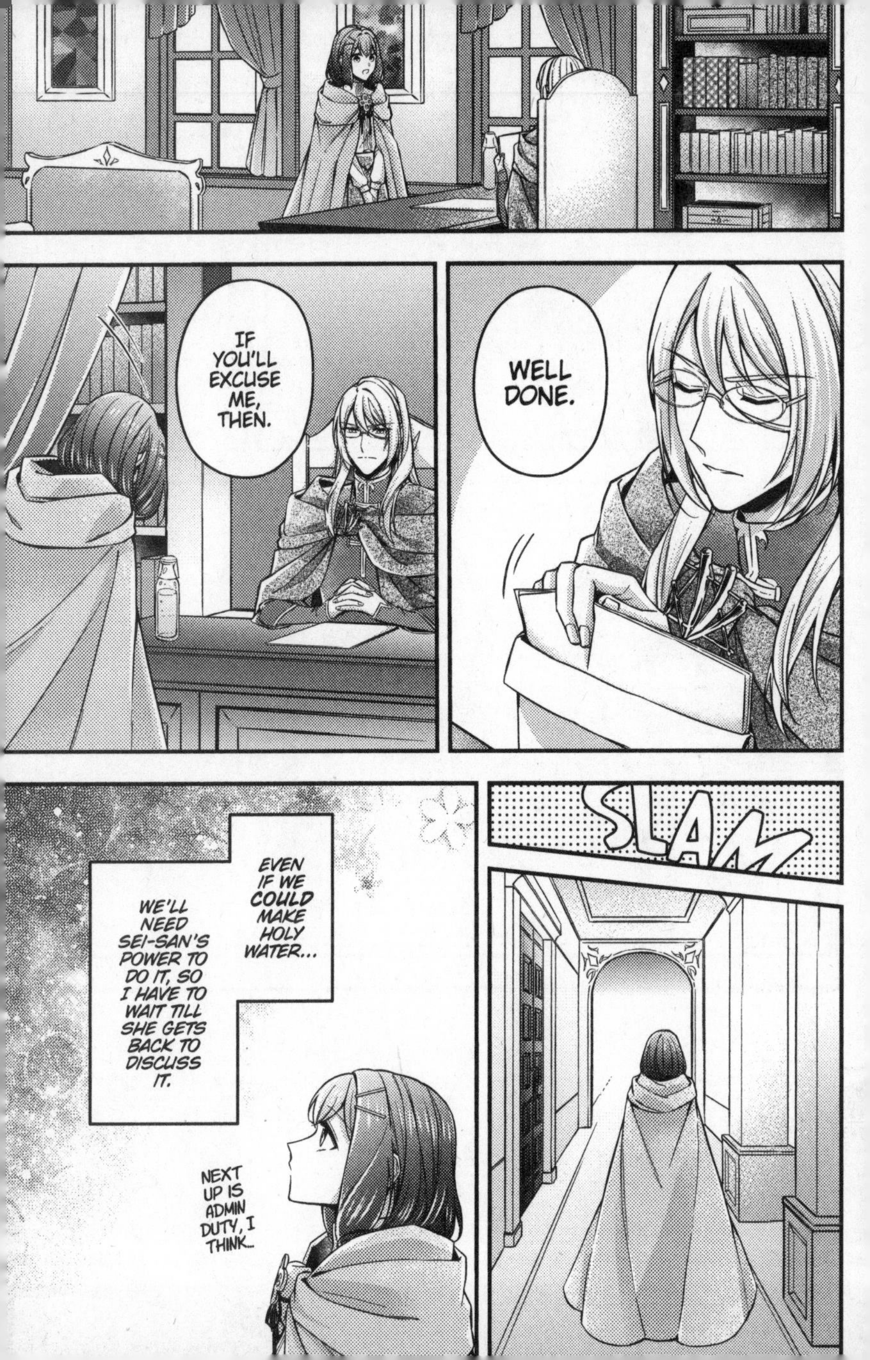
WELL DONE.
IF YOU'LL EXCUSE ME, THEN.
SLAM
EVEN IF WE COULD MAKE HOLY WATER...
WE'LL NEED SEI-SAN'S POWER TO DO IT, SO I HAVE TO WAIT TILL SHE GETS BACK TO DISCUSS IT.
NEXT UP IS ADMIN DUTY, I THINK...

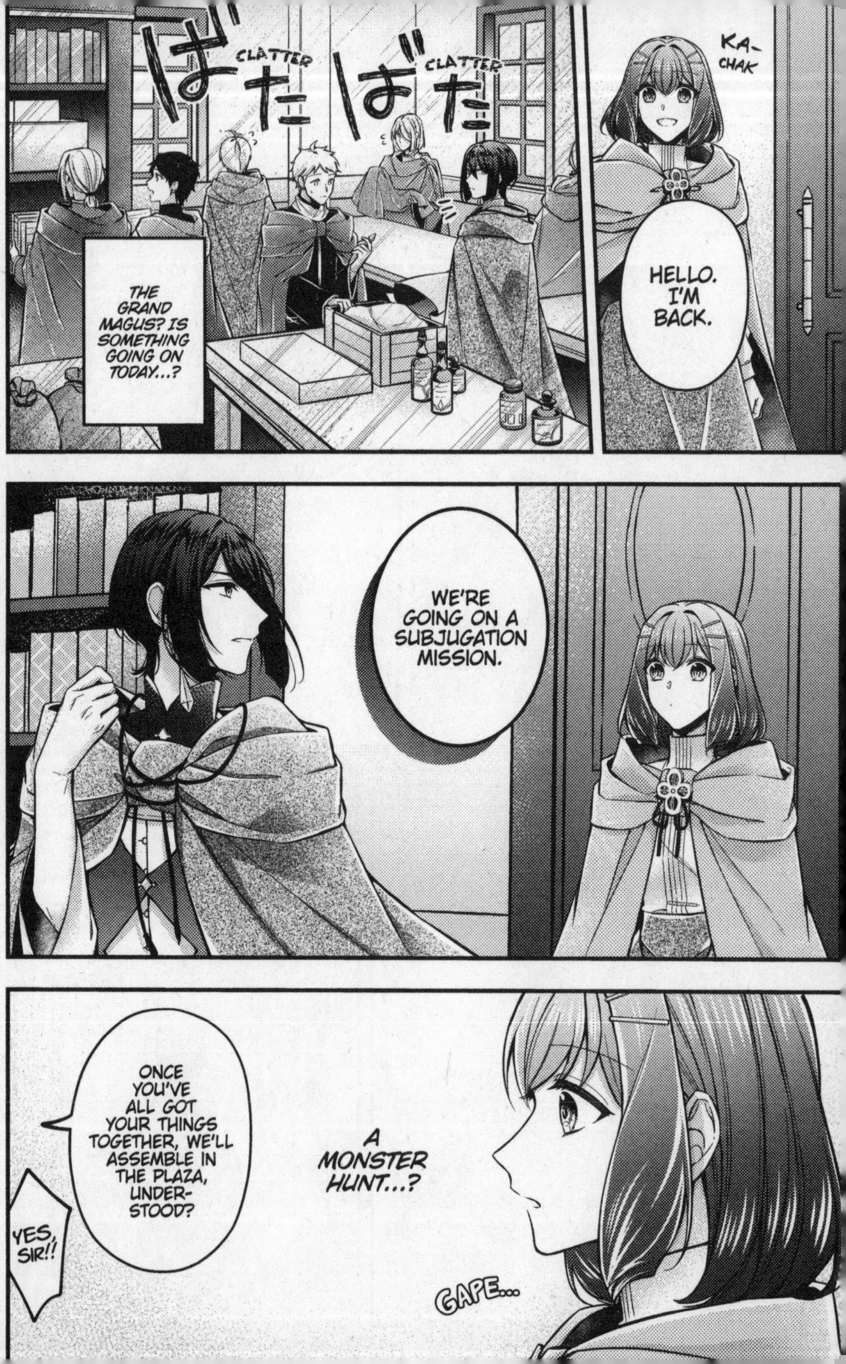
KA-CHAK
HELLO. I'M BACK.
ばたばた
CLATTER CLATTER
THE GRAND MAGUS? IS SOMETHING GOING ON TODAY...?
WE'RE GOING ON A SUBJUGATION MISSION.
A MONSTER HUNT...?
GAPE...
ONCE YOU'VE ALL GOT YOUR THINGS TOGETHER, WE'LL ASSEMBLE IN THE PLAZA, UNDER-STOOD?
YES, SIR!!

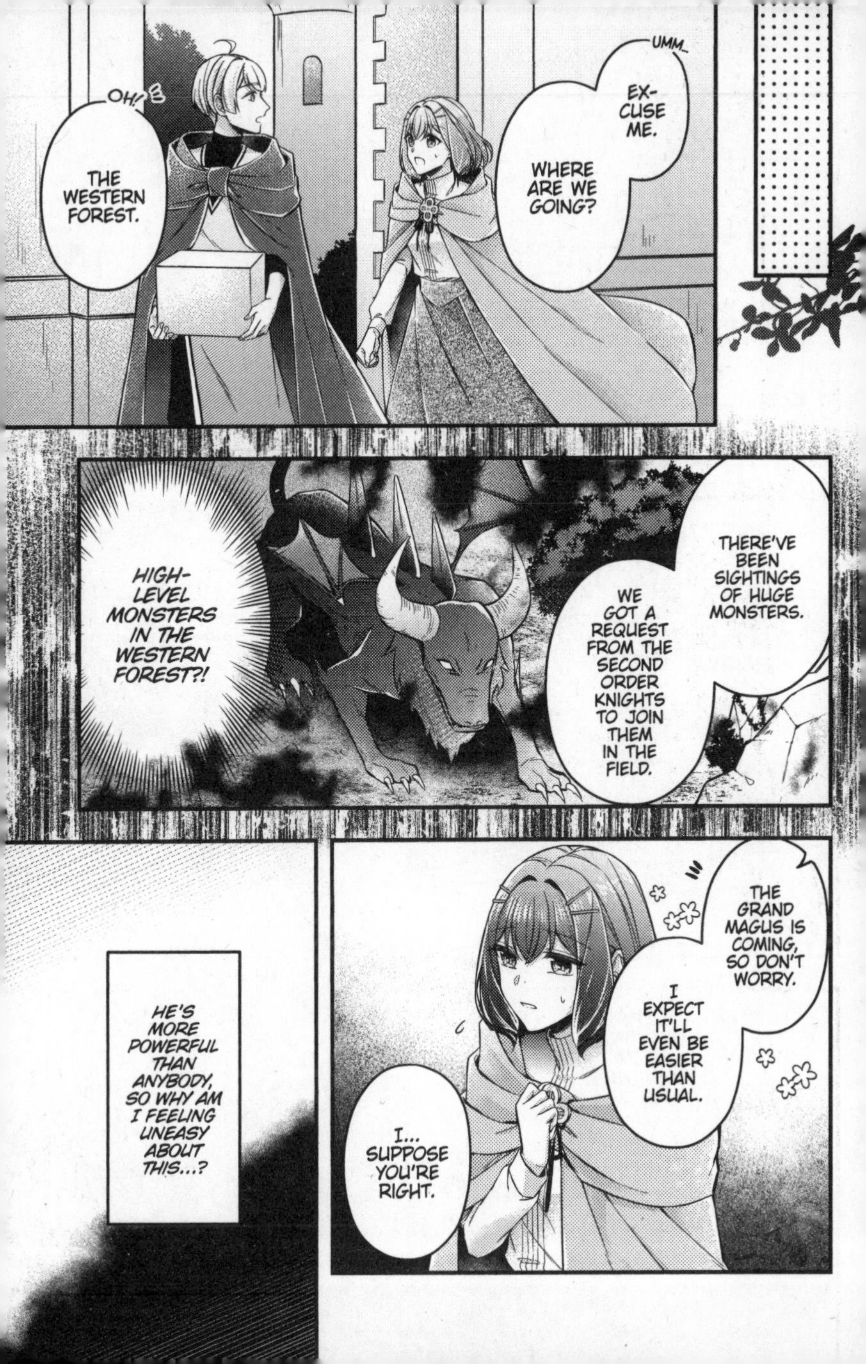
UMM...
EX-CUSE ME. WHERE ARE WE GOING?
OH!
THE WESTERN FOREST.
THERE'VE BEEN SIGHTINGS OF HUGE MONSTERS.
WE GOT A REQUEST FROM THE SECOND ORDER KNIGHTS TO JOIN THEM IN THE FIELD.
HIGH-LEVEL MONSTERS IN THE WESTERN FOREST?!
THE GRAND MAGUS IS COMING, SO DON'T WORRY.
I EXPECT IT'LL EVEN BE EASIER THAN USUAL.
I... SUPPOSE YOU'RE RIGHT.
HE'S MORE POWERFUL THAN ANYBODY, SO WHY AM I FEELING UNEASY ABOUT THIS...?

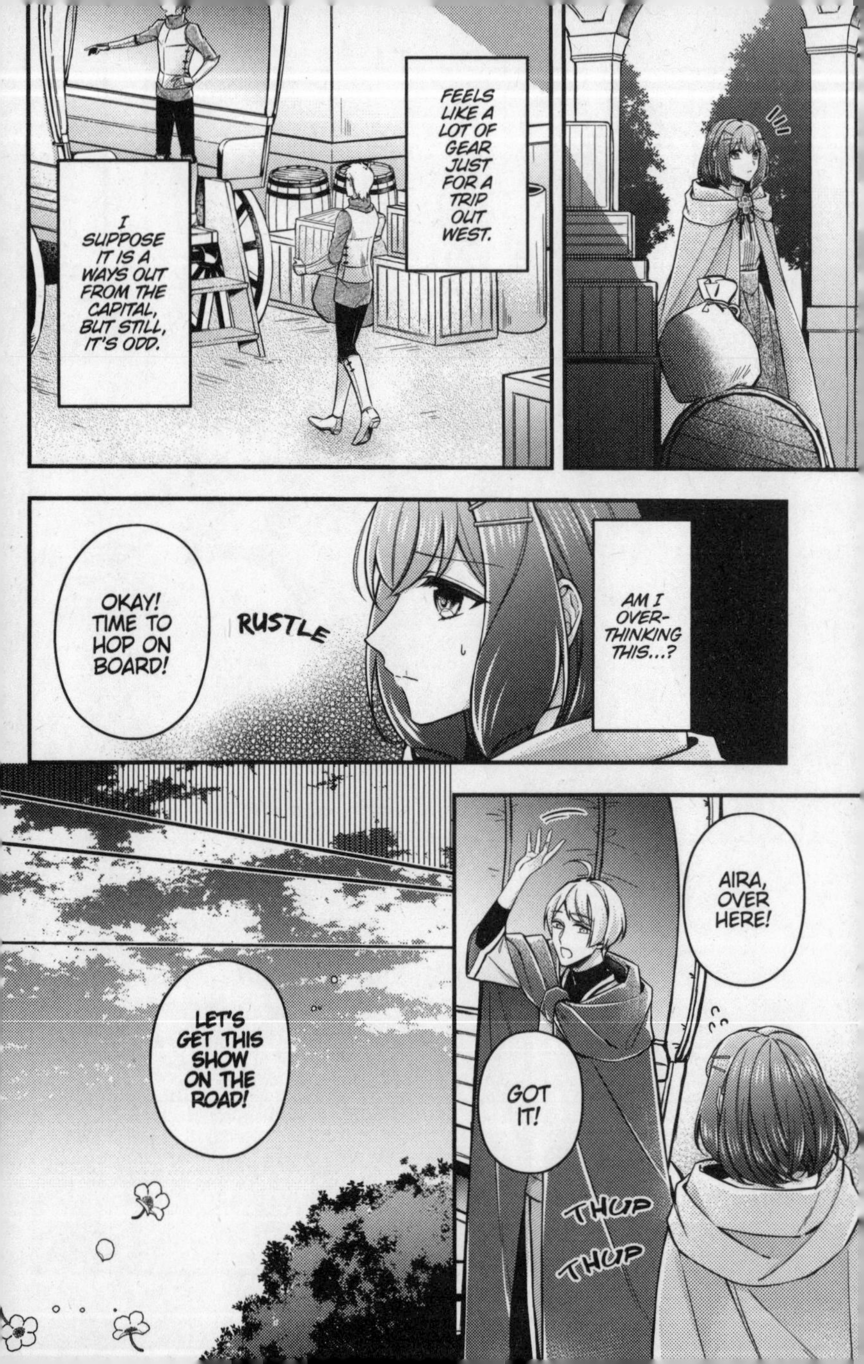
FEELS LIKE A LOT OF GEAR JUST FOR A TRIP OUT WEST.
I SUPPOSE IT IS A WAYS OUT FROM THE CAPITAL, BUT STILL, IT'S ODD.
AM I OVER-THINKING THIS...?
RUSTLE
OKAY! TIME TO HOP ON BOARD!
AIRA, OVER HERE!
GOT IT!
THUP THUP
LET'S GET THIS SHOW ON THE ROAD!

The **Saint's**
Magic Power is
Omnipotent
The Other Saint

The **Saint's** *Magic Power is * **Omnipotent**
~ The Other Saint ~

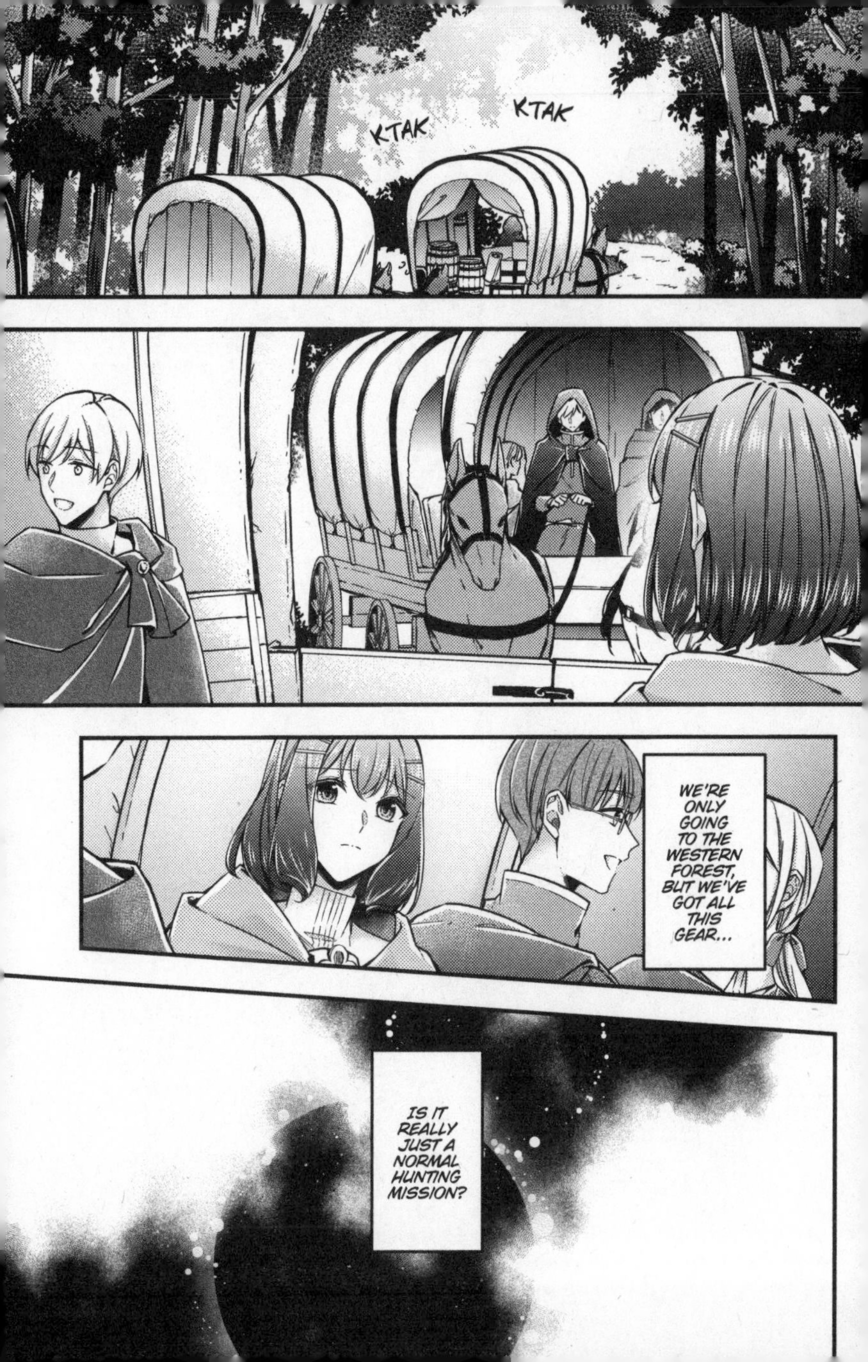
KTAK
KTAK
WE'RE ONLY GOING TO THE WESTERN FOREST, BUT WE'VE GOT ALL THIS GEAR...
IS IT REALLY JUST A NORMAL HUNTING MISSION?

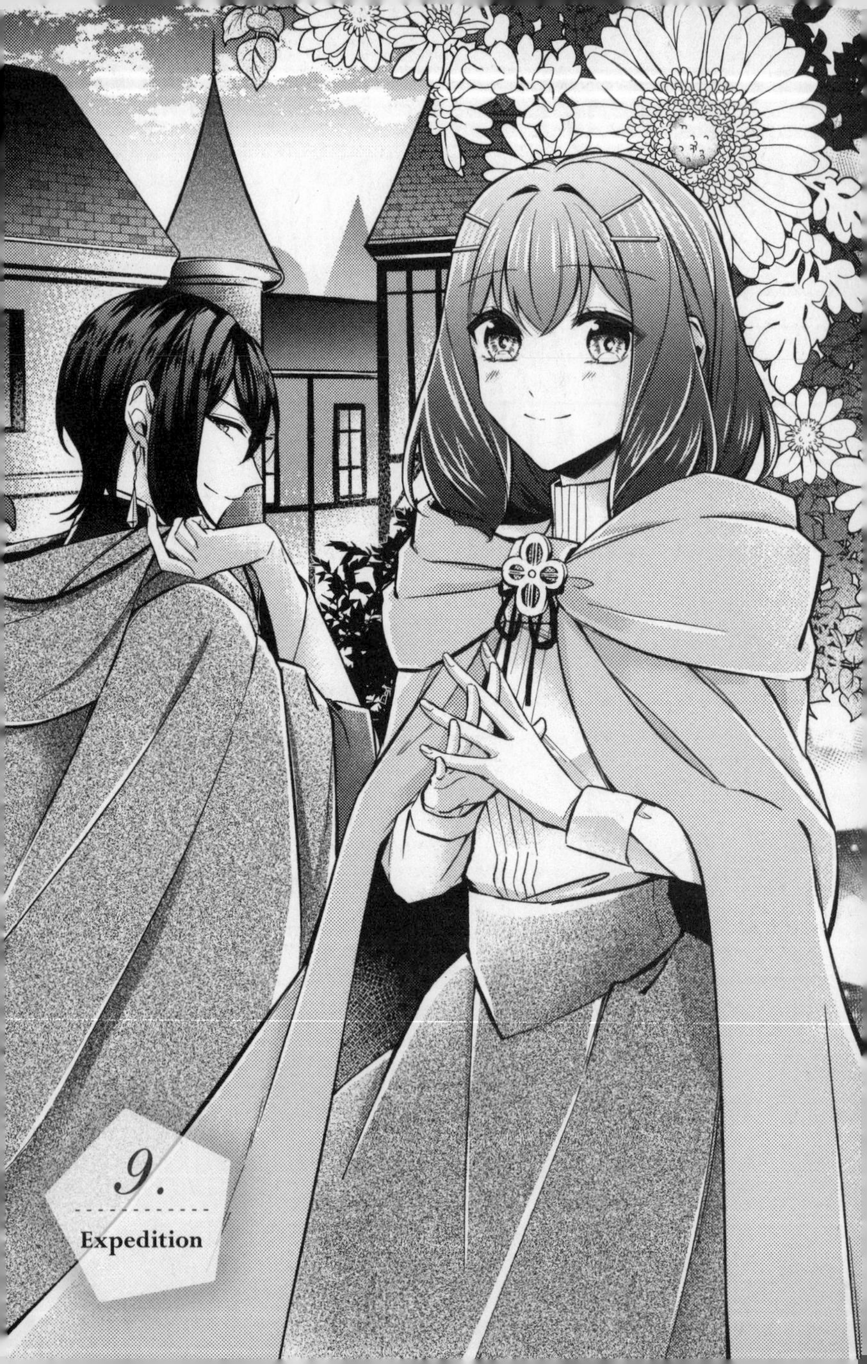
9.
Expedition

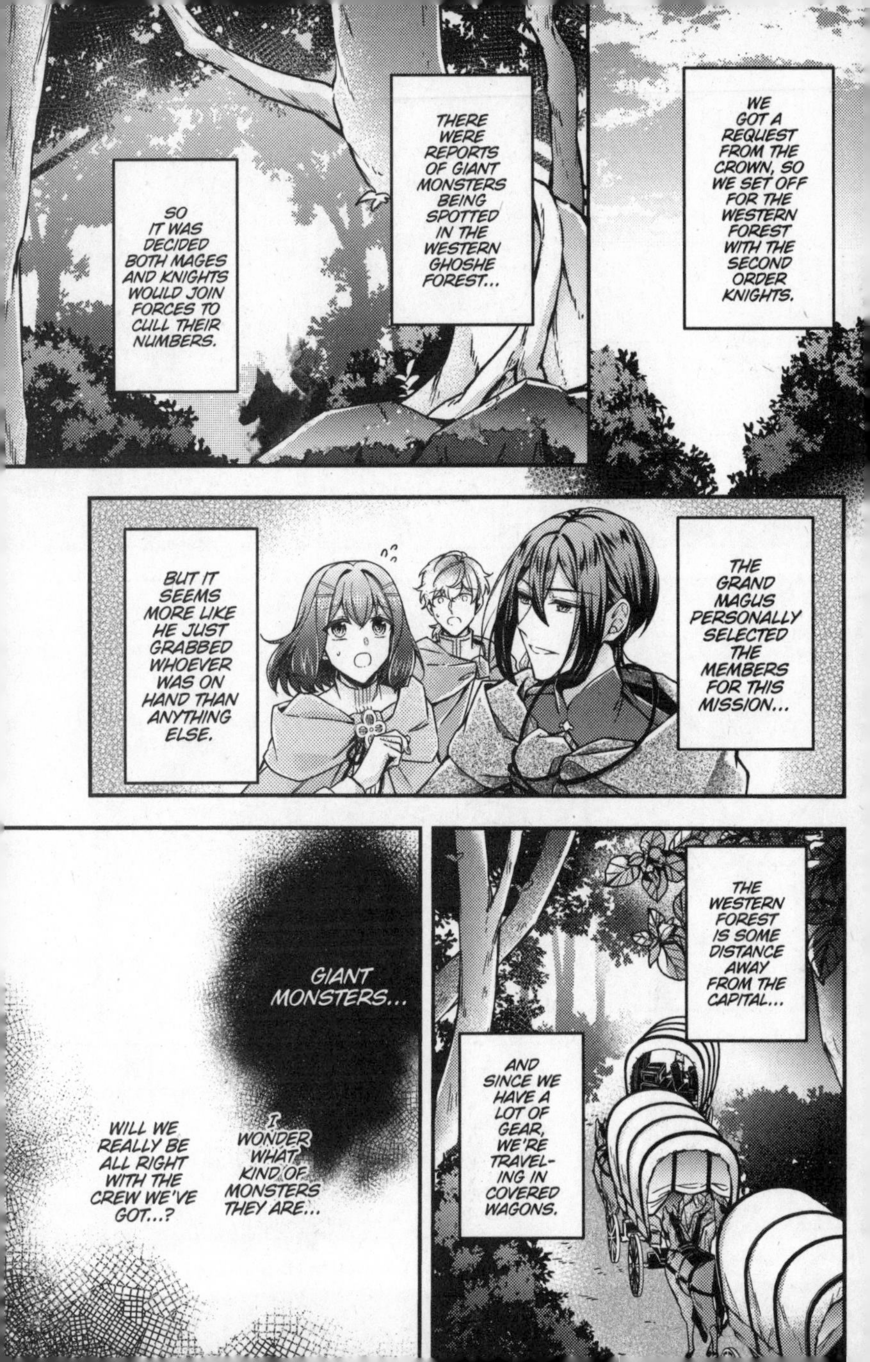
WE GOT A REQUEST FROM THE CROWN, SO WE SET OFF FOR THE WESTERN FOREST WITH THE SECOND ORDER KNIGHTS.
THERE WERE REPORTS OF GIANT MONSTERS BEING SPOTTED IN THE WESTERN GHOSHE FOREST...
SO IT WAS DECIDED BOTH MAGES AND KNIGHTS WOULD JOIN FORCES TO CULL THEIR NUMBERS.
THE GRAND MAGUS PERSONALLY SELECTED THE MEMBERS FOR THIS MISSION...
BUT IT SEEMS MORE LIKE HE JUST GRABBED WHOEVER WAS ON HAND THAN ANYTHING ELSE.
THE WESTERN FOREST IS SOME DISTANCE AWAY FROM THE CAPITAL...
AND SINCE WE HAVE A LOT OF GEAR, WE'RE TRAVEL-ING IN COVERED WAGONS.
GIANT MONSTERS...
I WONDER WHAT KIND OF MONSTERS THEY ARE...
WILL WE REALLY BE ALL RIGHT WITH THE CREW WE'VE GOT...?

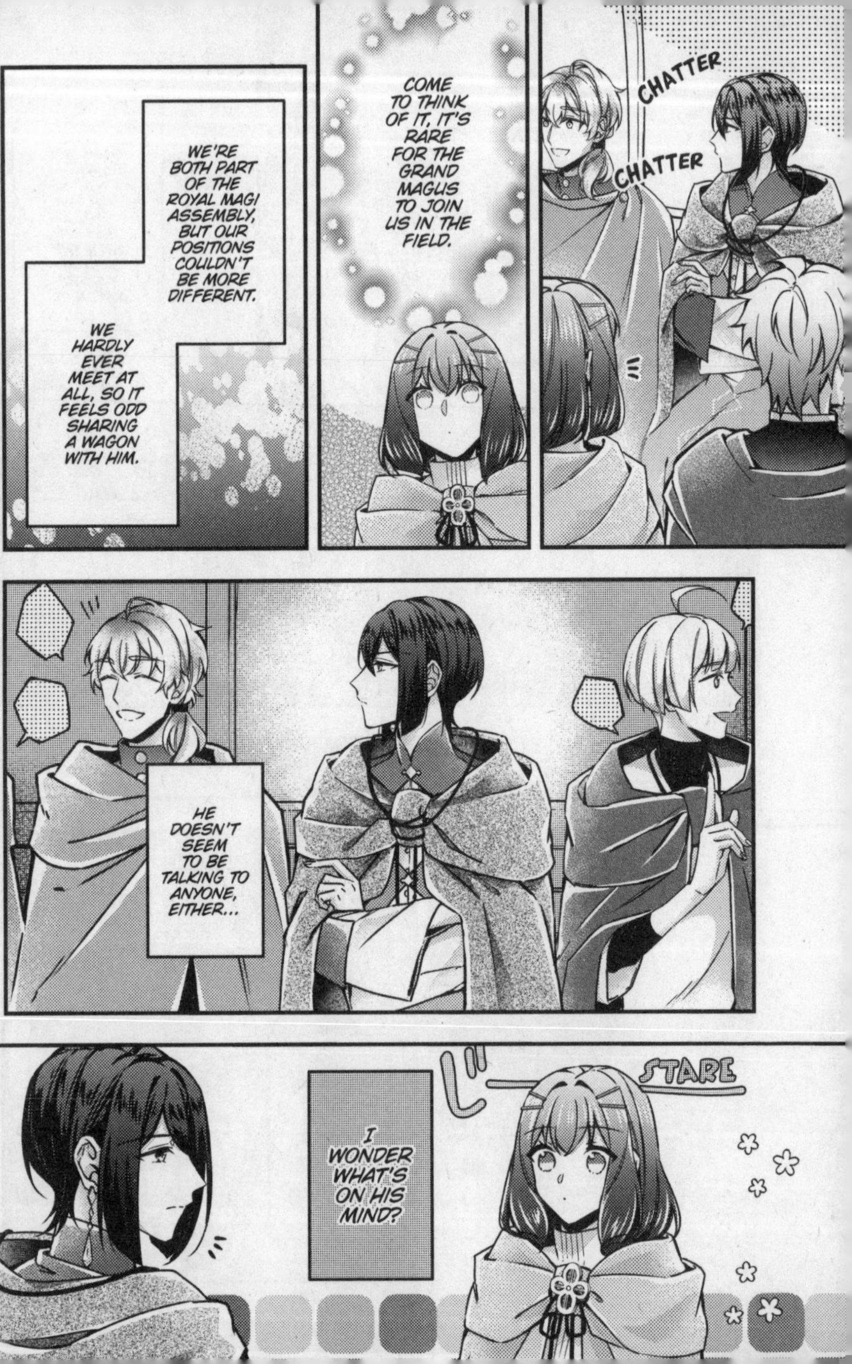
CHATTER
CHATTER
COME TO THINK OF IT, IT'S RARE FOR THE GRAND MAGUS TO JOIN US IN THE FIELD.
WE'RE BOTH PART OF THE ROYAL MAGI ASSEMBLY, BUT OUR POSITIONS COULDN'T BE MORE DIFFERENT.
WE HARDLY EVER MEET AT ALL, SO IT FEELS ODD SHARING A WAGON WITH HIM.
HE DOESN'T SEEM TO BE TALKING TO ANYONE, EITHER...
STARE
I WONDER WHAT'S ON HIS MIND?

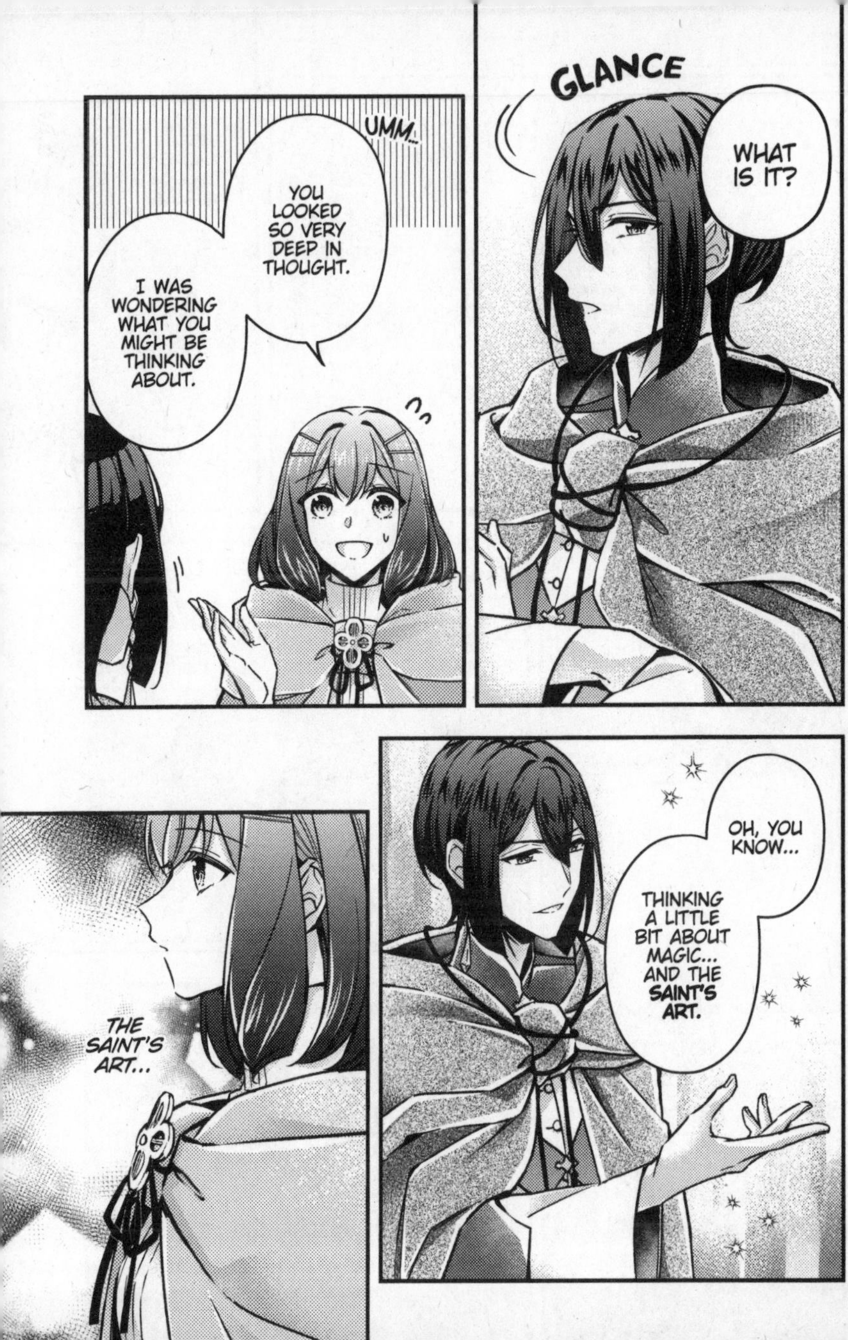
GLANCE
WHAT IS IT?
UMM...
YOU LOOKED SO VERY DEEP IN THOUGHT.
I WAS WONDERING WHAT YOU MIGHT BE THINKING ABOUT.
OH, YOU KNOW...
THINKING A LITTLE BIT ABOUT MAGIC... AND THE SAINT'S ART.
THE SAINT'S ART...

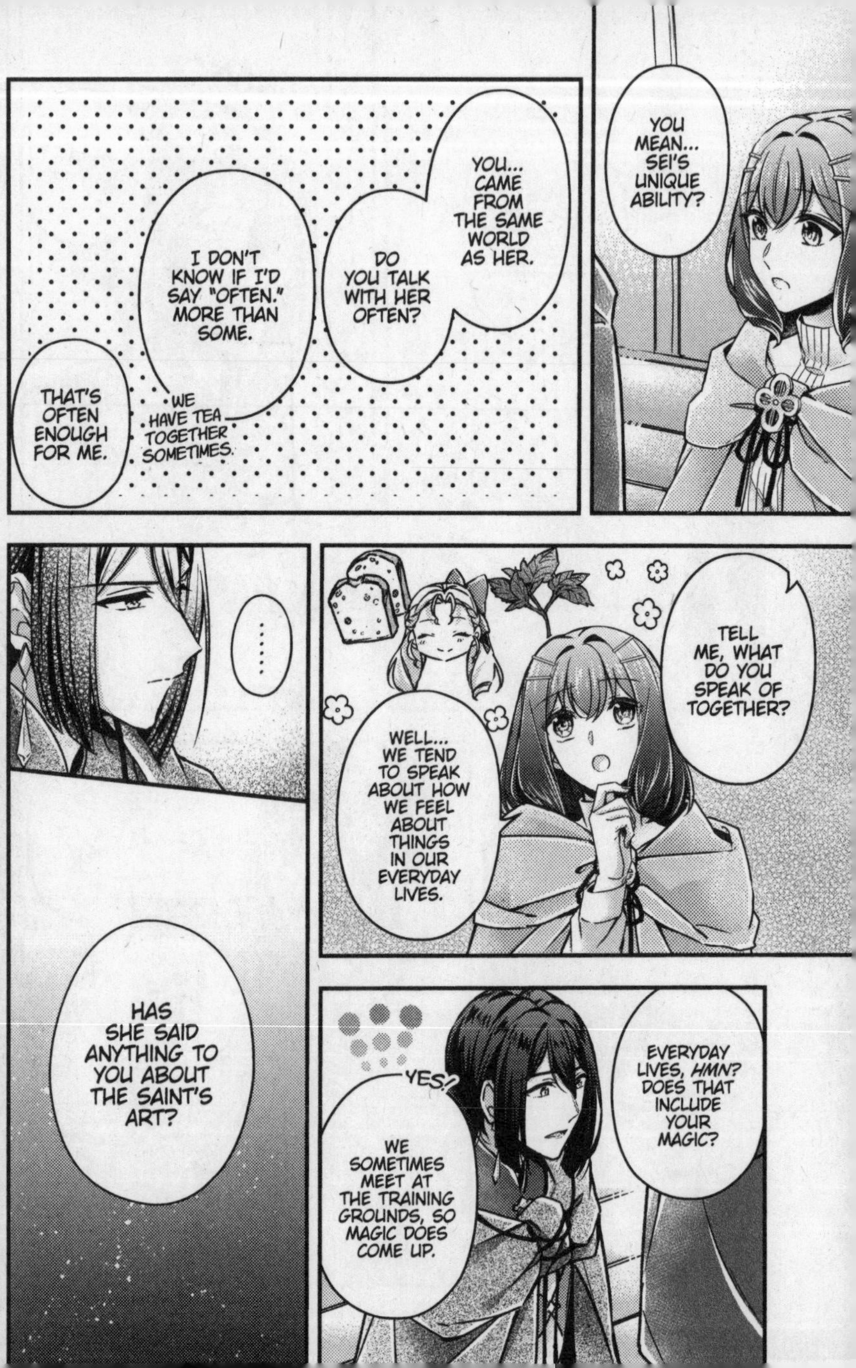
YOU MEAN... SEI'S UNIQUE ABILITY?
YOU... CAME FROM THE SAME WORLD AS HER.
DO YOU TALK WITH HER OFTEN?
I DON'T KNOW IF I'D SAY "OFTEN." MORE THAN SOME.
WE HAVE TEA TOGETHER SOMETIMES.
THAT'S OFTEN ENOUGH FOR ME.
TELL ME, WHAT DO YOU SPEAK OF TOGETHER?
WELL... WE TEND TO SPEAK ABOUT HOW WE FEEL ABOUT THINGS IN OUR EVERYDAY LIVES.
EVERYDAY LIVES, *HMN*? DOES THAT INCLUDE YOUR MAGIC?
YES!
WE SOMETIMES MEET AT THE TRAINING GROUNDS, SO MAGIC DOES COME UP.
......
HAS SHE SAID ANYTHING TO YOU ABOUT THE SAINT'S ART?

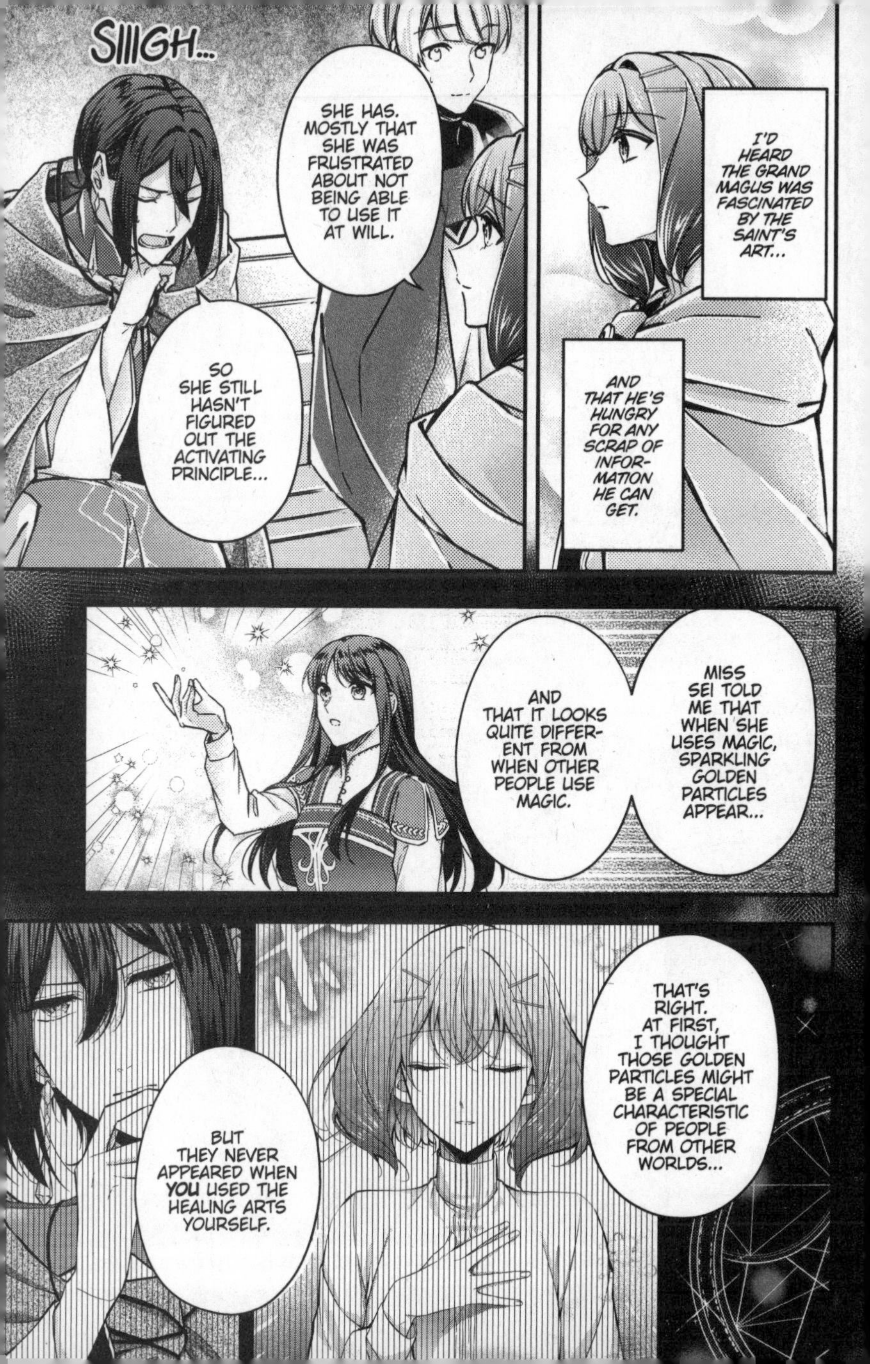
I'D HEARD THE GRAND MAGUS WAS FASCINATED BY THE SAINT'S ART...
AND THAT HE'S HUNGRY FOR ANY SCRAP OF INFORMATION HE CAN GET.
SHE HAS. MOSTLY THAT SHE WAS FRUSTRATED ABOUT NOT BEING ABLE TO USE IT AT WILL.
SIIIGH...
SO SHE STILL HASN'T FIGURED OUT THE ACTIVATING PRINCIPLE...
MISS SEI TOLD ME THAT WHEN SHE USES MAGIC, SPARKLING GOLDEN PARTICLES APPEAR...
AND THAT IT LOOKS QUITE DIFFERENT FROM WHEN OTHER PEOPLE USE MAGIC.
THAT'S RIGHT. AT FIRST, I THOUGHT THOSE GOLDEN PARTICLES MIGHT BE A SPECIAL CHARACTERISTIC OF PEOPLE FROM OTHER WORLDS...
BUT THEY NEVER APPEARED WHEN YOU USED THE HEALING ARTS YOURSELF.

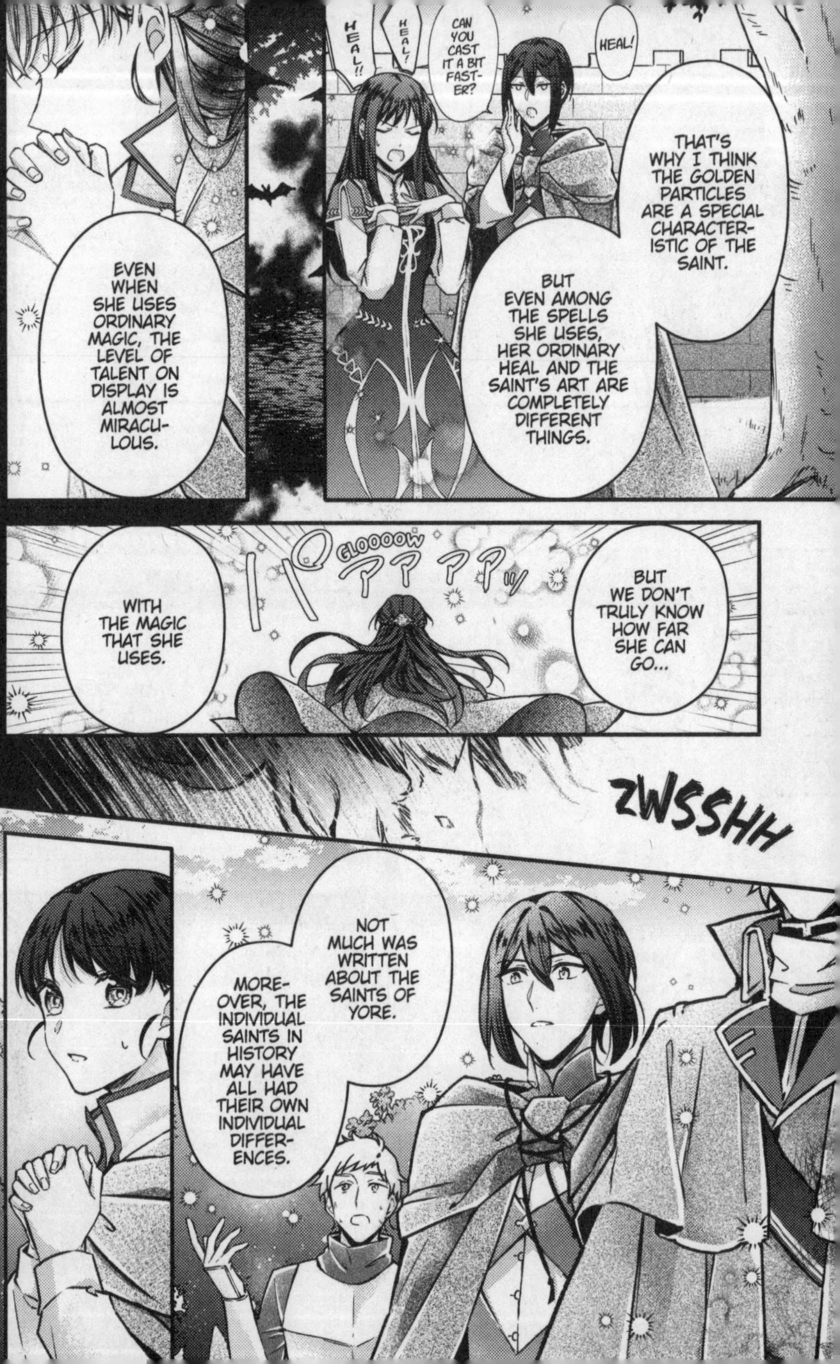
HEAL!
CAN YOU CAST IT A BIT FASTER?
HEAL!
HEAL!!
THAT'S WHY I THINK THE GOLDEN PARTICLES ARE A SPECIAL CHARACTERISTIC OF THE SAINT.
BUT EVEN AMONG THE SPELLS SHE USES, HER ORDINARY HEAL AND THE SAINT'S ART ARE COMPLETELY DIFFERENT THINGS.
EVEN WHEN SHE USES ORDINARY MAGIC, THE LEVEL OF TALENT ON DISPLAY IS ALMOST MIRACULOUS.
BUT WE DON'T TRULY KNOW HOW FAR SHE CAN GO...
GLOOOOW
WITH THE MAGIC THAT SHE USES.
ZWSSHH
NOT MUCH WAS WRITTEN ABOUT THE SAINTS OF YORE.
MOREOVER, THE INDIVIDUAL SAINTS IN HISTORY MAY HAVE ALL HAD THEIR OWN INDIVIDUAL DIFFERENCES.

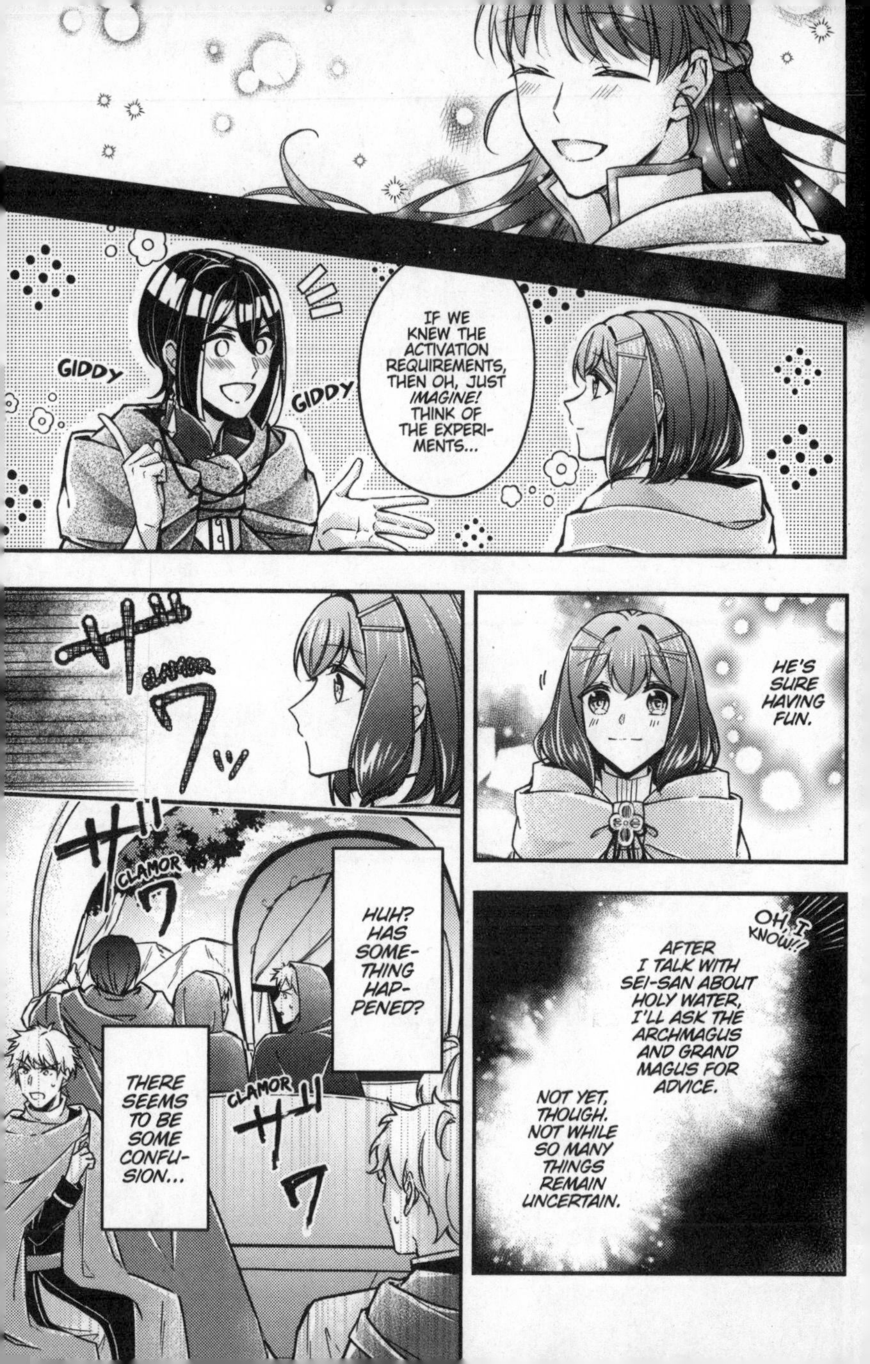
GIDDY
IF WE KNEW THE ACTIVATION REQUIREMENTS, THEN OH, JUST *IMAGINE!* THINK OF THE EXPERIMENTS...
GIDDY
HE'S SURE HAVING FUN.
CLAMOR
OH, I KNOW!!
AFTER I TALK WITH SEI-SAN ABOUT HOLY WATER, I'LL ASK THE ARCHMAGUS AND GRAND MAGUS FOR ADVICE.
NOT YET, THOUGH. NOT WHILE SO MANY THINGS REMAIN UNCERTAIN.
CLAMOR
HUH? HAS SOMETHING HAPPENED?
CLAMOR
THERE SEEMS TO BE SOME CONFUSION...

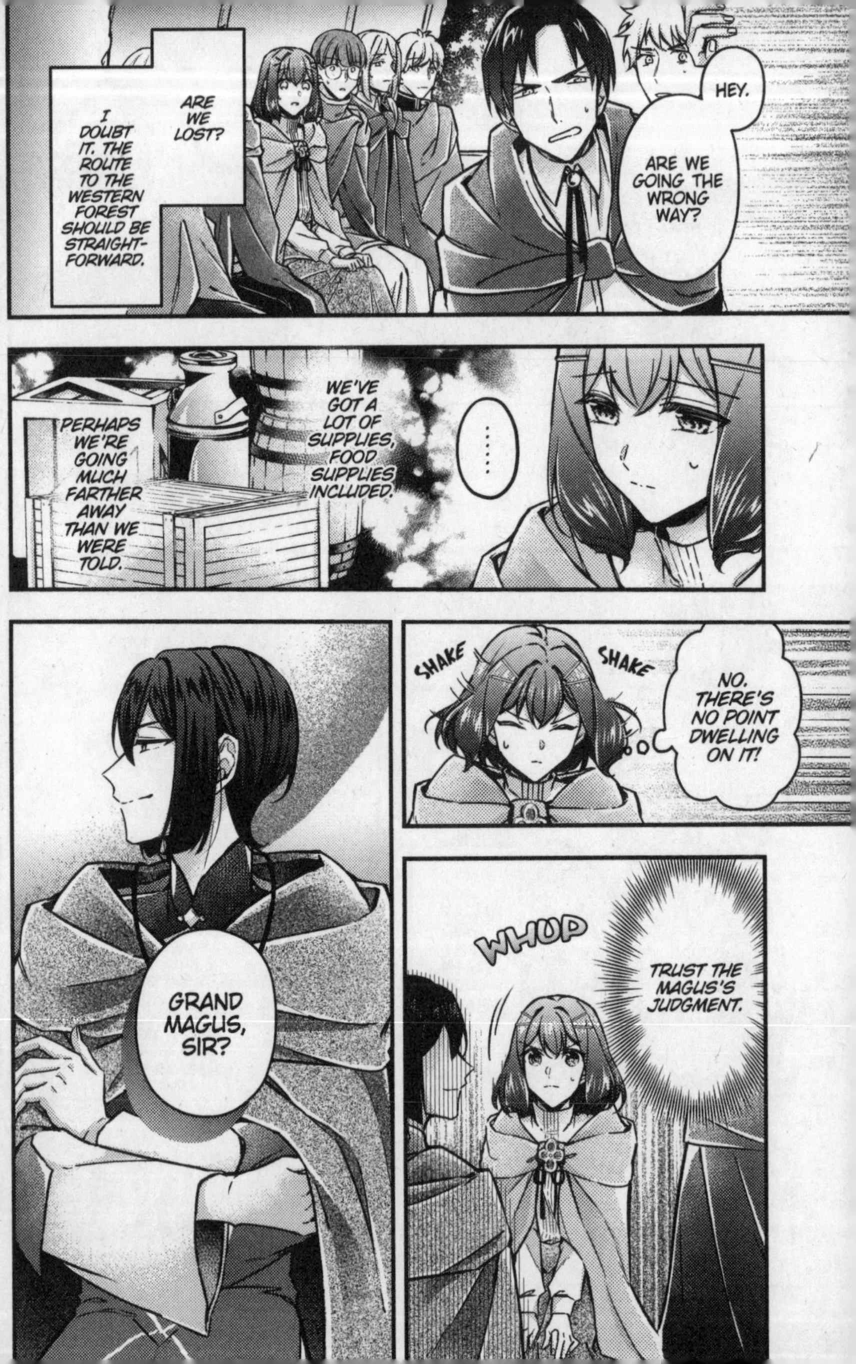
HEY.
ARE WE GOING THE WRONG WAY?
ARE WE LOST?
I DOUBT IT. THE ROUTE TO THE WESTERN FOREST SHOULD BE STRAIGHT-FORWARD.
......
WE'VE GOT A LOT OF SUPPLIES, FOOD SUPPLIES INCLUDED.
PERHAPS WE'RE GOING MUCH FARTHER AWAY THAN WE WERE TOLD.
SHAKE
SHAKE
NO. THERE'S NO POINT DWELLING ON IT!
WHUP
TRUST THE MAGUS'S JUDGMENT.
GRAND MAGUS, SIR?

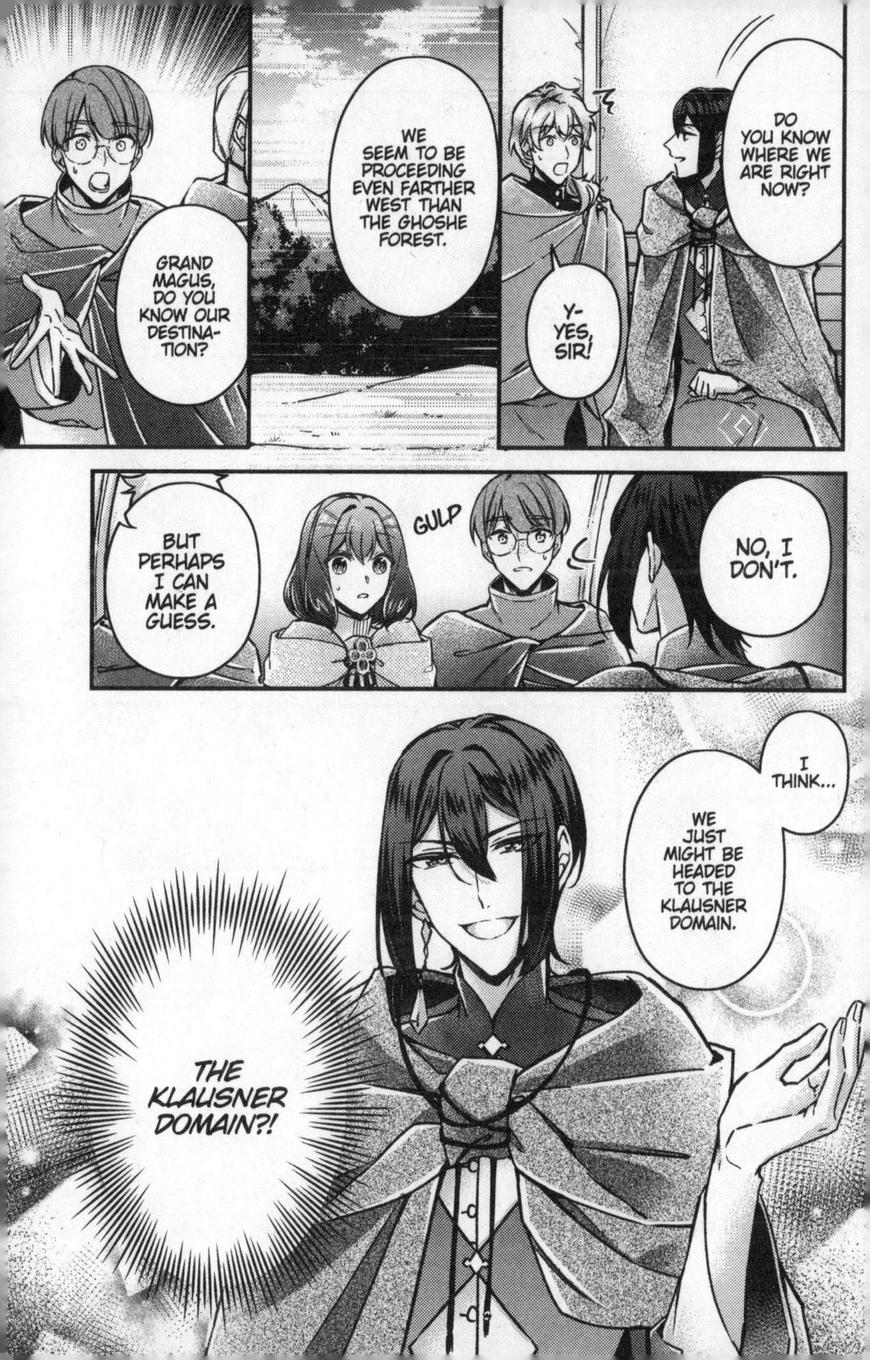
DO YOU KNOW WHERE WE ARE RIGHT NOW?
Y-YES, SIR!
WE SEEM TO BE PROCEEDING EVEN FARTHER WEST THAN THE GHOSHE FOREST.
GRAND MAGUS, DO YOU KNOW OUR DESTINATION?
NO, I DON'T.
GULP
BUT PERHAPS I CAN MAKE A GUESS.
I THINK...
WE JUST MIGHT BE HEADED TO THE KLAUSNER DOMAIN.
THE KLAUSNER DOMAIN?!

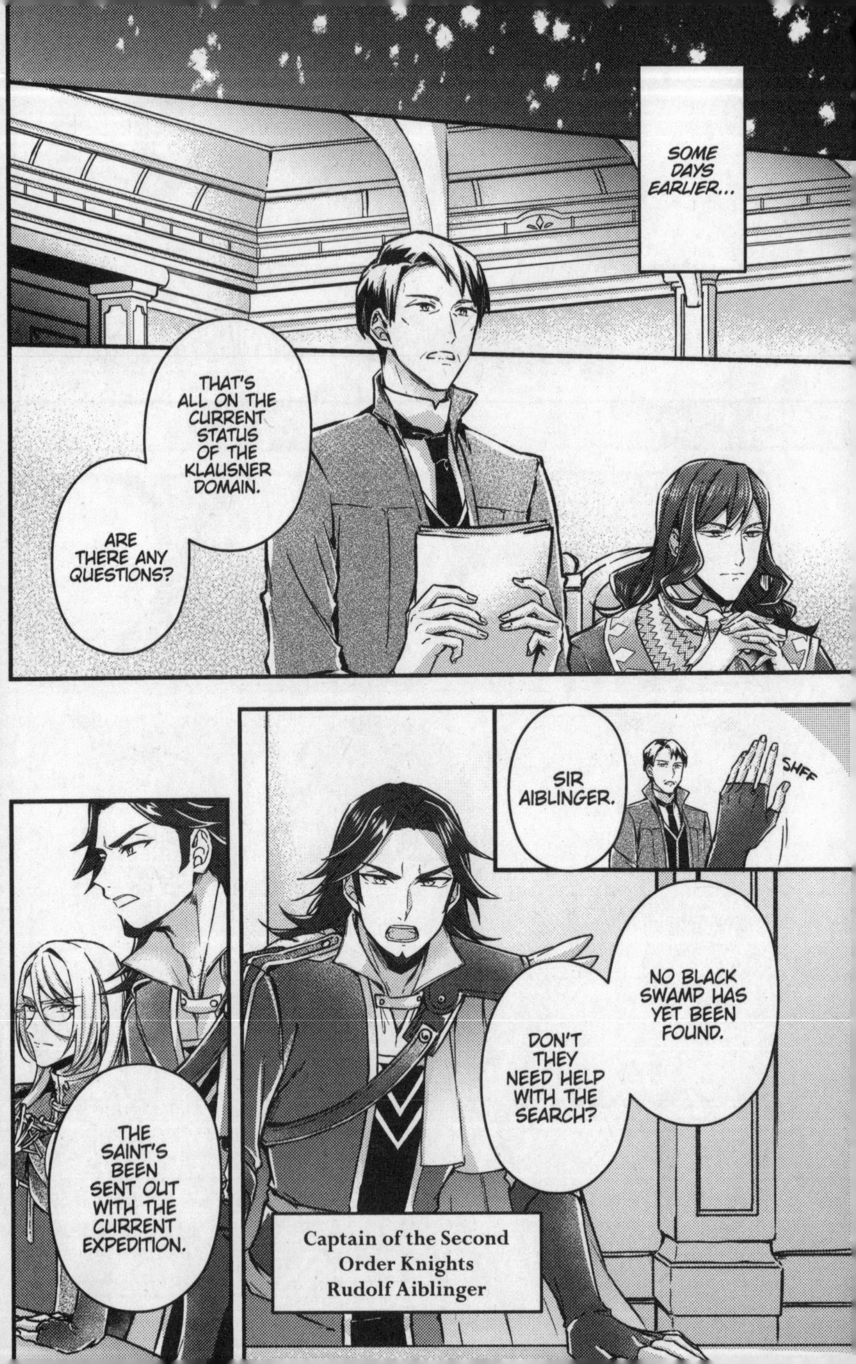
SOME DAYS EARLIER...
THAT'S ALL ON THE CURRENT STATUS OF THE KLAUSNER DOMAIN.
ARE THERE ANY QUESTIONS?
SIR AIBLINGER.
SHFF
NO BLACK SWAMP HAS YET BEEN FOUND.
DON'T THEY NEED HELP WITH THE SEARCH?
Captain of the Second Order Knights Rudolf Aiblinger
THE SAINT'S BEEN SENT OUT WITH THE CURRENT EXPEDITION.

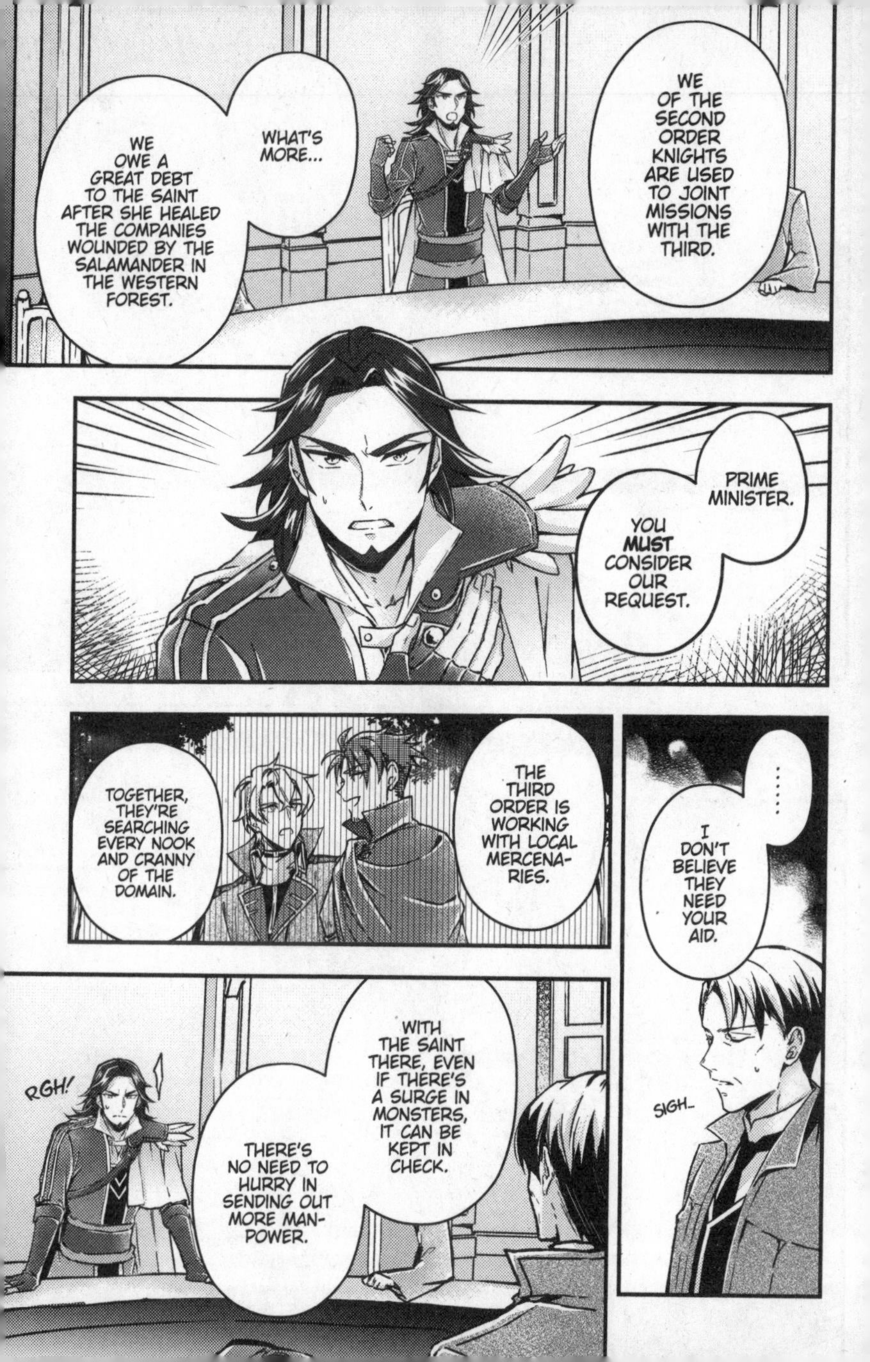
WE OF THE SECOND ORDER KNIGHTS ARE USED TO JOINT MISSIONS WITH THE THIRD.
WHAT'S MORE...
WE OWE A GREAT DEBT TO THE SAINT AFTER SHE HEALED THE COMPANIES WOUNDED BY THE SALAMANDER IN THE WESTERN FOREST.
PRIME MINISTER.
YOU **MUST** CONSIDER OUR REQUEST.
......
I DON'T BELIEVE THEY NEED YOUR AID.
SIGH...
THE THIRD ORDER IS WORKING WITH LOCAL MERCENA-RIES.
TOGETHER, THEY'RE SEARCHING EVERY NOOK AND CRANNY OF THE DOMAIN.
WITH THE SAINT THERE, EVEN IF THERE'S A SURGE IN MONSTERS, IT CAN BE KEPT IN CHECK.
THERE'S NO NEED TO HURRY IN SENDING OUT MORE MAN-POWER.
RGH!

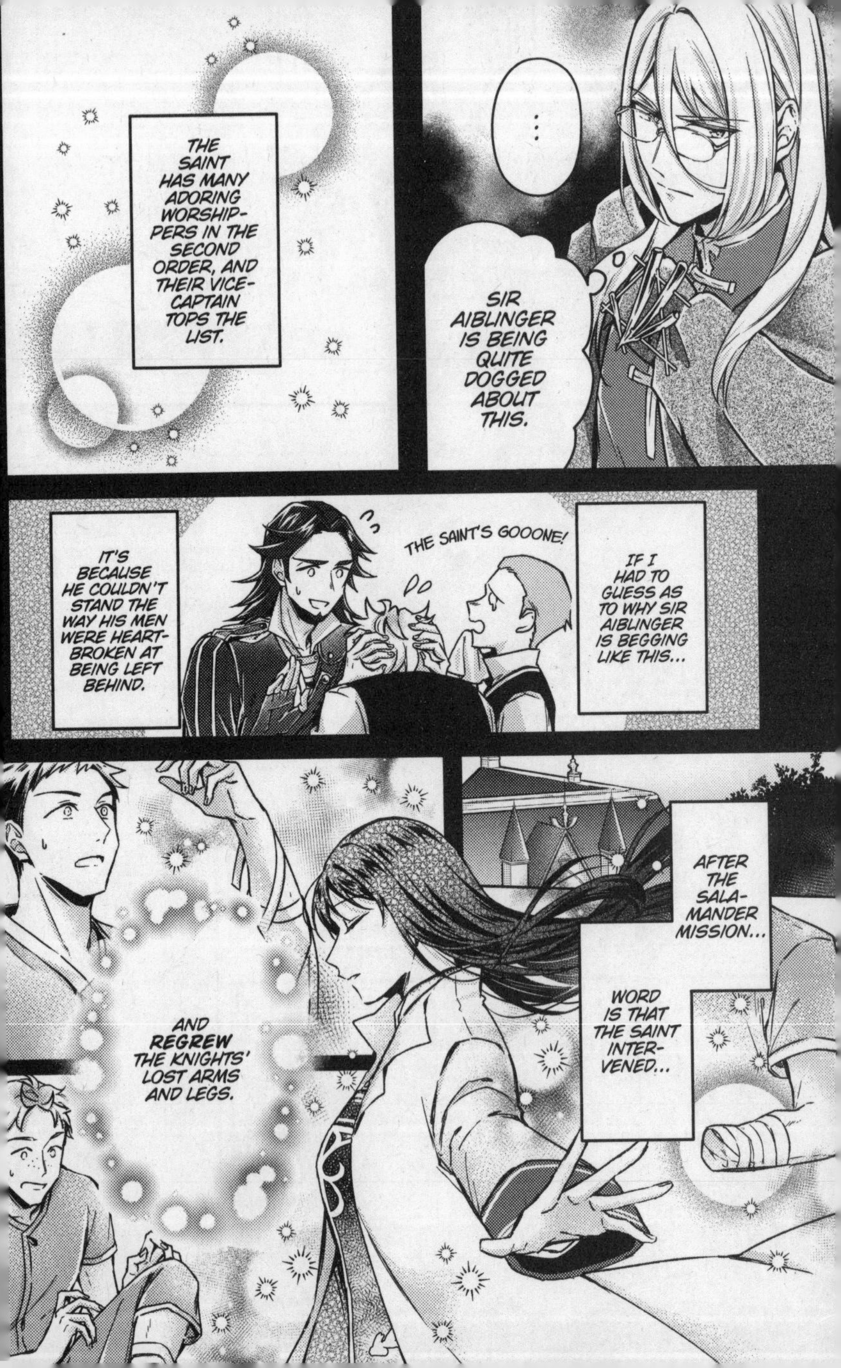
...
SIR AIBLINGER IS BEING QUITE DOGGED ABOUT THIS.
THE SAINT HAS MANY ADORING WORSHIPPERS IN THE SECOND ORDER, AND THEIR VICE-CAPTAIN TOPS THE LIST.
IF I HAD TO GUESS AS TO WHY SIR AIBLINGER IS BEGGING LIKE THIS...
THE SAINT'S GOOONE!
IT'S BECAUSE HE COULDN'T STAND THE WAY HIS MEN WERE HEART-BROKEN AT BEING LEFT BEHIND.
AFTER THE SALAMANDER MISSION...
WORD IS THAT THE SAINT INTERVENED...
AND **REGREW** THE KNIGHTS' LOST ARMS AND LEGS.

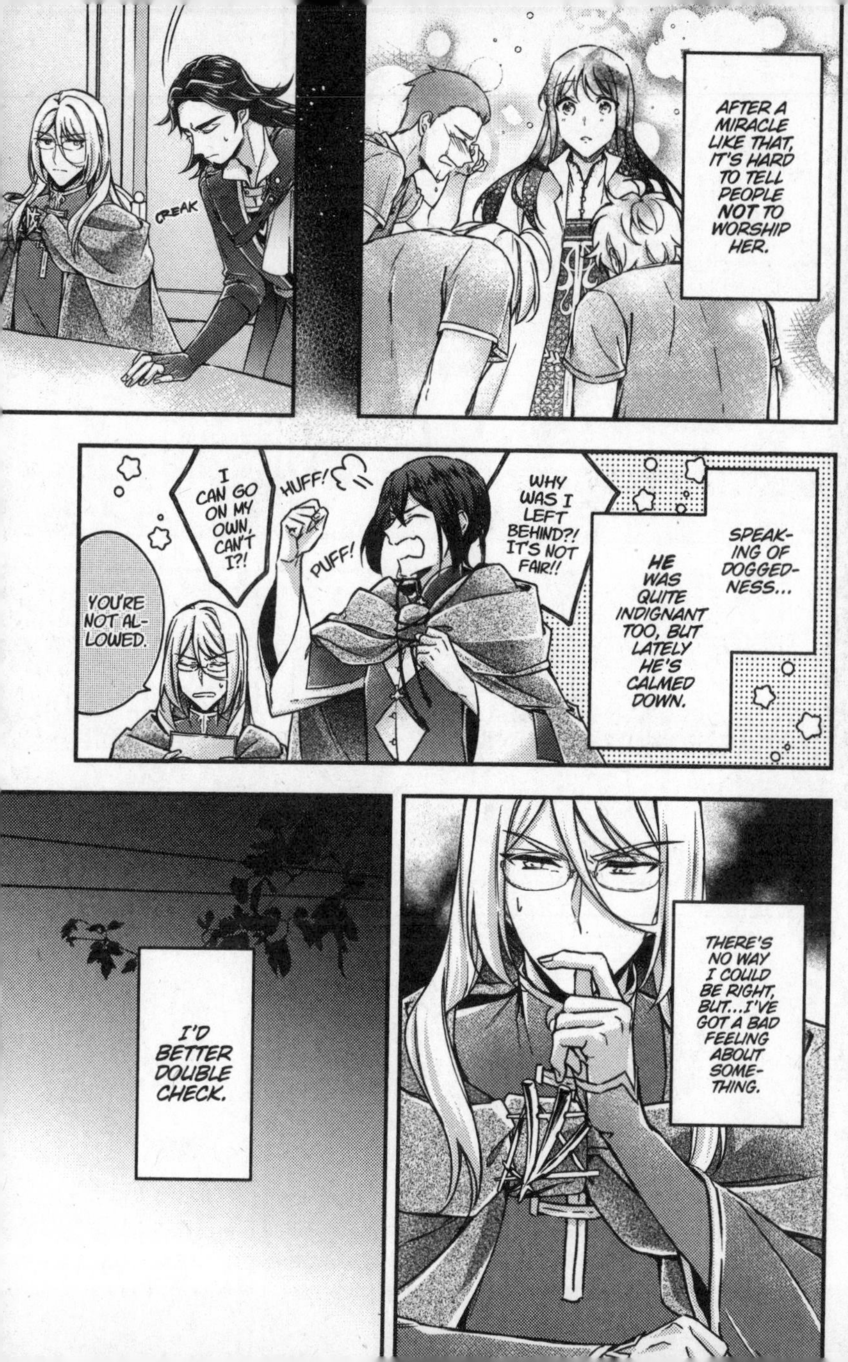
AFTER A MIRACLE LIKE THAT, IT'S HARD TO TELL PEOPLE NOT TO WORSHIP HER.
CREAK
SPEAK-ING OF DOGGED-NESS...
HE WAS QUITE INDIGNANT TOO, BUT LATELY HE'S CALMED DOWN.
WHY WAS I LEFT BEHIND?! IT'S NOT FAIR!!
HUFF!
PUFF!
I CAN GO ON MY OWN, CAN'T I?!
YOU'RE NOT AL-LOWED.
THERE'S NO WAY I COULD BE RIGHT, BUT...I'VE GOT A BAD FEELING ABOUT SOME-THING.
I'D BETTER DOUBLE CHECK.

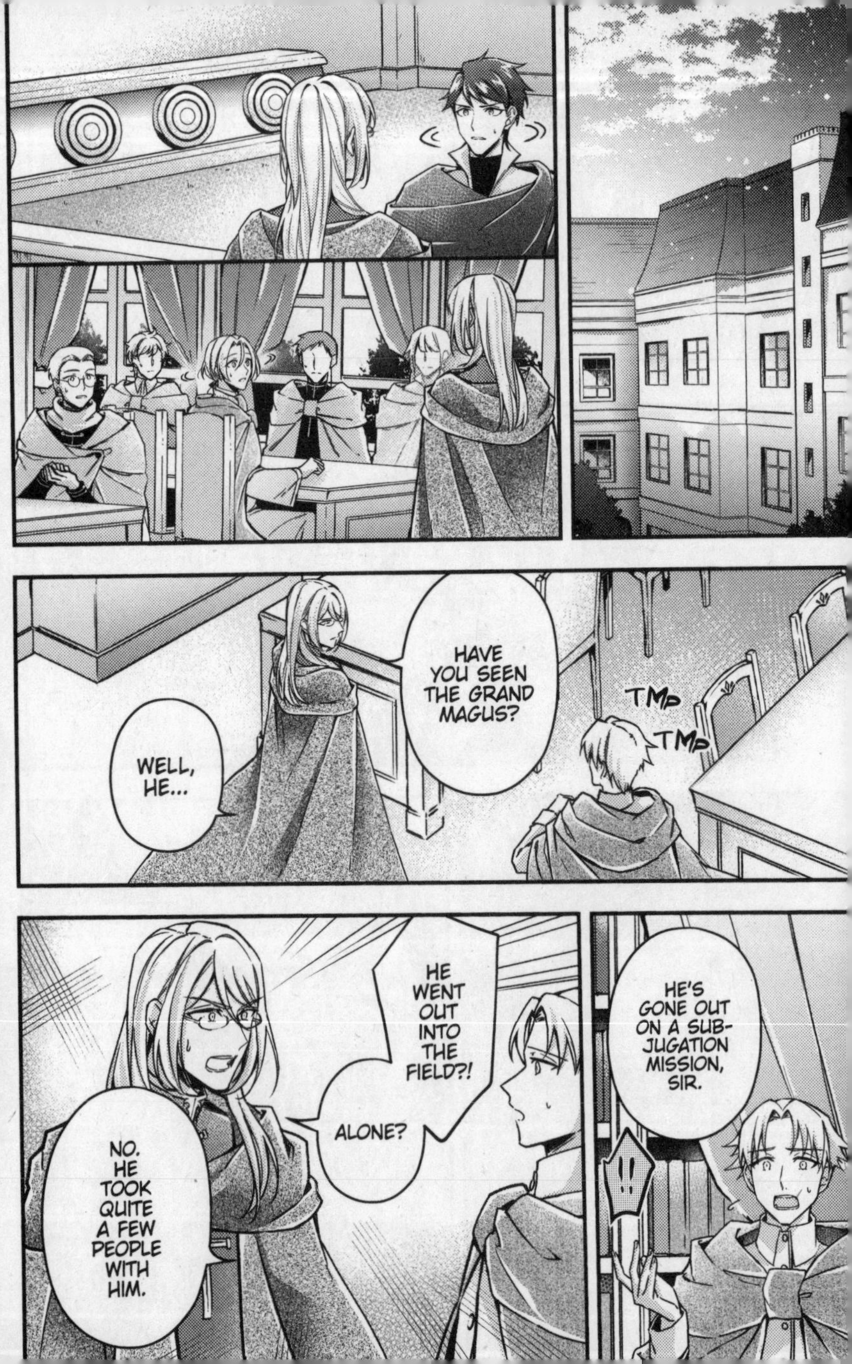
TMP
TMP
HAVE YOU SEEN THE GRAND MAGUS?
WELL, HE...
HE'S GONE OUT ON A SUB-JUGATION MISSION, SIR.
!!
HE WENT OUT INTO THE FIELD?!
ALONE?
NO. HE TOOK QUITE A FEW PEOPLE WITH HIM.

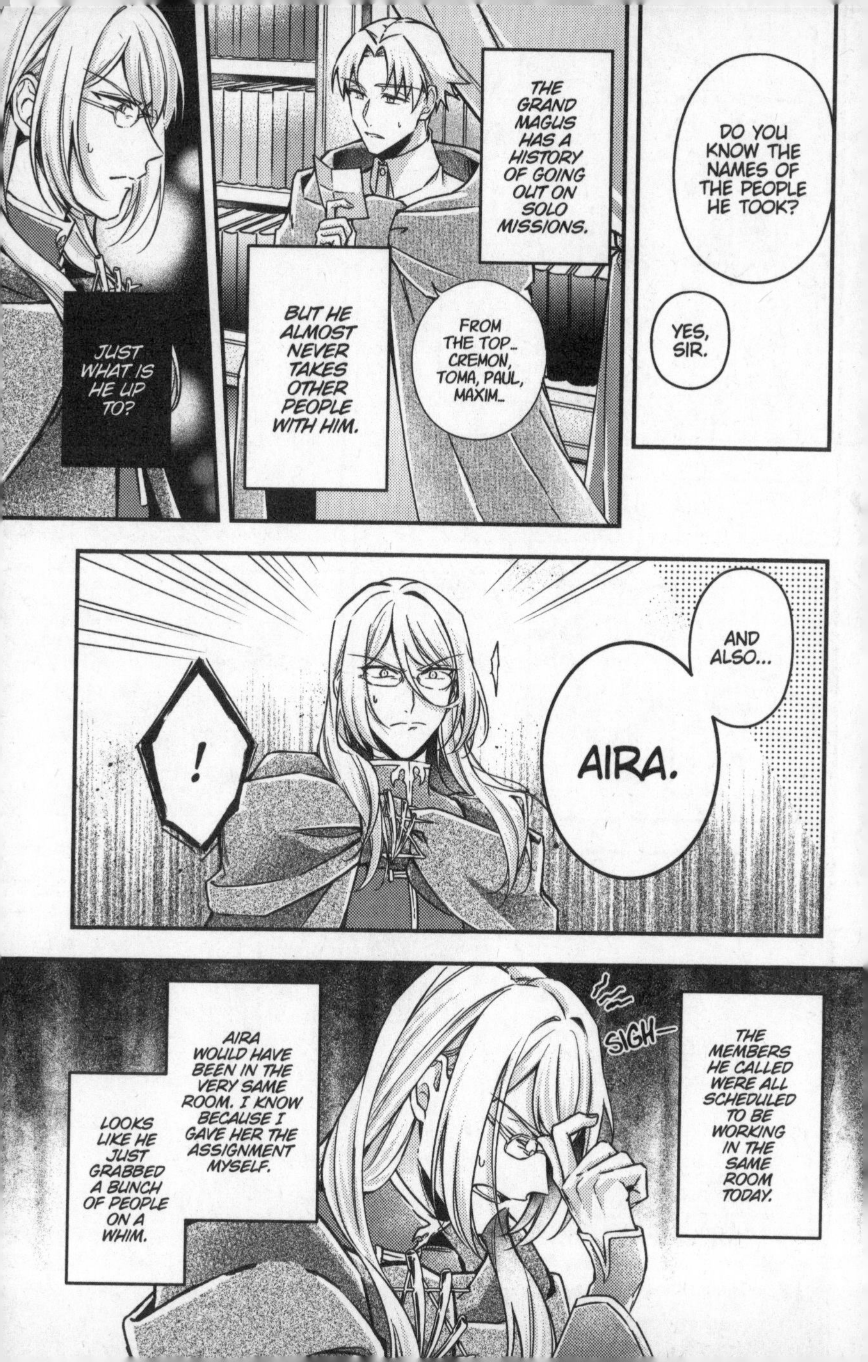
DO YOU KNOW THE NAMES OF THE PEOPLE HE TOOK?
YES, SIR.
THE GRAND MAGUS HAS A HISTORY OF GOING OUT ON SOLO MISSIONS.
FROM THE TOP... CREMON, TOMA, PAUL, MAXIM...
BUT HE ALMOST NEVER TAKES OTHER PEOPLE WITH HIM.
JUST WHAT IS HE UP TO?
AND ALSO...
AIRA.
!
SIGH—
THE MEMBERS HE CALLED WERE ALL SCHEDULED TO BE WORKING IN THE SAME ROOM TODAY.
AIRA WOULD HAVE BEEN IN THE VERY SAME ROOM. I KNOW BECAUSE I GAVE HER THE ASSIGNMENT MYSELF.
LOOKS LIKE HE JUST GRABBED A BUNCH OF PEOPLE ON A WHIM.

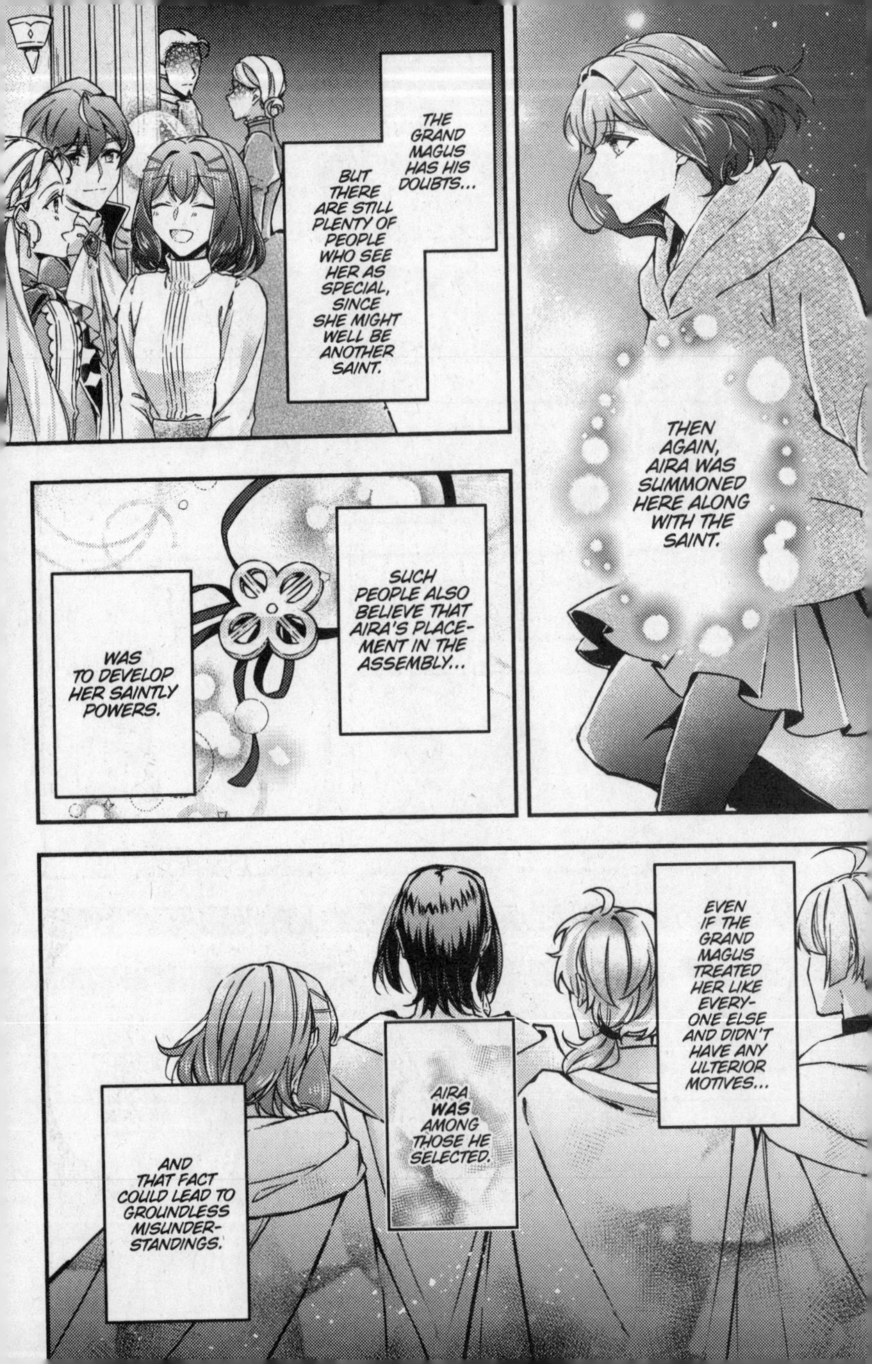
THE GRAND MAGUS HAS HIS DOUBTS...
BUT THERE ARE STILL PLENTY OF PEOPLE WHO SEE HER AS SPECIAL, SINCE SHE MIGHT WELL BE ANOTHER SAINT.
THEN AGAIN, AIRA WAS SUMMONED HERE ALONG WITH THE SAINT.
SUCH PEOPLE ALSO BELIEVE THAT AIRA'S PLACEMENT IN THE ASSEMBLY...
WAS TO DEVELOP HER SAINTLY POWERS.
EVEN IF THE GRAND MAGUS TREATED HER LIKE EVERYONE ELSE AND DIDN'T HAVE ANY ULTERIOR MOTIVES...
AIRA WAS AMONG THOSE HE SELECTED.
AND THAT FACT COULD LEAD TO GROUNDLESS MISUNDERSTANDINGS.

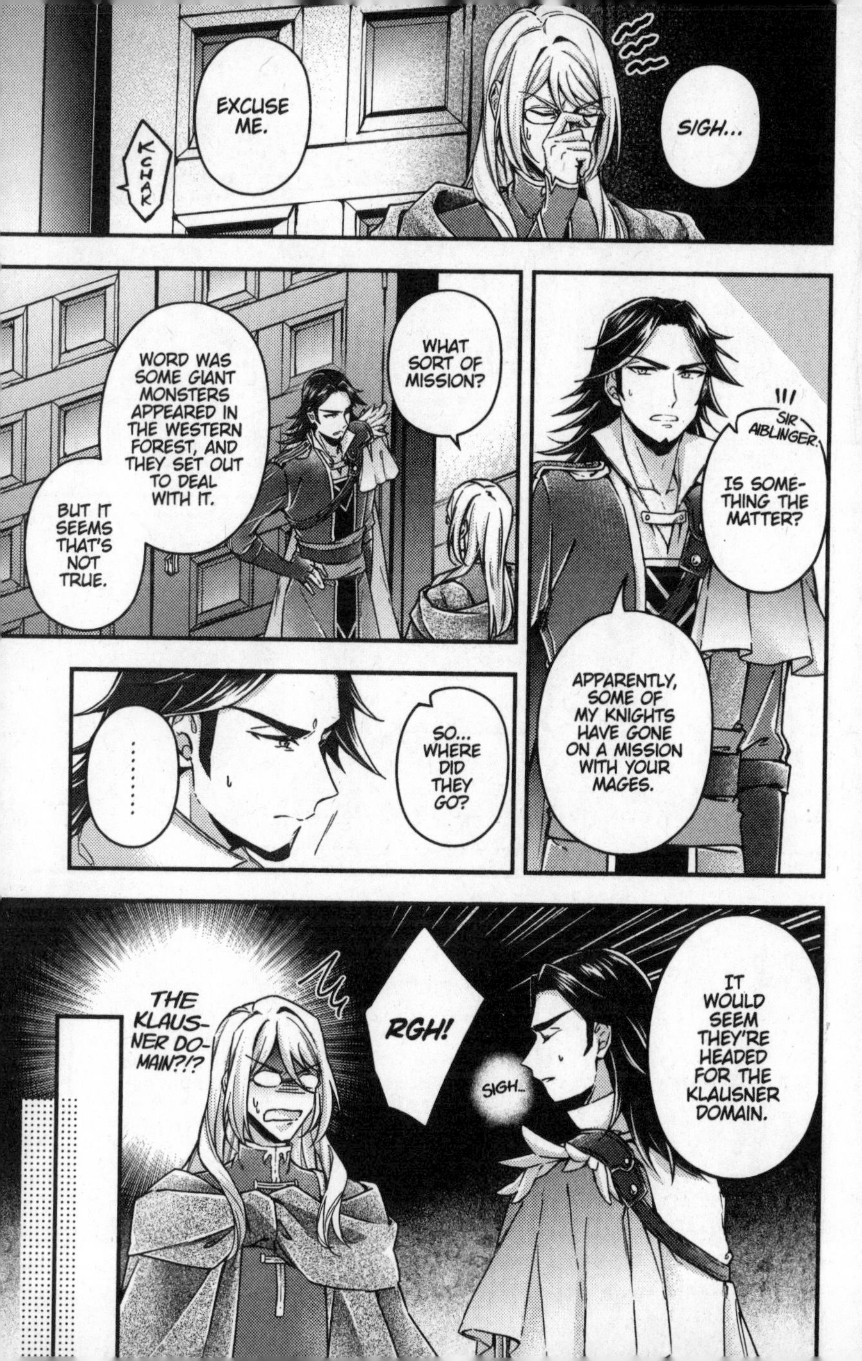
SIGH...
EXCUSE ME.
KCHAK
!!!
SIR AIBLINGER.
IS SOMETHING THE MATTER?
APPARENTLY, SOME OF MY KNIGHTS HAVE GONE ON A MISSION WITH YOUR MAGES.
WHAT SORT OF MISSION?
WORD WAS SOME GIANT MONSTERS APPEARED IN THE WESTERN FOREST, AND THEY SET OUT TO DEAL WITH IT.
BUT IT SEEMS THAT'S NOT TRUE.
SO... WHERE DID THEY GO?
......
IT WOULD SEEM THEY'RE HEADED FOR THE KLAUSNER DOMAIN.
SIGH...
RGH!
THE KLAUSNER DOMAIN?!?

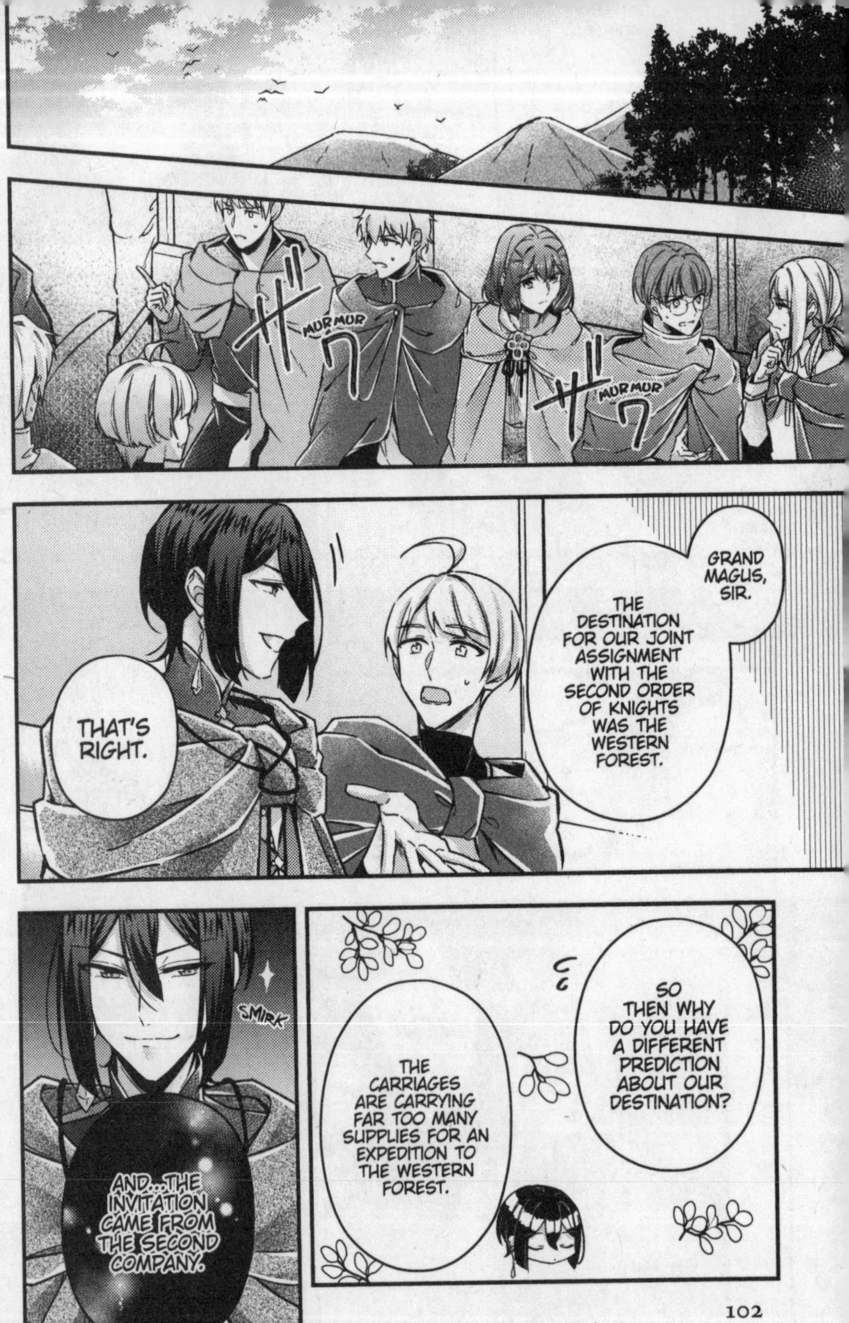
MURMUR
MURMUR
GRAND MAGUS, SIR.
THE DESTINATION FOR OUR JOINT ASSIGNMENT WITH THE SECOND ORDER OF KNIGHTS WAS THE WESTERN FOREST.
THAT'S RIGHT.
SO THEN WHY DO YOU HAVE A DIFFERENT PREDICTION ABOUT OUR DESTINATION?
THE CARRIAGES ARE CARRYING FAR TOO MANY SUPPLIES FOR AN EXPEDITION TO THE WESTERN FOREST.
SMIRK
AND...THE INVITATION CAME FROM THE SECOND COMPANY.

WHEN THE ASSIGNMENT CAME IN, IT CAUGHT MY EYE FOR SOME REASON OR OTHER, AND I AGREED TO JOIN.

I'M GLAD I DID.

HOW COME WE WEREN'T CHOSEN?!

IT CAN'T BE TRUE... THE SAINT WA—

SEE, A LOT OF PEOPLE IN THE SECOND ORDER ABSOLUTELY LOVE THE SAINT.

THEY MUST BE JUST SHATTERED THAT THEY DIDN'T GET TAKEN TO THE KLAUSNER DOMAIN ALONG WITH HER.

. . . . . .

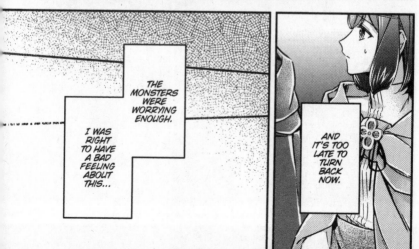

THE MONSTERS WERE WORRYING ENOUGH.

I WAS RIGHT TO HAVE A BAD FEELING ABOUT THIS...

AND IT'S TOO LATE TO TURN BACK NOW.

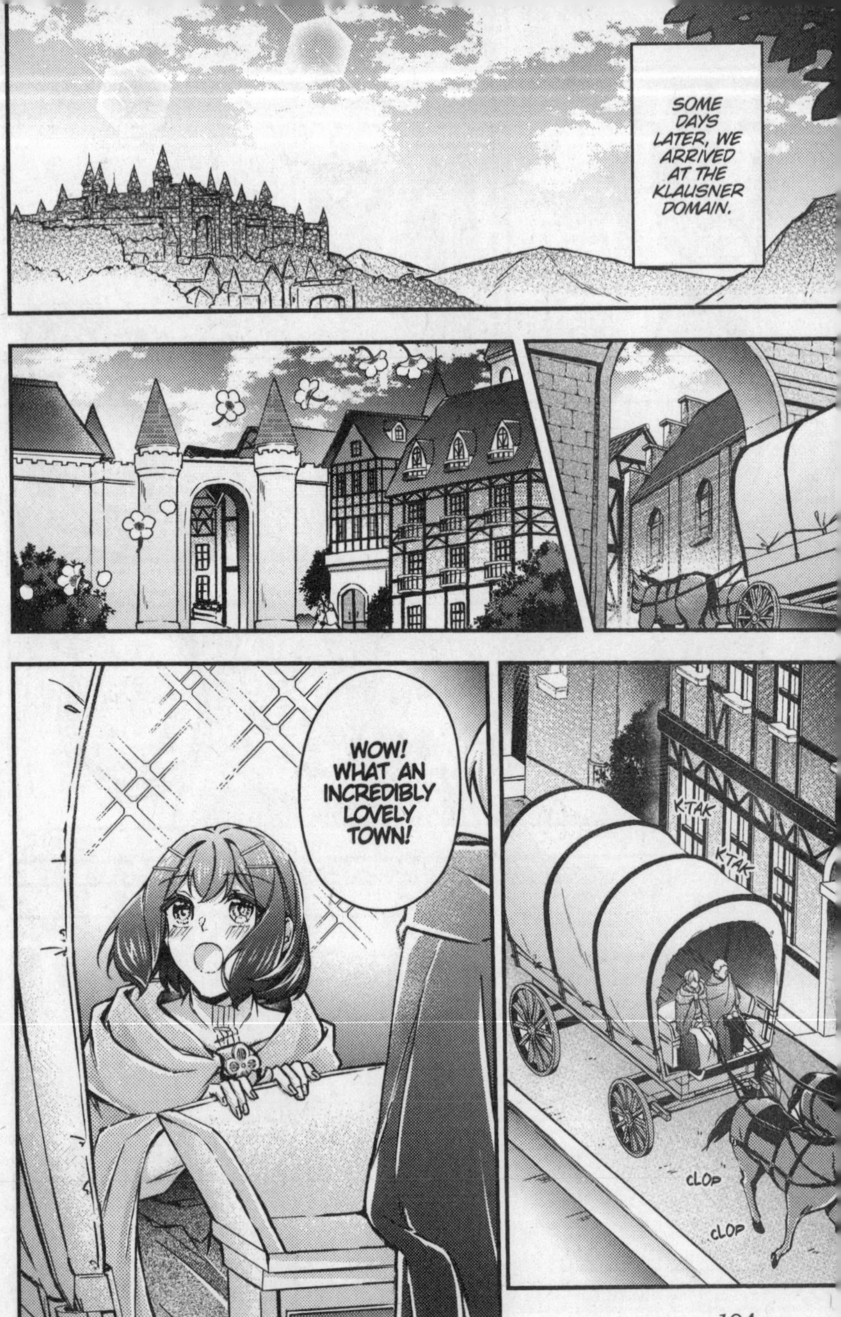
SOME DAYS LATER, WE ARRIVED AT THE KLAUSNER DOMAIN.
K-TAK
K-TAK
CLOP
CLOP
WOW! WHAT AN INCREDIBLY LOVELY TOWN!

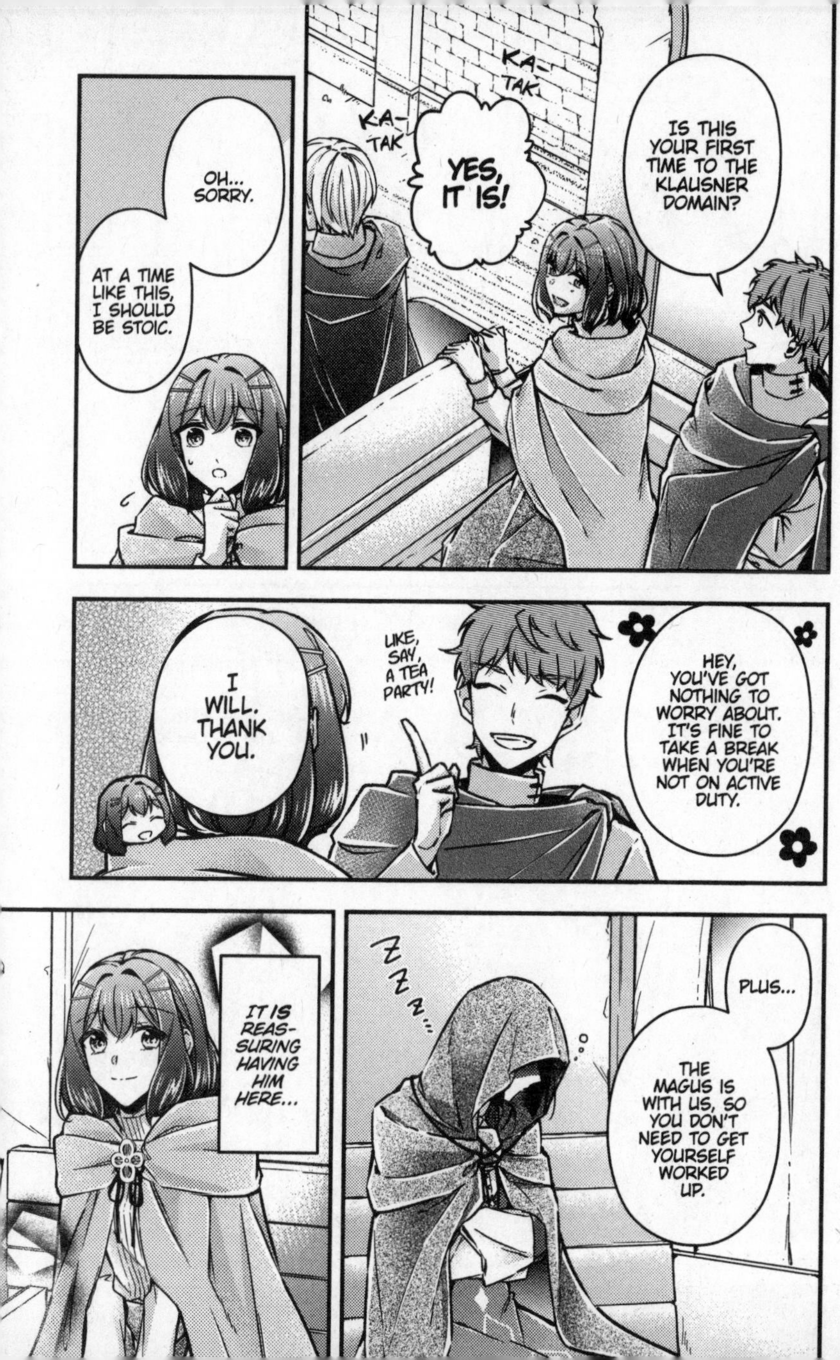
IS THIS YOUR FIRST TIME TO THE KLAUSNER DOMAIN?
KA-TAK
YES, IT IS!
KA-TAK
OH... SORRY.
AT A TIME LIKE THIS, I SHOULD BE STOIC.
HEY, YOU'VE GOT NOTHING TO WORRY ABOUT. IT'S FINE TO TAKE A BREAK WHEN YOU'RE NOT ON ACTIVE DUTY.
LIKE, SAY, A TEA PARTY!
I WILL. THANK YOU.
PLUS...
THE MAGUS IS WITH US, SO YOU DON'T NEED TO GET YOURSELF WORKED UP.
ZZZ...
IT IS REAS-SURING HAVING HIM HERE...

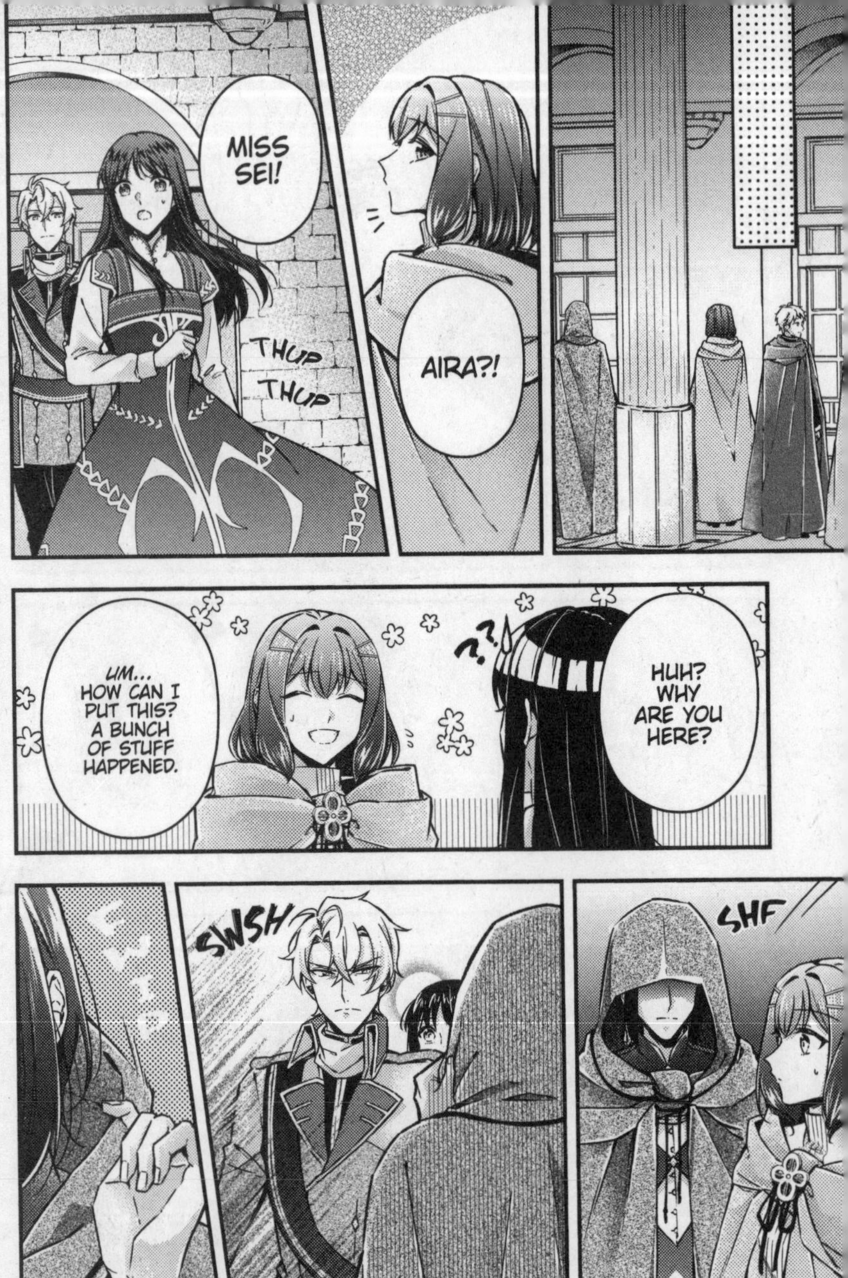
AIRA?!
MISS SEI!
THUP THUP
HUH? WHY ARE YOU HERE?
??
UM... HOW CAN I PUT THIS? A BUNCH OF STUFF HAPPENED.
SHF
SWSH

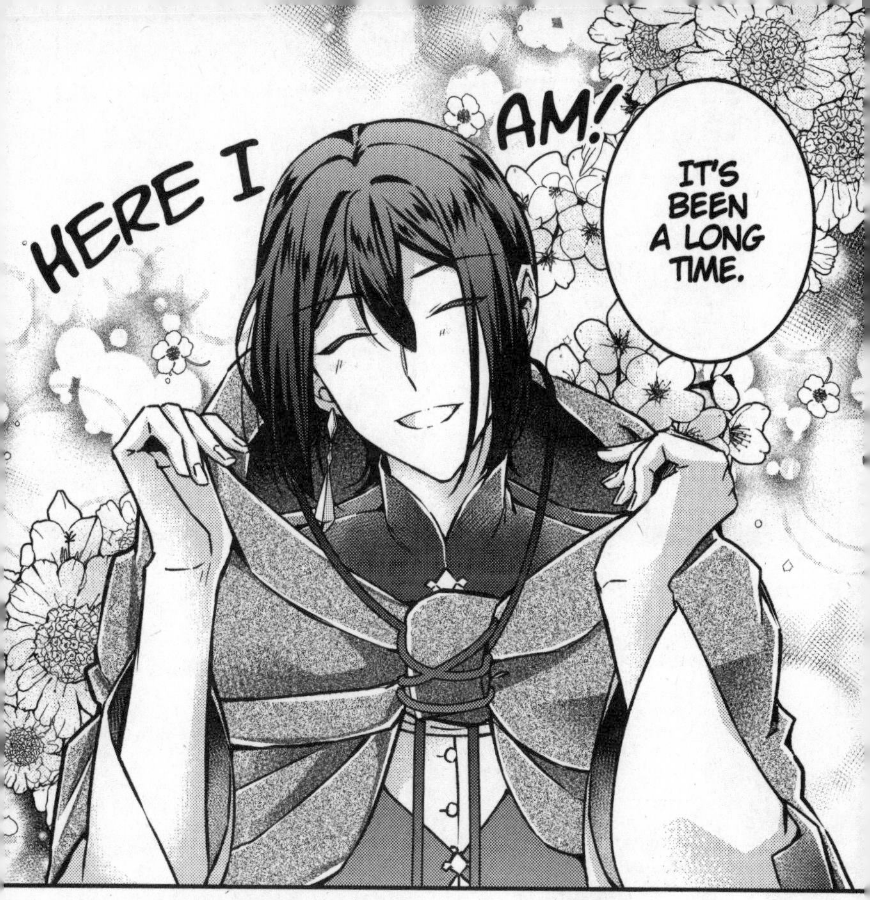
HERE I AM!
IT'S BEEN A LONG TIME.
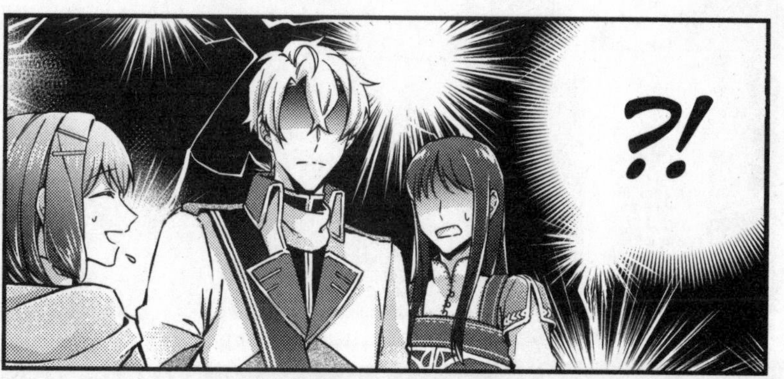
?!

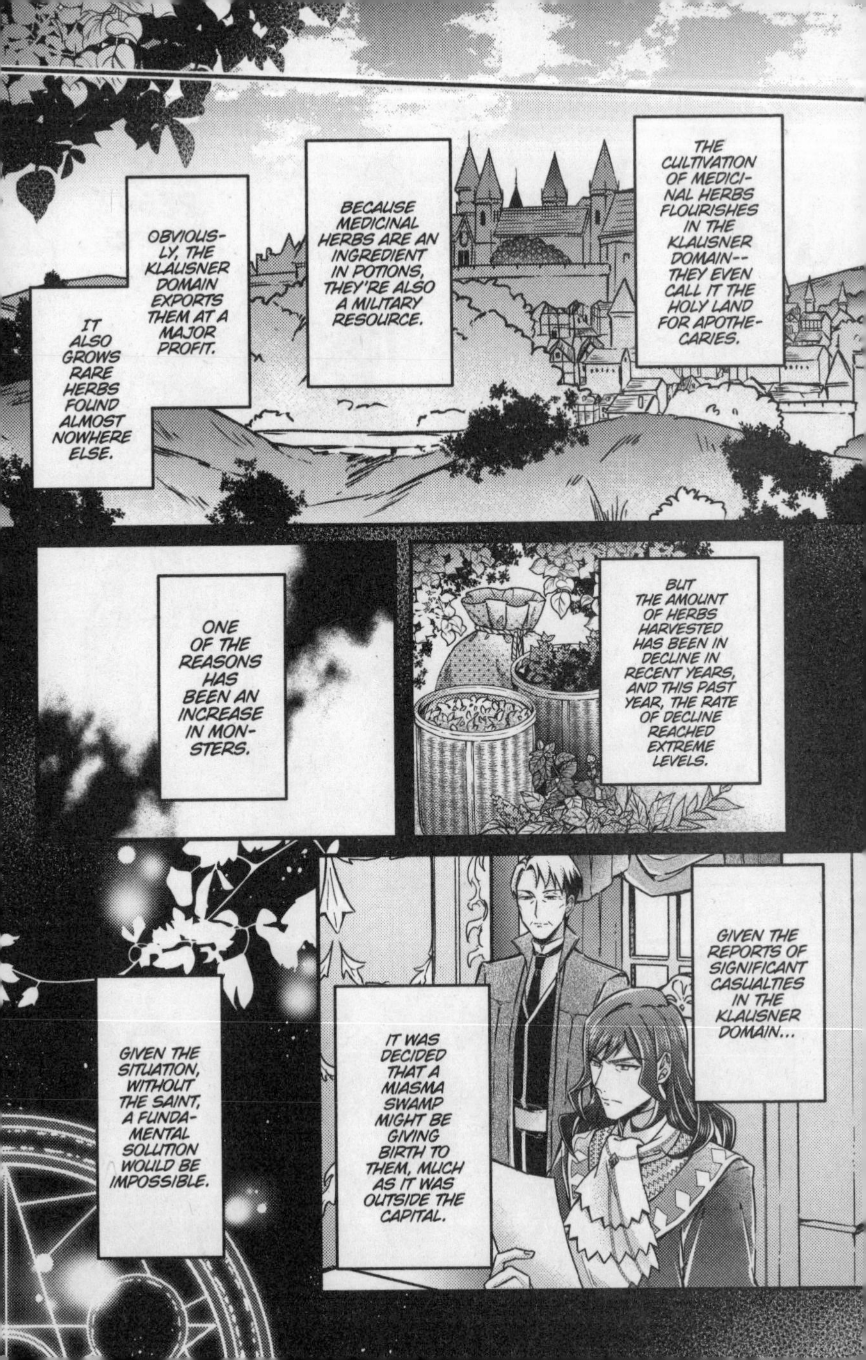
THE CULTIVATION OF MEDICINAL HERBS FLOURISHES IN THE KLAUSNER DOMAIN-- THEY EVEN CALL IT THE HOLY LAND FOR APOTHECARIES.
BECAUSE MEDICINAL HERBS ARE AN INGREDIENT IN POTIONS, THEY'RE ALSO A MILITARY RESOURCE.
OBVIOUSLY, THE KLAUSNER DOMAIN EXPORTS THEM AT A MAJOR PROFIT.
IT ALSO GROWS RARE HERBS FOUND ALMOST NOWHERE ELSE.
BUT THE AMOUNT OF HERBS HARVESTED HAS BEEN IN DECLINE IN RECENT YEARS, AND THIS PAST YEAR, THE RATE OF DECLINE REACHED EXTREME LEVELS.
ONE OF THE REASONS HAS BEEN AN INCREASE IN MONSTERS.
GIVEN THE REPORTS OF SIGNIFICANT CASUALTIES IN THE KLAUSNER DOMAIN...
IT WAS DECIDED THAT A MIASMA SWAMP MIGHT BE GIVING BIRTH TO THEM, MUCH AS IT WAS OUTSIDE THE CAPITAL.
GIVEN THE SITUATION, WITHOUT THE SAINT, A FUNDAMENTAL SOLUTION WOULD BE IMPOSSIBLE.

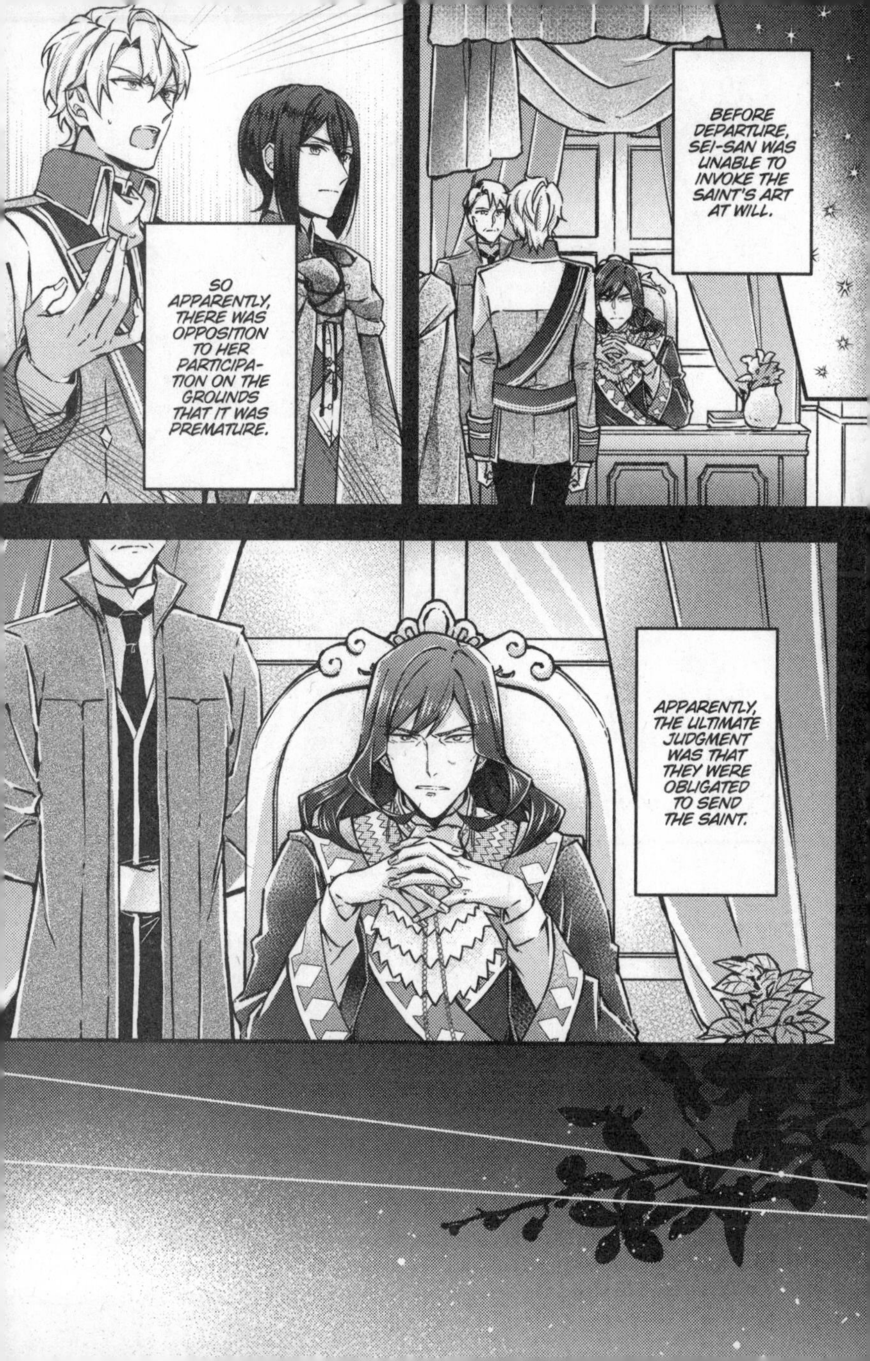
BEFORE DEPARTURE, SEI-SAN WAS UNABLE TO INVOKE THE SAINT'S ART AT WILL.
SO APPARENTLY, THERE WAS OPPOSITION TO HER PARTICIPATION ON THE GROUNDS THAT IT WAS PREMATURE.
APPARENTLY, THE ULTIMATE JUDGMENT WAS THAT THEY WERE OBLIGATED TO SEND THE SAINT.

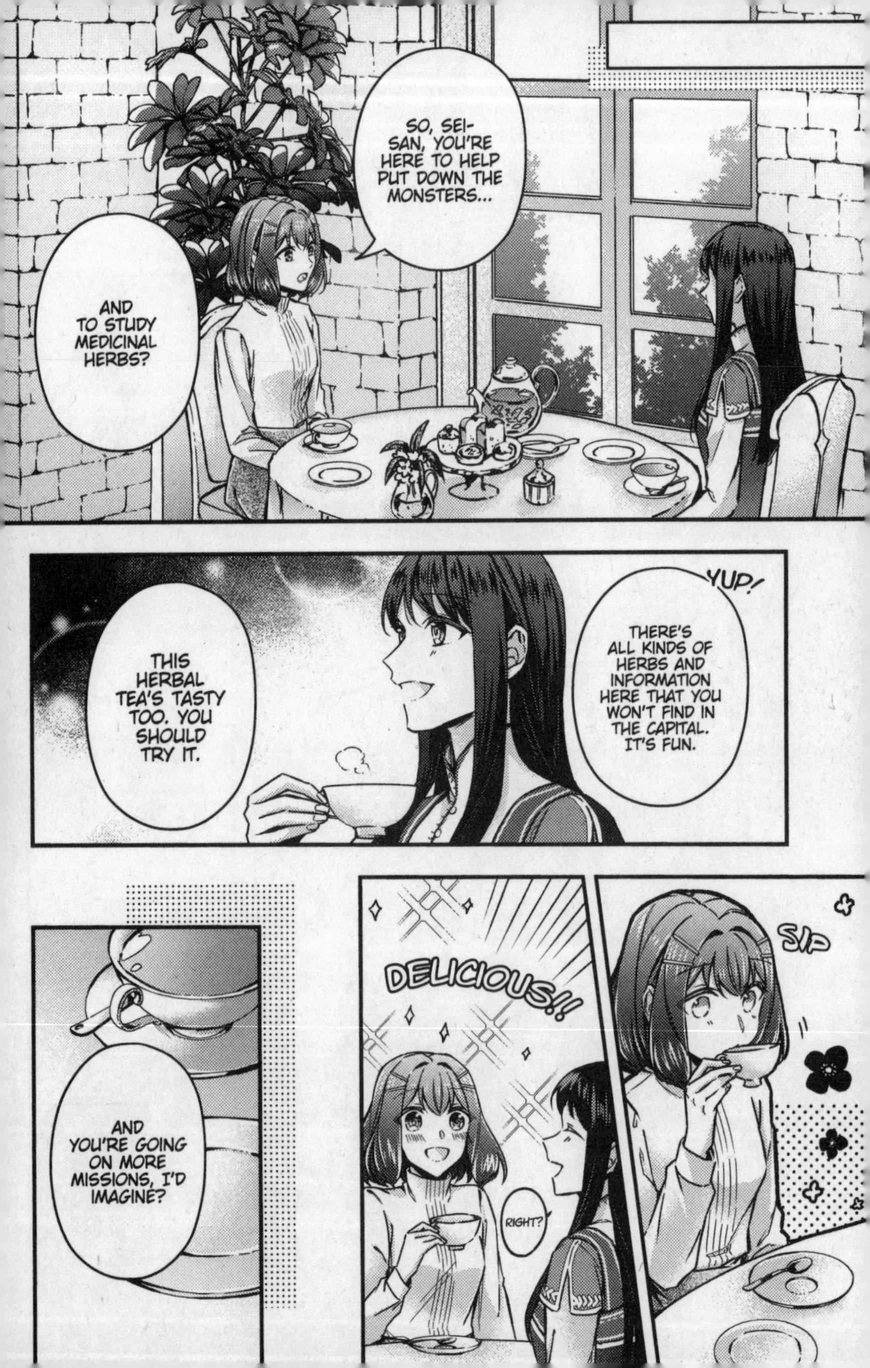
SO, SEI-SAN, YOU'RE HERE TO HELP PUT DOWN THE MONSTERS...
AND TO STUDY MEDICINAL HERBS?
YUP!
THERE'S ALL KINDS OF HERBS AND INFORMATION HERE THAT YOU WON'T FIND IN THE CAPITAL. IT'S FUN.
THIS HERBAL TEA'S TASTY TOO. YOU SHOULD TRY IT.
SIP
DELICIOUS!!
RIGHT?
AND YOU'RE GOING ON MORE MISSIONS, I'D IMAGINE?

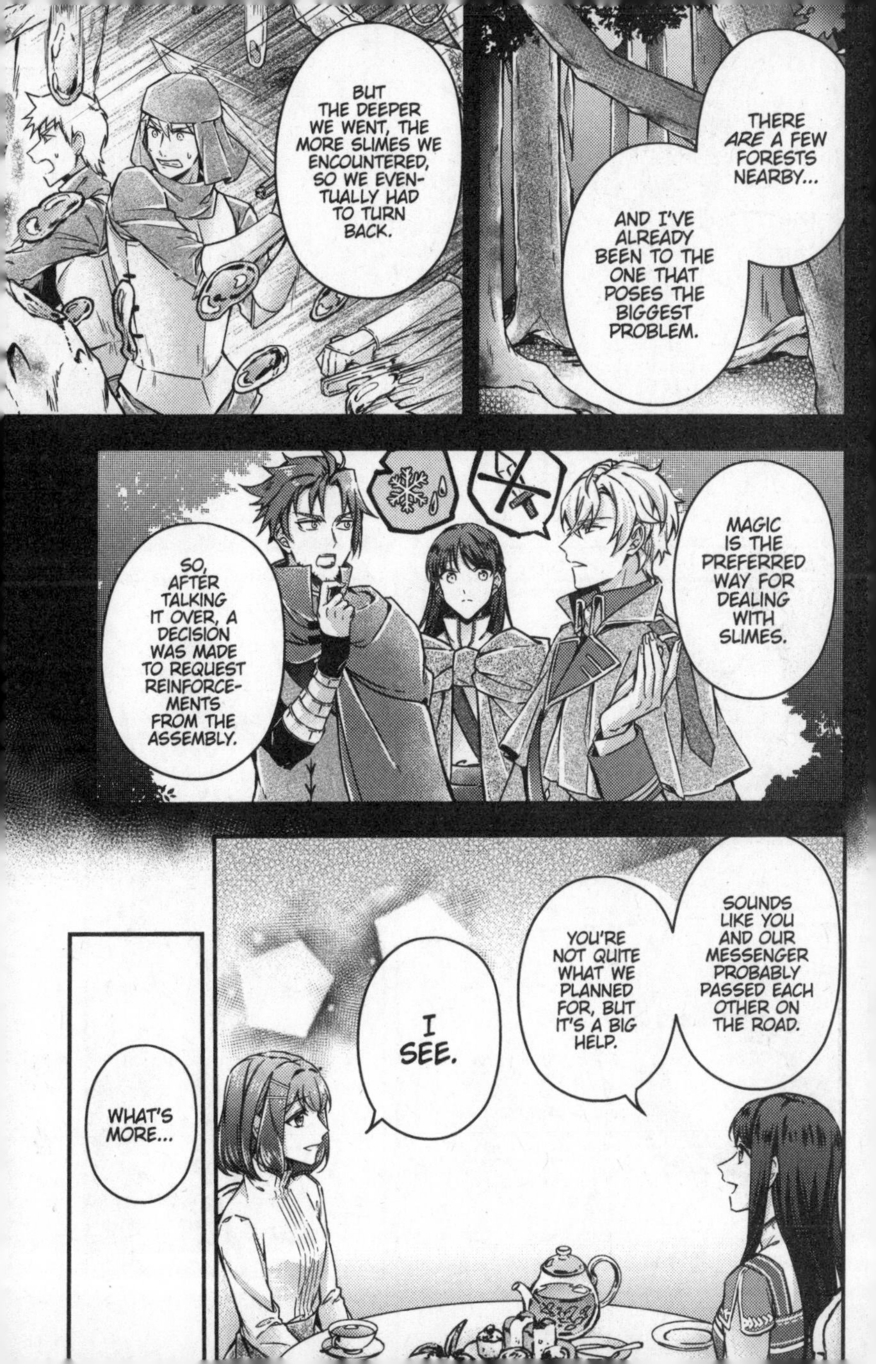

THERE ARE A FEW FORESTS NEARBY...
AND I'VE ALREADY BEEN TO THE ONE THAT POSES THE BIGGEST PROBLEM.
BUT THE DEEPER WE WENT, THE MORE SLIMES WE ENCOUNTERED, SO WE EVEN-TUALLY HAD TO TURN BACK.
MAGIC IS THE PREFERRED WAY FOR DEALING WITH SLIMES.
SO, AFTER TALKING IT OVER, A DECISION WAS MADE TO REQUEST REINFORCE-MENTS FROM THE ASSEMBLY.
SOUNDS LIKE YOU AND OUR MESSENGER PROBABLY PASSED EACH OTHER ON THE ROAD.
YOU'RE NOT QUITE WHAT WE PLANNED FOR, BUT IT'S A BIG HELP.
I SEE.
WHAT'S MORE...

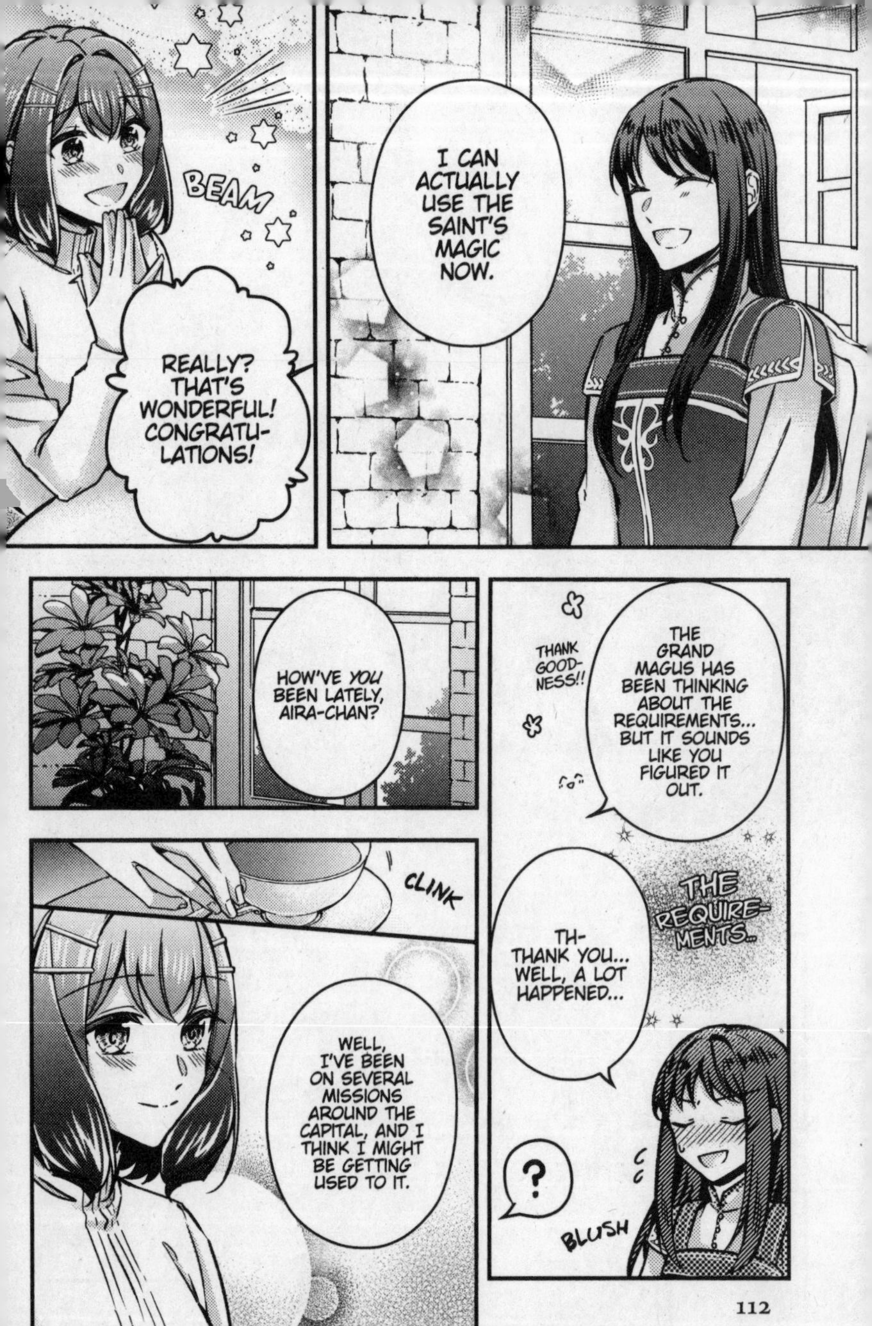
I CAN ACTUALLY USE THE SAINT'S MAGIC NOW.
BEAM
REALLY? THAT'S WONDERFUL! CONGRATU-LATIONS!
THE GRAND MAGUS HAS BEEN THINKING ABOUT THE REQUIREMENTS... BUT IT SOUNDS LIKE YOU FIGURED IT OUT.
THANK GOOD-NESS!!
THE REQUIRE-MENTS...
TH-THANK YOU... WELL, A LOT HAPPENED...
?
BLUSH
HOW'VE *YOU* BEEN LATELY, AIRA-CHAN?
CLINK
WELL, I'VE BEEN ON SEVERAL MISSIONS AROUND THE CAPITAL, AND I THINK I MIGHT BE GETTING USED TO IT.

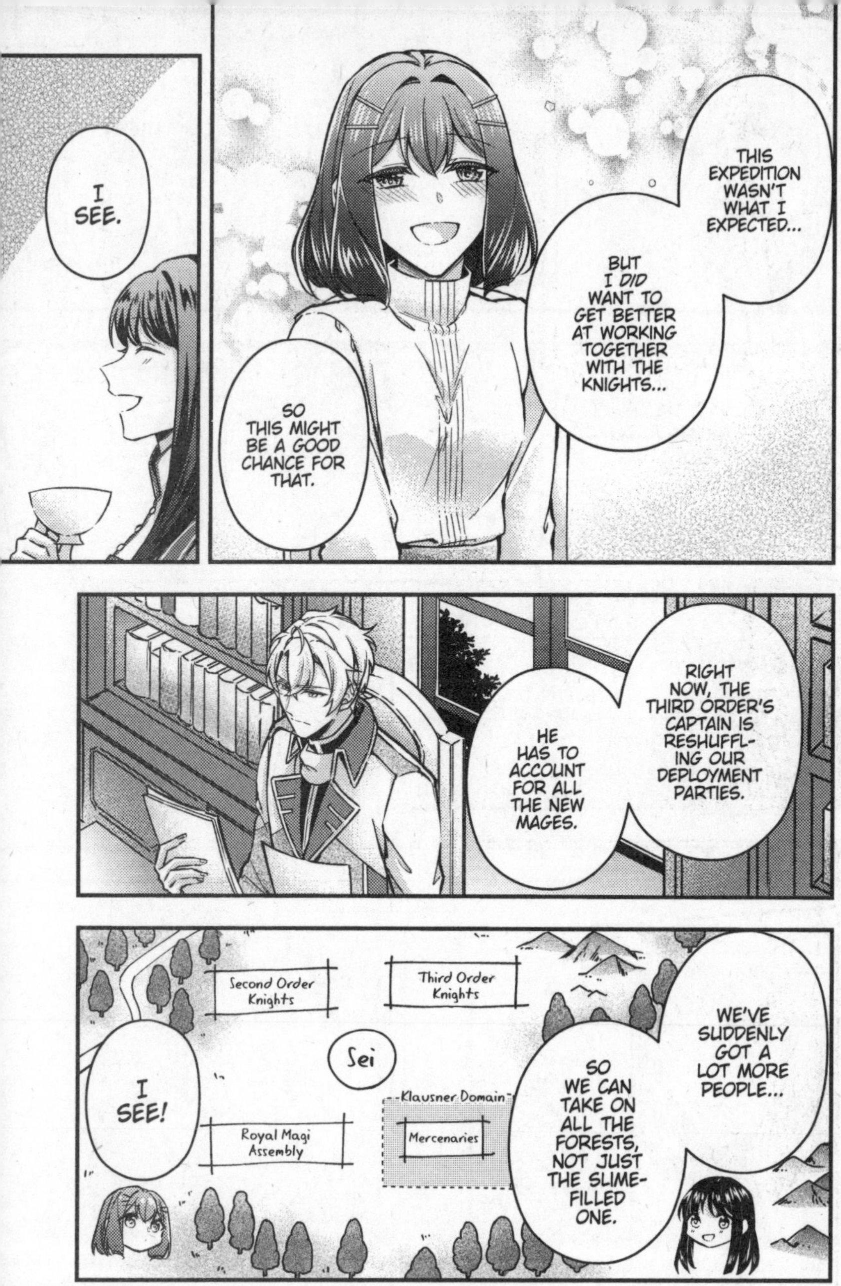
THIS EXPEDITION WASN'T WHAT I EXPECTED...
BUT I *DID* WANT TO GET BETTER AT WORKING TOGETHER WITH THE KNIGHTS...
SO THIS MIGHT BE A GOOD CHANCE FOR THAT.
I SEE.
RIGHT NOW, THE THIRD ORDER'S CAPTAIN IS RESHUFFLING OUR DEPLOYMENT PARTIES.
HE HAS TO ACCOUNT FOR ALL THE NEW MAGES.
WE'VE SUDDENLY GOT A LOT MORE PEOPLE...
SO WE CAN TAKE ON ALL THE FORESTS, NOT JUST THE SLIME-FILLED ONE.
Third Order Knights
Second Order Knights
Sei
Klausner Domain
Mercenaries
Royal Magi Assembly
I SEE!

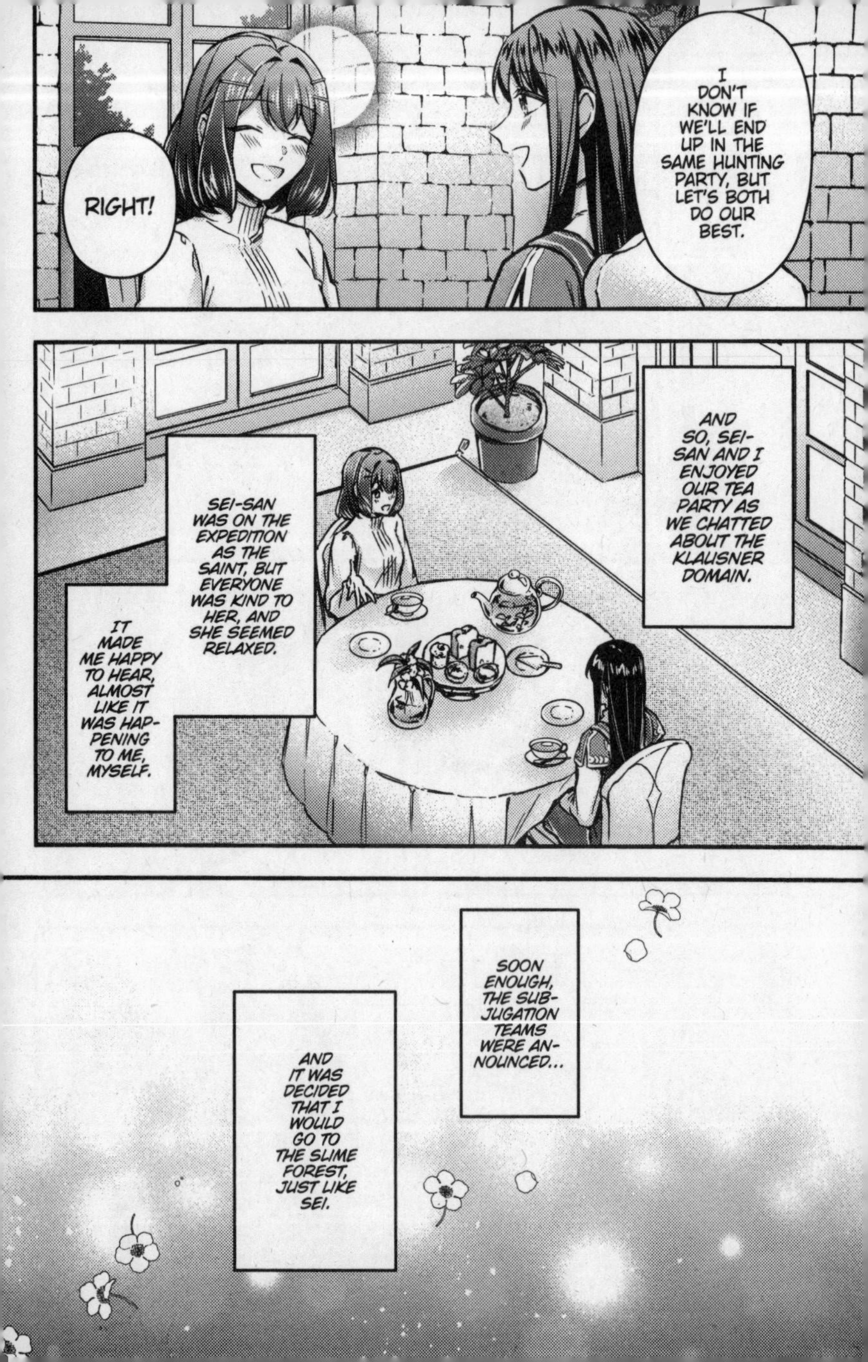
I DON'T KNOW IF WE'LL END UP IN THE SAME HUNTING PARTY, BUT LET'S BOTH DO OUR BEST.
RIGHT!
AND SO, SEI-SAN AND I ENJOYED OUR TEA PARTY AS WE CHATTED ABOUT THE KLAUSNER DOMAIN.
SEI-SAN WAS ON THE EXPEDITION AS THE SAINT, BUT EVERYONE WAS KIND TO HER, AND SHE SEEMED RELAXED.
IT MADE ME HAPPY TO HEAR, ALMOST LIKE IT WAS HAP-PENING TO ME, MYSELF.
SOON ENOUGH, THE SUB-JUGATION TEAMS WERE AN-NOUNCED...
AND IT WAS DECIDED THAT I WOULD GO TO THE SLIME FOREST, JUST LIKE SEI.

The **Saint's**
Magic Power is
Omnipotent
— The Other Saint —

The **Saint's**
Magic Power is
Omnipotent
— The Other Saint —

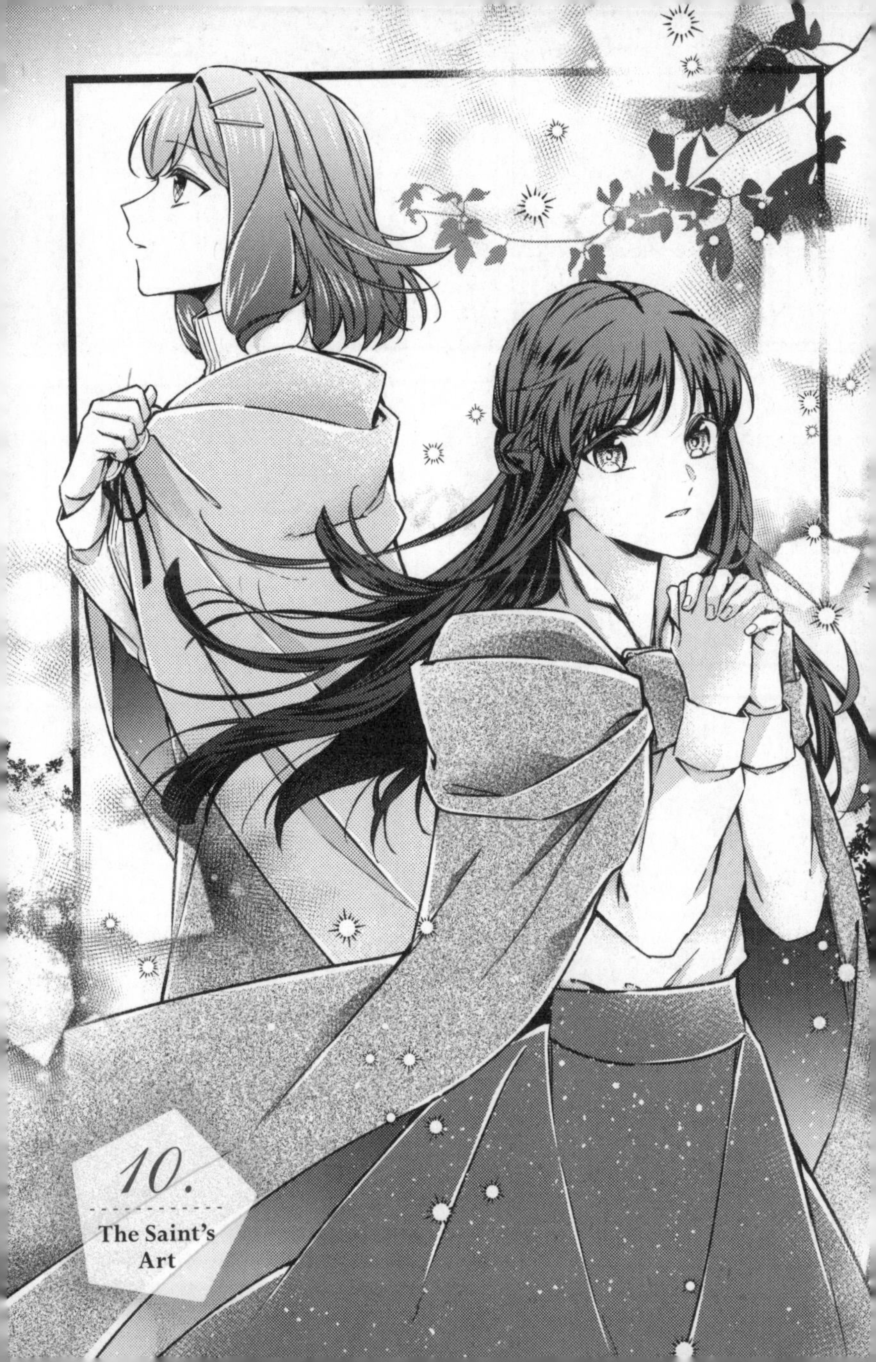
10.
The Saint's Art

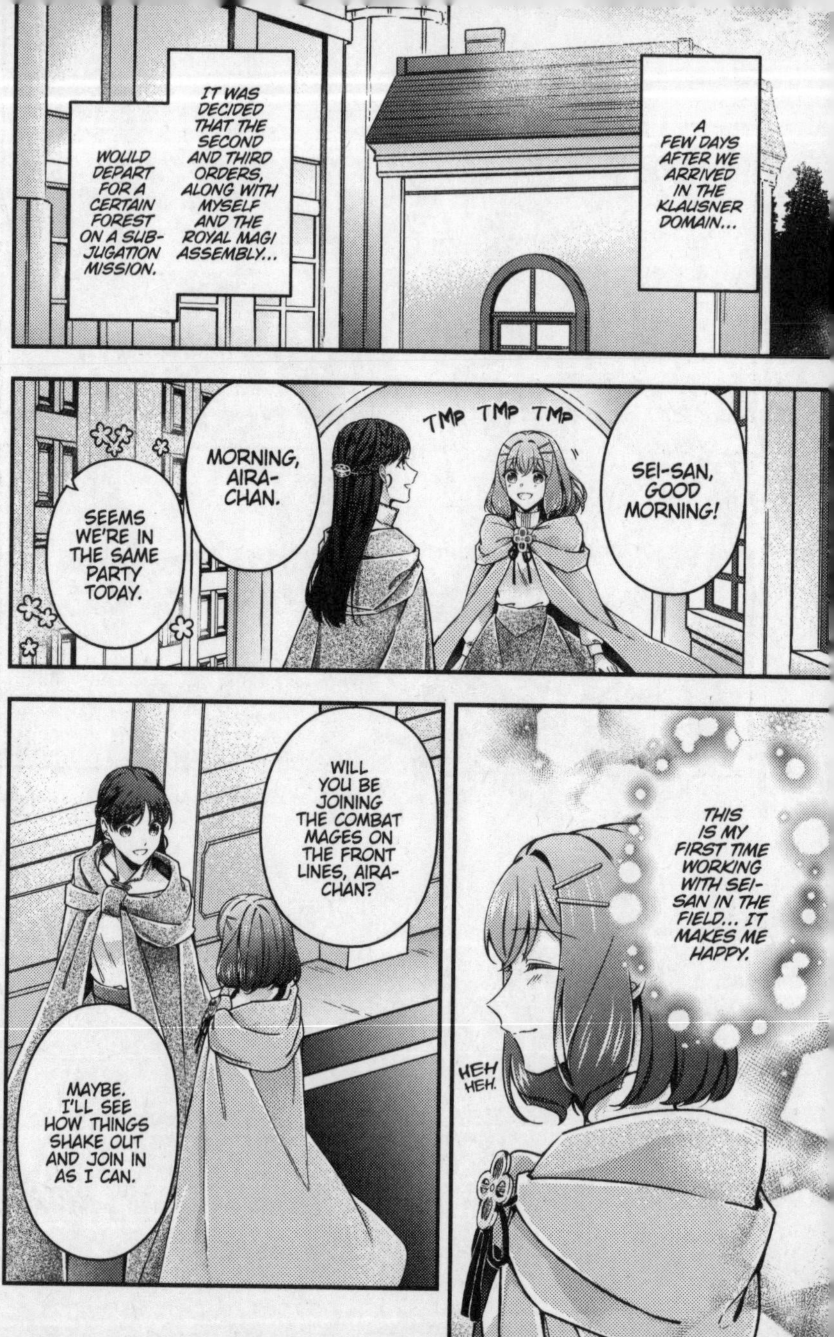
A FEW DAYS AFTER WE ARRIVED IN THE KLAUSNER DOMAIN...
IT WAS DECIDED THAT THE SECOND AND THIRD ORDERS, ALONG WITH MYSELF AND THE ROYAL MAGI ASSEMBLY...
WOULD DEPART FOR A CERTAIN FOREST ON A SUB-JUGATION MISSION.
SEI-SAN, GOOD MORNING!
TMP TMP TMP
MORNING, AIRA-CHAN.
SEEMS WE'RE IN THE SAME PARTY TODAY.
THIS IS MY FIRST TIME WORKING WITH SEI-SAN IN THE FIELD... IT MAKES ME HAPPY.
HEH HEH.
WILL YOU BE JOINING THE COMBAT MAGES ON THE FRONT LINES, AIRA-CHAN?
MAYBE. I'LL SEE HOW THINGS SHAKE OUT AND JOIN IN AS I CAN.

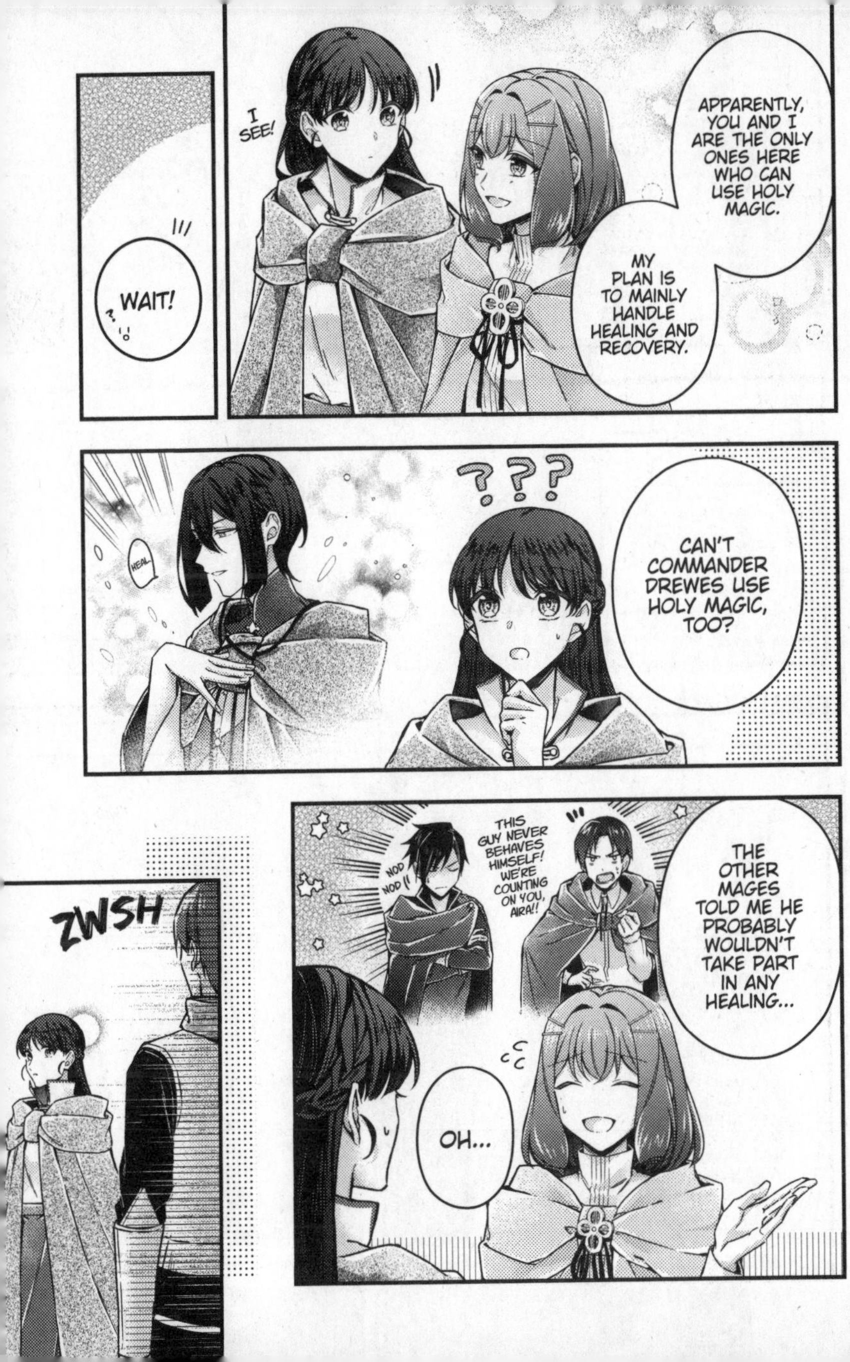
APPARENTLY, YOU AND I ARE THE ONLY ONES HERE WHO CAN USE HOLY MAGIC.
MY PLAN IS TO MAINLY HANDLE HEALING AND RECOVERY.
I SEE!
WAIT!
???
CAN'T COMMANDER DREWES USE HOLY MAGIC, TOO?
HEAL
THE OTHER MAGES TOLD ME HE PROBABLY WOULDN'T TAKE PART IN ANY HEALING...
THIS GUY NEVER BEHAVES HIMSELF! WE'RE COUNTING ON YOU, AIRA!!
NOD NOD
OH...
ZWSH

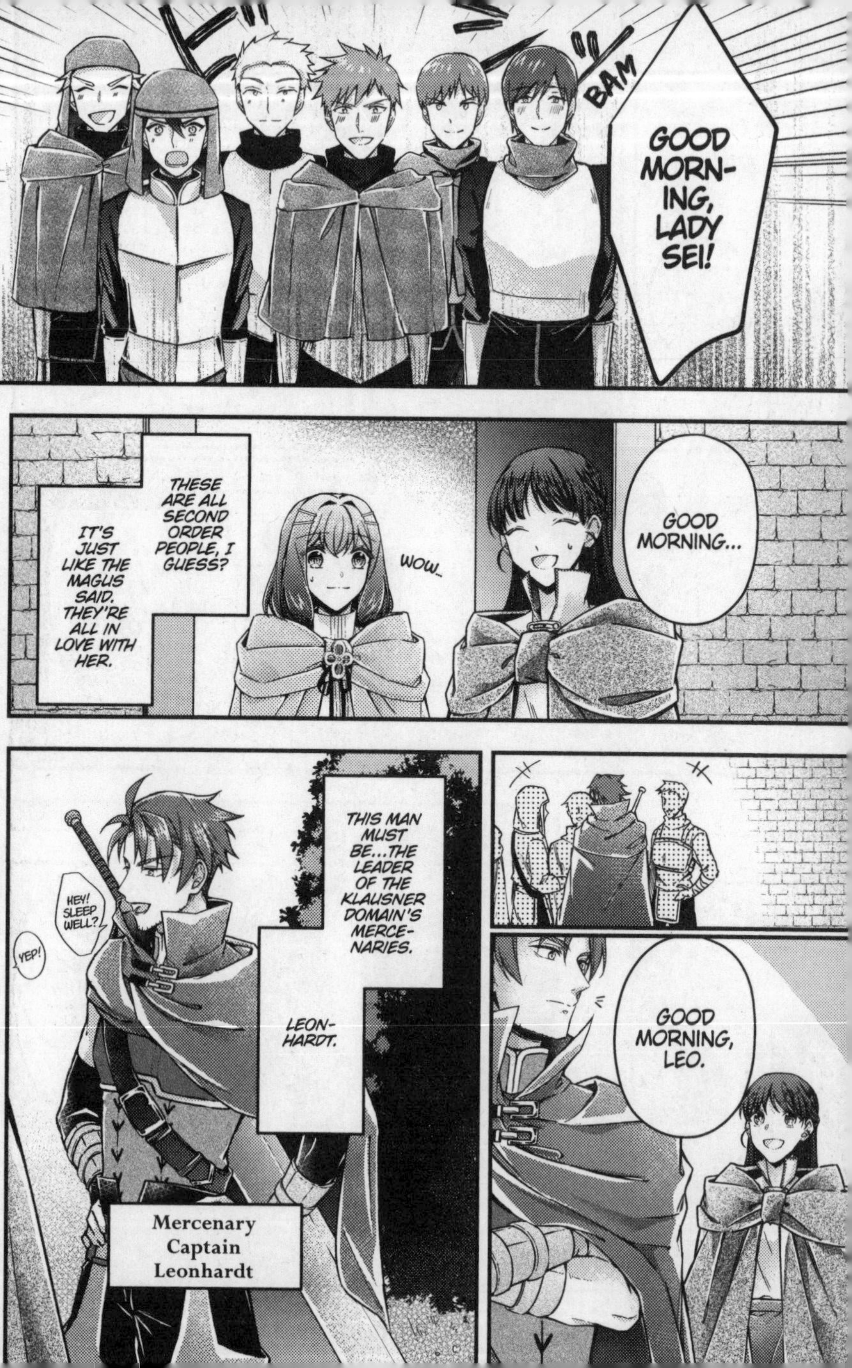
BAM
GOOD MORNING, LADY SEI!
GOOD MORNING...
WOW..
THESE ARE ALL SECOND ORDER PEOPLE, I GUESS?
IT'S JUST LIKE THE MAGUS SAID. THEY'RE ALL IN LOVE WITH HER.
GOOD MORNING, LEO.
THIS MAN MUST BE...THE LEADER OF THE KLAUSNER DOMAIN'S MERCENARIES.
LEONHARDT.
HEY! SLEEP WELL?
YEP!
Mercenary Captain Leonhardt

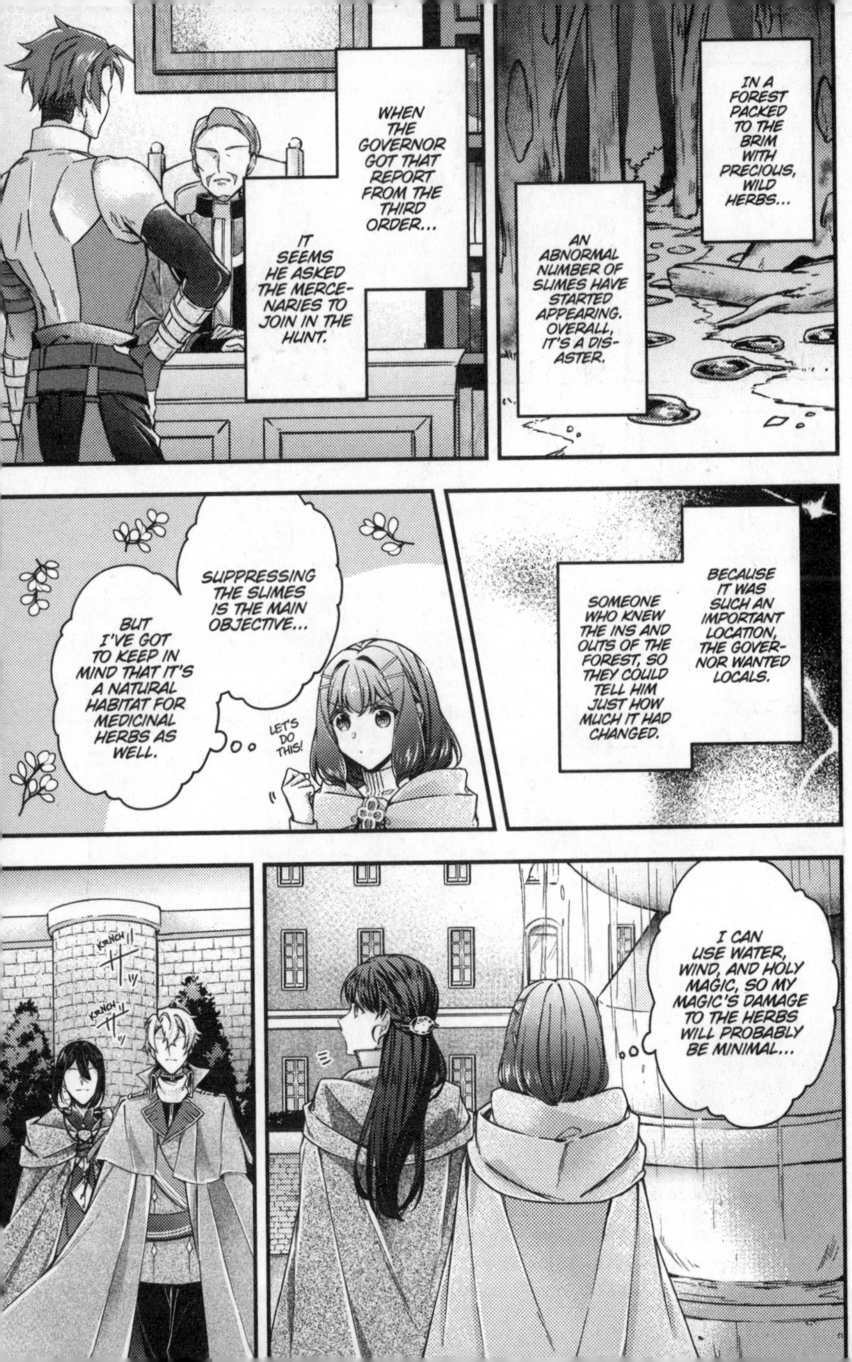
IN A FOREST PACKED TO THE BRIM WITH PRECIOUS, WILD HERBS...
AN ABNORMAL NUMBER OF SLIMES HAVE STARTED APPEARING. OVERALL, IT'S A DISASTER.
WHEN THE GOVERNOR GOT THAT REPORT FROM THE THIRD ORDER...
IT SEEMS HE ASKED THE MERCENARIES TO JOIN IN THE HUNT.
BECAUSE IT WAS SUCH AN IMPORTANT LOCATION, THE GOVERNOR WANTED LOCALS.
SOMEONE WHO KNEW THE INS AND OUTS OF THE FOREST, SO THEY COULD TELL HIM JUST HOW MUCH IT HAD CHANGED.
SUPPRESSING THE SLIMES IS THE MAIN OBJECTIVE...
BUT I'VE GOT TO KEEP IN MIND THAT IT'S A NATURAL HABITAT FOR MEDICINAL HERBS AS WELL.
LET'S DO THIS!
I CAN USE WATER, WIND, AND HOLY MAGIC, SO MY MAGIC'S DAMAGE TO THE HERBS WILL PROBABLY BE MINIMAL...
KRNCH
KRNCH

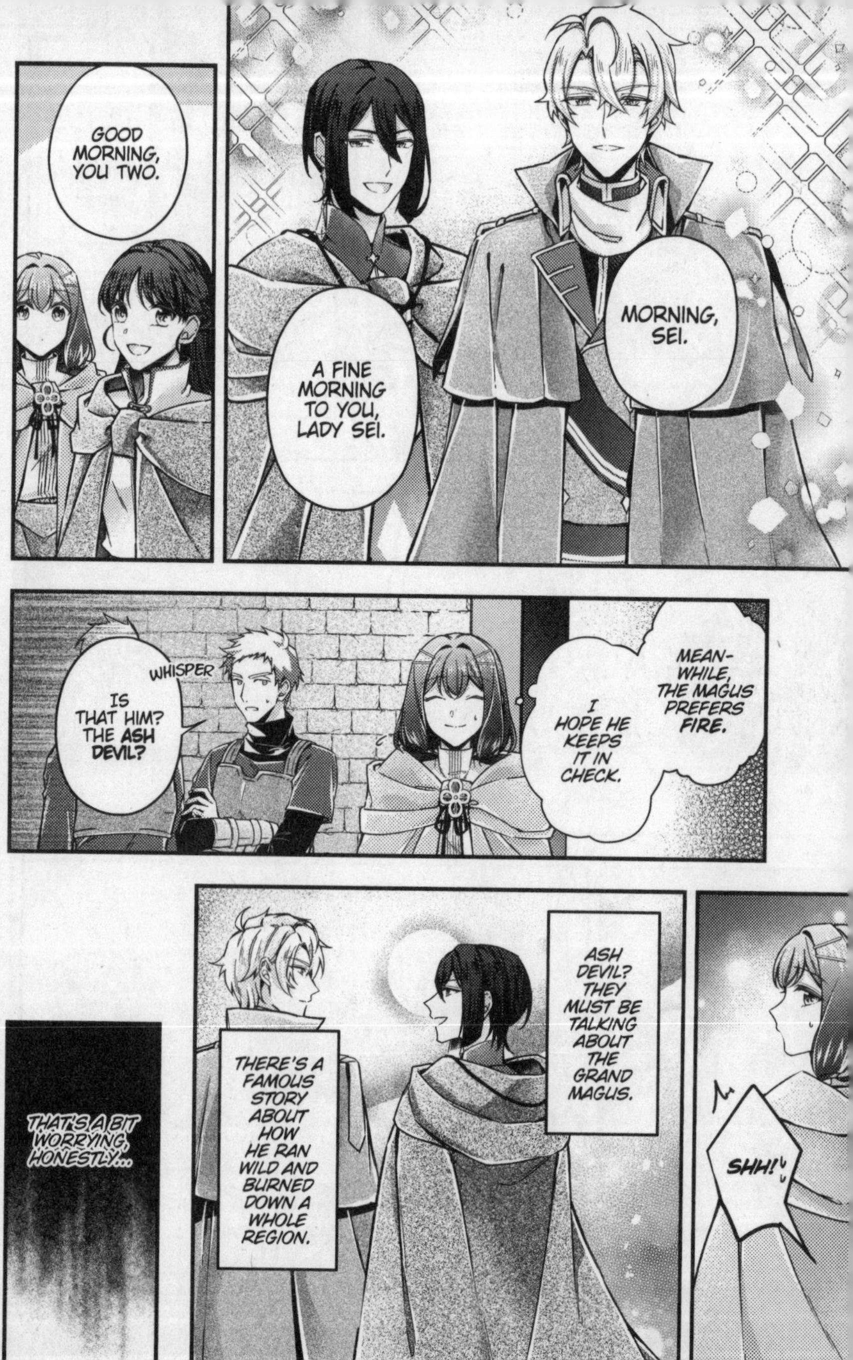
MORNING, SEI.
A FINE MORNING TO YOU, LADY SEI.
GOOD MORNING, YOU TWO.
MEAN-WHILE, THE MAGUS PREFERS FIRE.
I HOPE HE KEEPS IT IN CHECK.
WHISPER
IS THAT HIM? THE ASH DEVIL?
SHH!
ASH DEVIL? THEY MUST BE TALKING ABOUT THE GRAND MAGUS.
THERE'S A FAMOUS STORY ABOUT HOW HE RAN WILD AND BURNED DOWN A WHOLE REGION.
THAT'S A BIT WORRYING, HONESTLY...

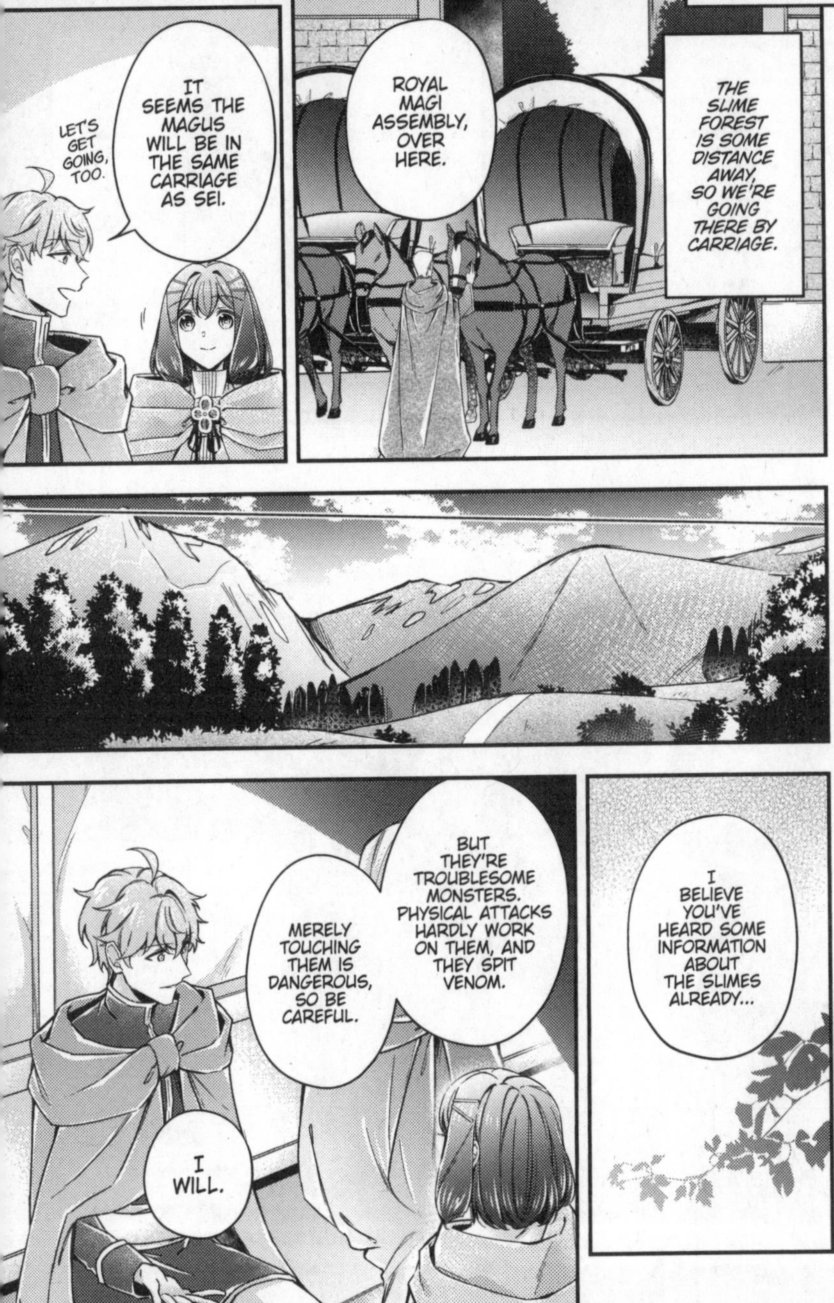
THE SLIME FOREST IS SOME DISTANCE AWAY, SO WE'RE GOING THERE BY CARRIAGE.
ROYAL MAGI ASSEMBLY, OVER HERE.
IT SEEMS THE MAGUS WILL BE IN THE SAME CARRIAGE AS SEI.
LET'S GET GOING, TOO.
I BELIEVE YOU'VE HEARD SOME INFORMATION ABOUT THE SLIMES ALREADY...
BUT THEY'RE TROUBLESOME MONSTERS. PHYSICAL ATTACKS HARDLY WORK ON THEM, AND THEY SPIT VENOM.
MERELY TOUCHING THEM IS DANGEROUS, SO BE CAREFUL.
I WILL.

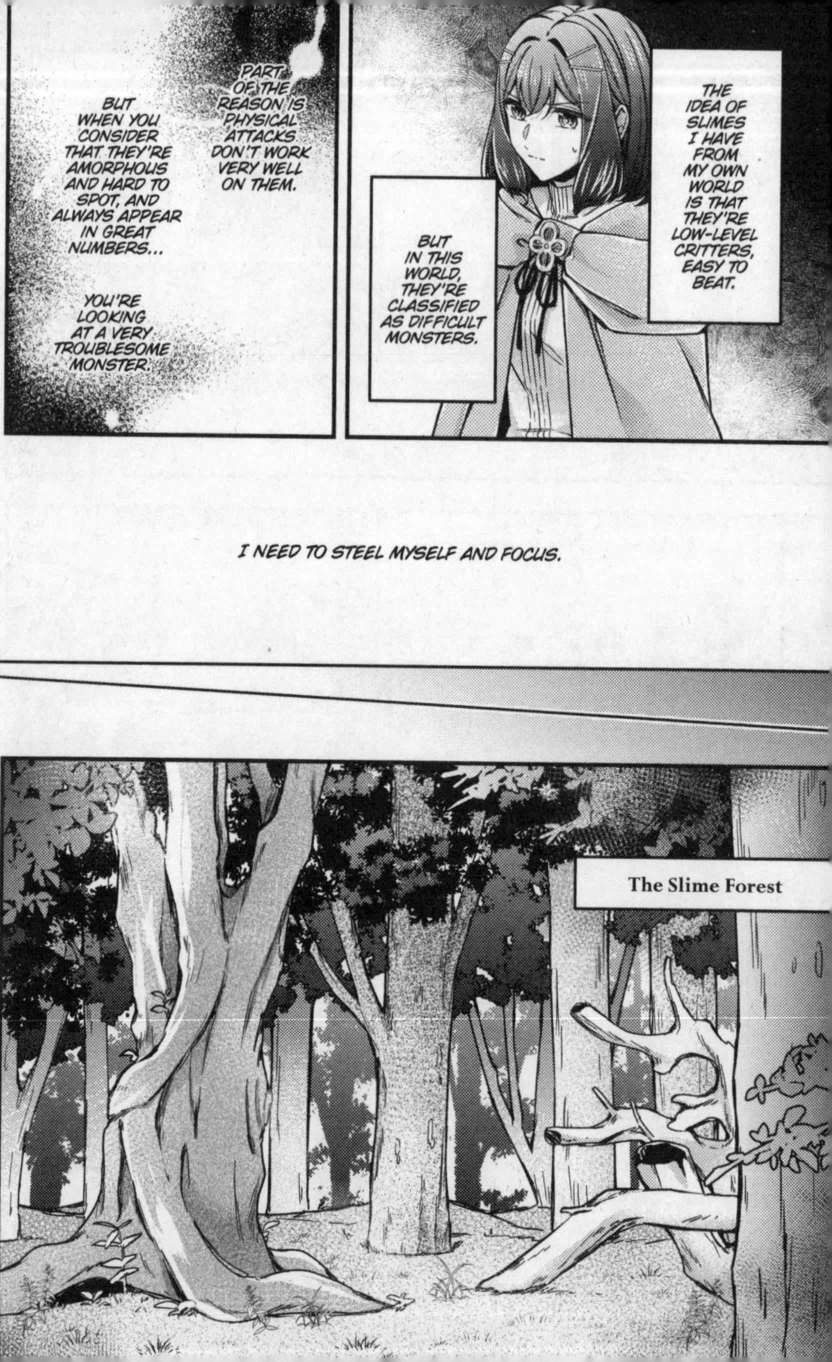
THE IDEA OF SLIMES I HAVE FROM MY OWN WORLD IS THAT THEY'RE LOW-LEVEL CRITTERS, EASY TO BEAT.
BUT IN THIS WORLD, THEY'RE CLASSIFIED AS DIFFICULT MONSTERS.
PART OF THE REASON IS PHYSICAL ATTACKS DON'T WORK VERY WELL ON THEM.
BUT WHEN YOU CONSIDER THAT THEY'RE AMORPHOUS AND HARD TO SPOT, AND ALWAYS APPEAR IN GREAT NUMBERS...
YOU'RE LOOKING AT A VERY TROUBLESOME MONSTER.
I NEED TO STEEL MYSELF AND FOCUS.
The Slime Forest

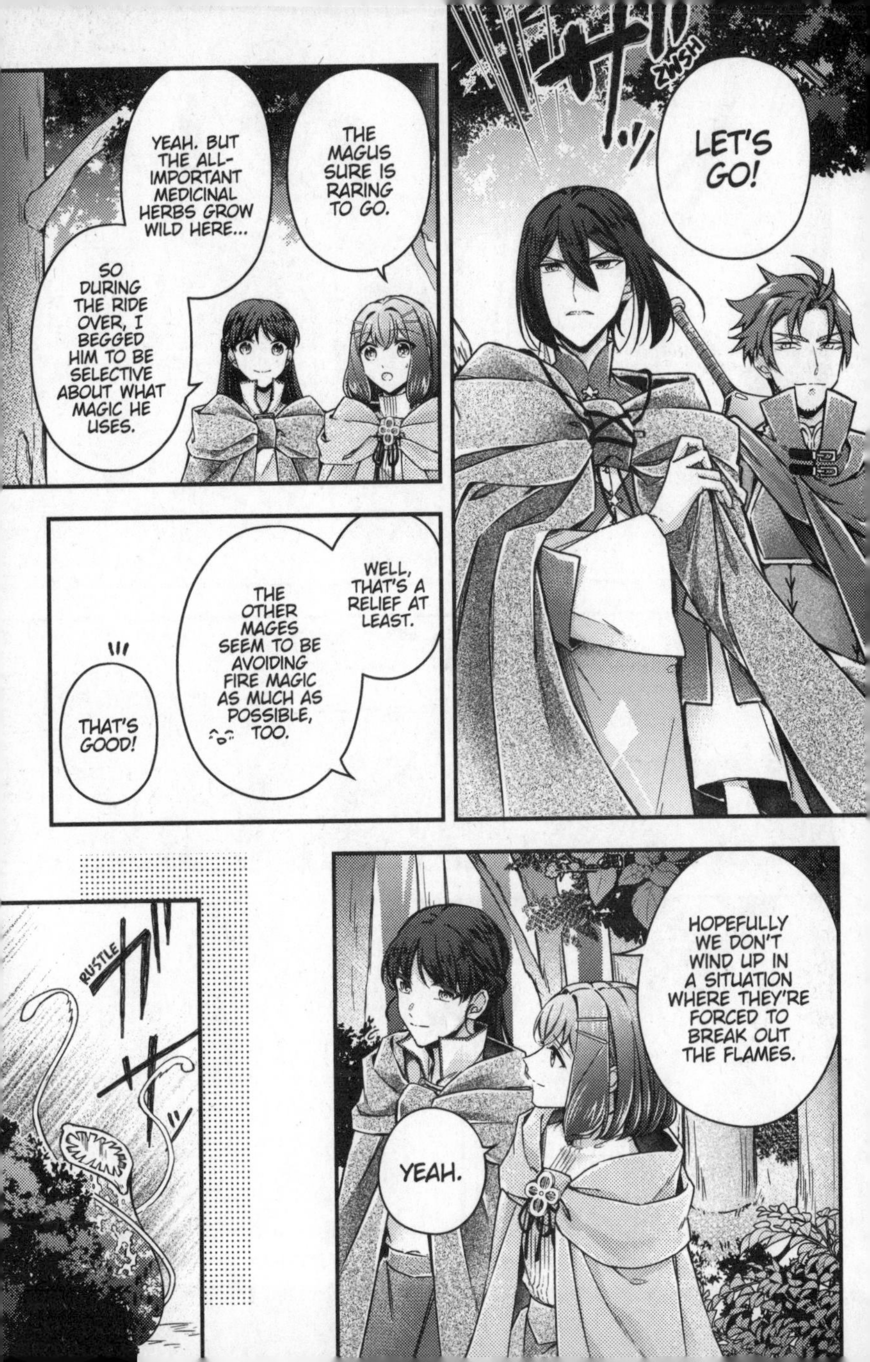
ZWSH
LET'S GO!
THE MAGUS SURE IS RARING TO GO.
YEAH. BUT THE ALL-IMPORTANT MEDICINAL HERBS GROW WILD HERE...
SO DURING THE RIDE OVER, I BEGGED HIM TO BE SELECTIVE ABOUT WHAT MAGIC HE USES.
WELL, THAT'S A RELIEF AT LEAST.
THE OTHER MAGES SEEM TO BE AVOIDING FIRE MAGIC AS MUCH AS POSSIBLE, TOO.
THAT'S GOOD!
HOPEFULLY WE DON'T WIND UP IN A SITUATION WHERE THEY'RE FORCED TO BREAK OUT THE FLAMES.
YEAH.
RUSTLE

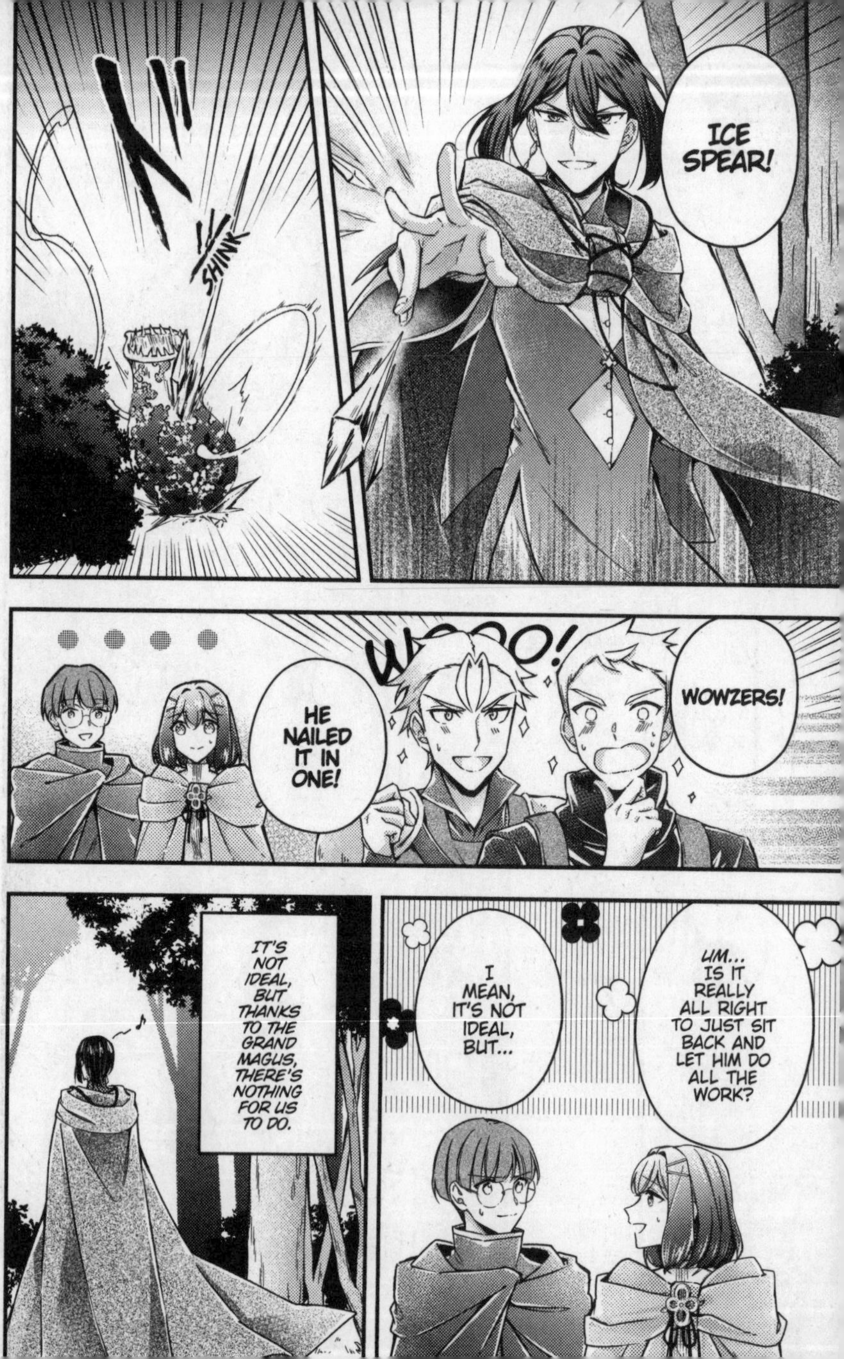
ICE SPEAR!
SHINK
WOWZERS!
HE NAILED IT IN ONE!
UM... IS IT REALLY ALL RIGHT TO JUST SIT BACK AND LET HIM DO ALL THE WORK?
I MEAN, IT'S NOT IDEAL, BUT...
IT'S NOT IDEAL, BUT THANKS TO THE GRAND MAGUS, THERE'S NOTHING FOR US TO DO.

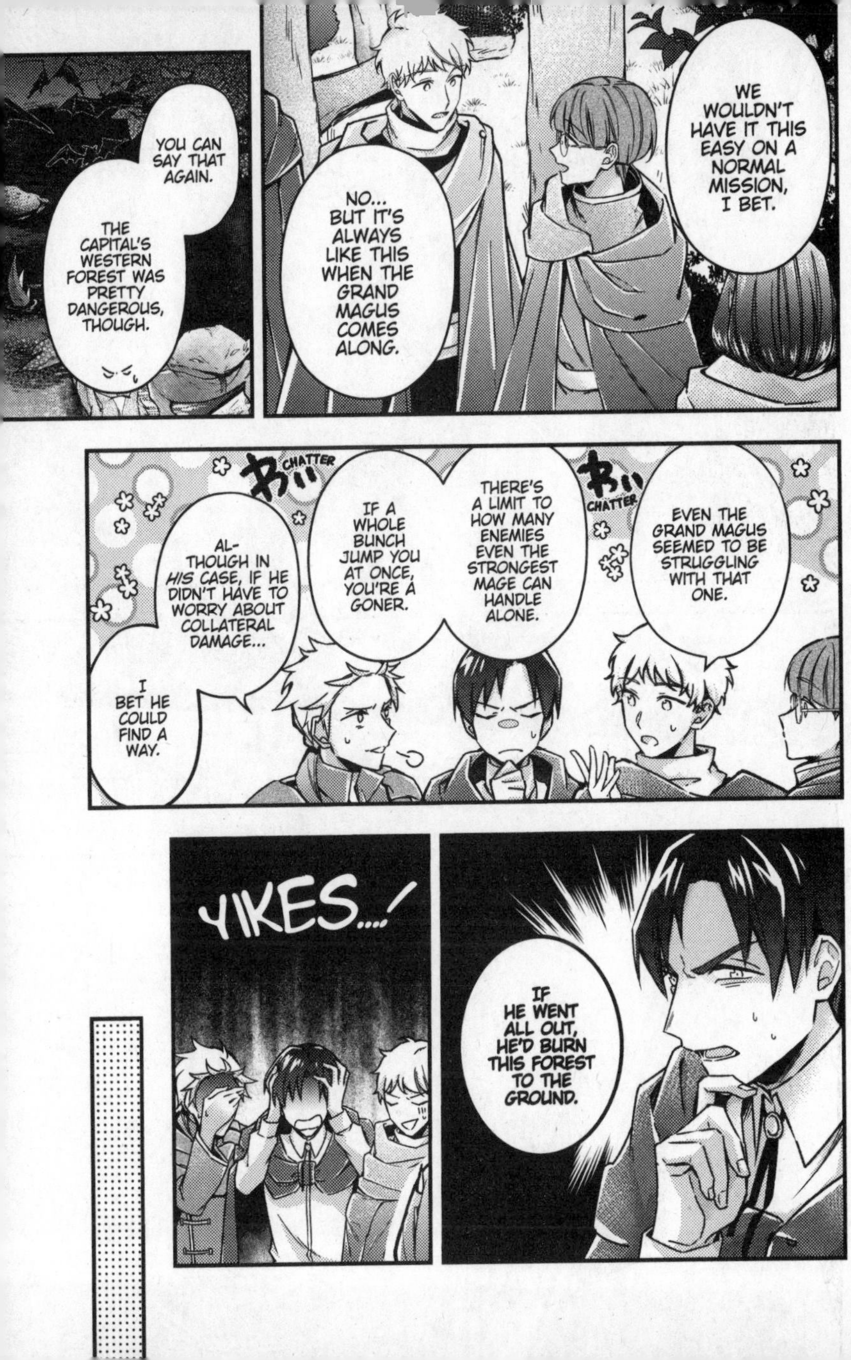
WE WOULDN'T HAVE IT THIS EASY ON A NORMAL MISSION, I BET.
NO... BUT IT'S ALWAYS LIKE THIS WHEN THE GRAND MAGUS COMES ALONG.
YOU CAN SAY THAT AGAIN.
THE CAPITAL'S WESTERN FOREST WAS PRETTY DANGEROUS, THOUGH.
EVEN THE GRAND MAGUS SEEMED TO BE STRUGGLING WITH THAT ONE.
CHATTER
THERE'S A LIMIT TO HOW MANY ENEMIES EVEN THE STRONGEST MAGE CAN HANDLE ALONE.
IF A WHOLE BUNCH JUMP YOU AT ONCE, YOU'RE A GONER.
CHATTER
AL-THOUGH IN *HIS* CASE, IF HE DIDN'T HAVE TO WORRY ABOUT COLLATERAL DAMAGE...
I BET HE COULD FIND A WAY.
IF HE WENT ALL OUT, HE'D BURN THIS FOREST TO THE GROUND.
YIKES...!

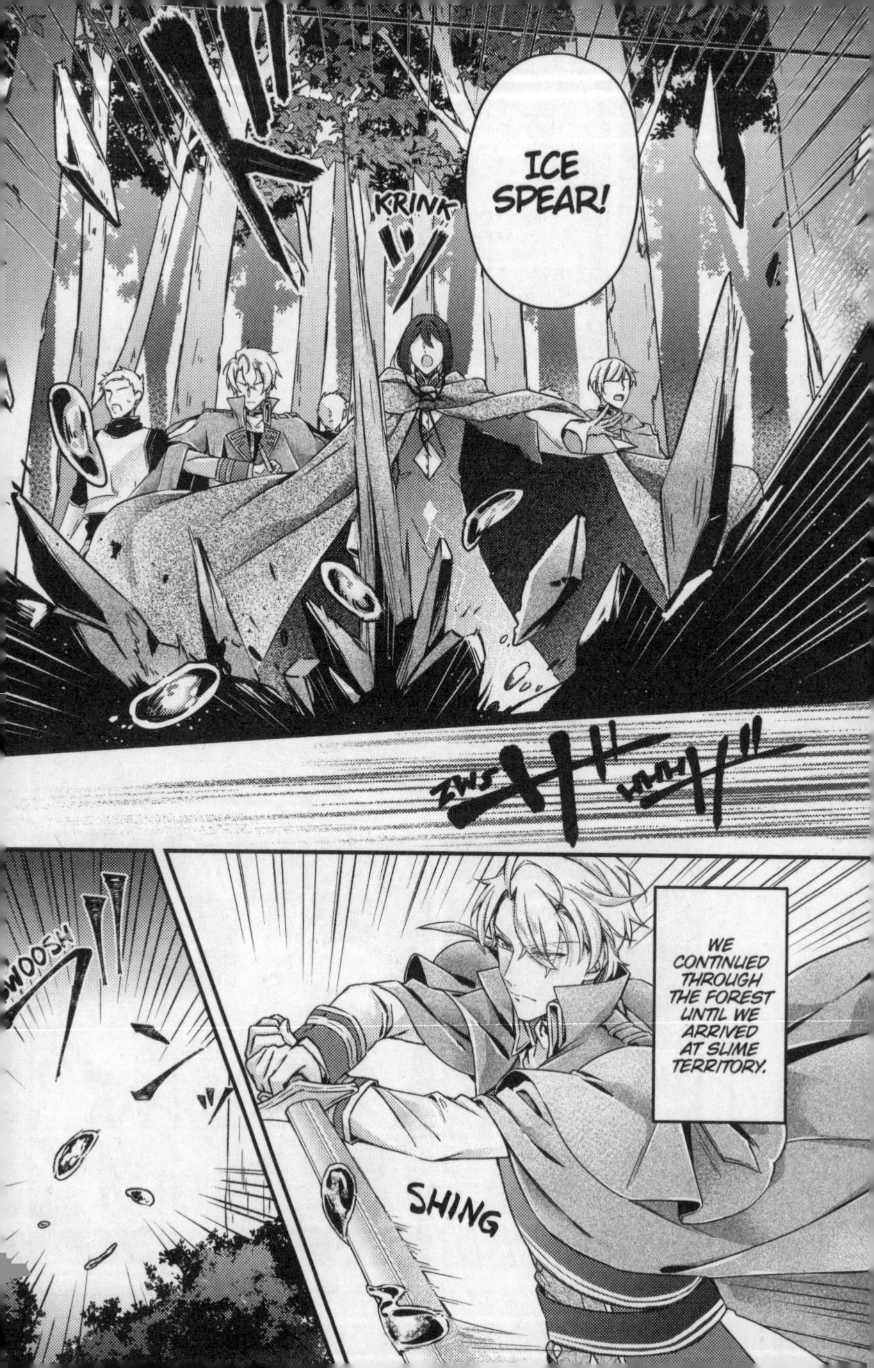
ICE SPEAR!
KRINK
WE CONTINUED THROUGH THE FOREST UNTIL WE ARRIVED AT SLIME TERRITORY.
SHING
WOOSH

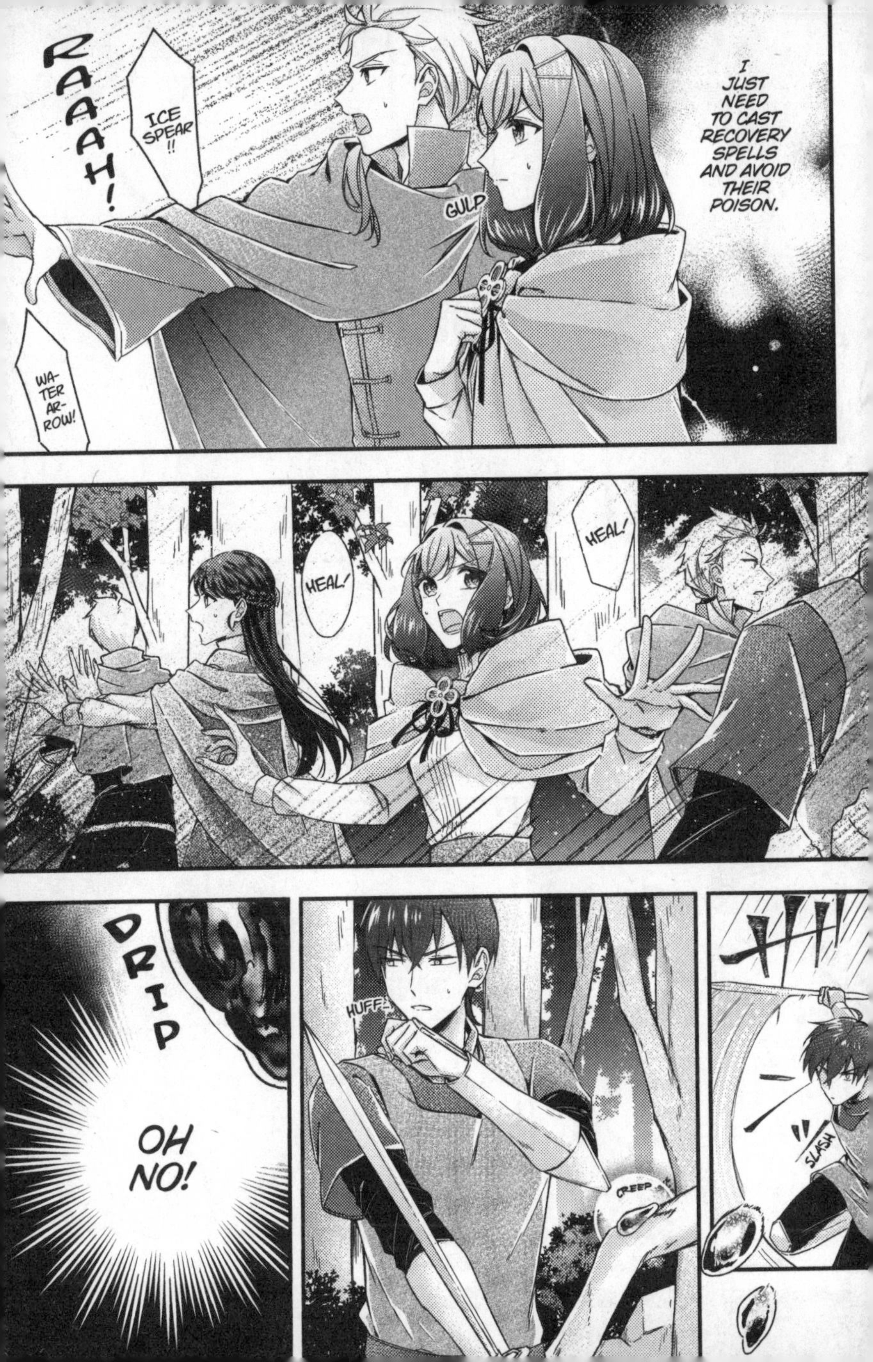
I JUST NEED TO CAST RECOVERY SPELLS AND AVOID THEIR POISON.
GULP
ICE SPEAR!!
RAAAAH!
WATER ARROW!
HEAL!
HEAL!
SLASH
HUFF
CREEP
DRIP
OH NO!

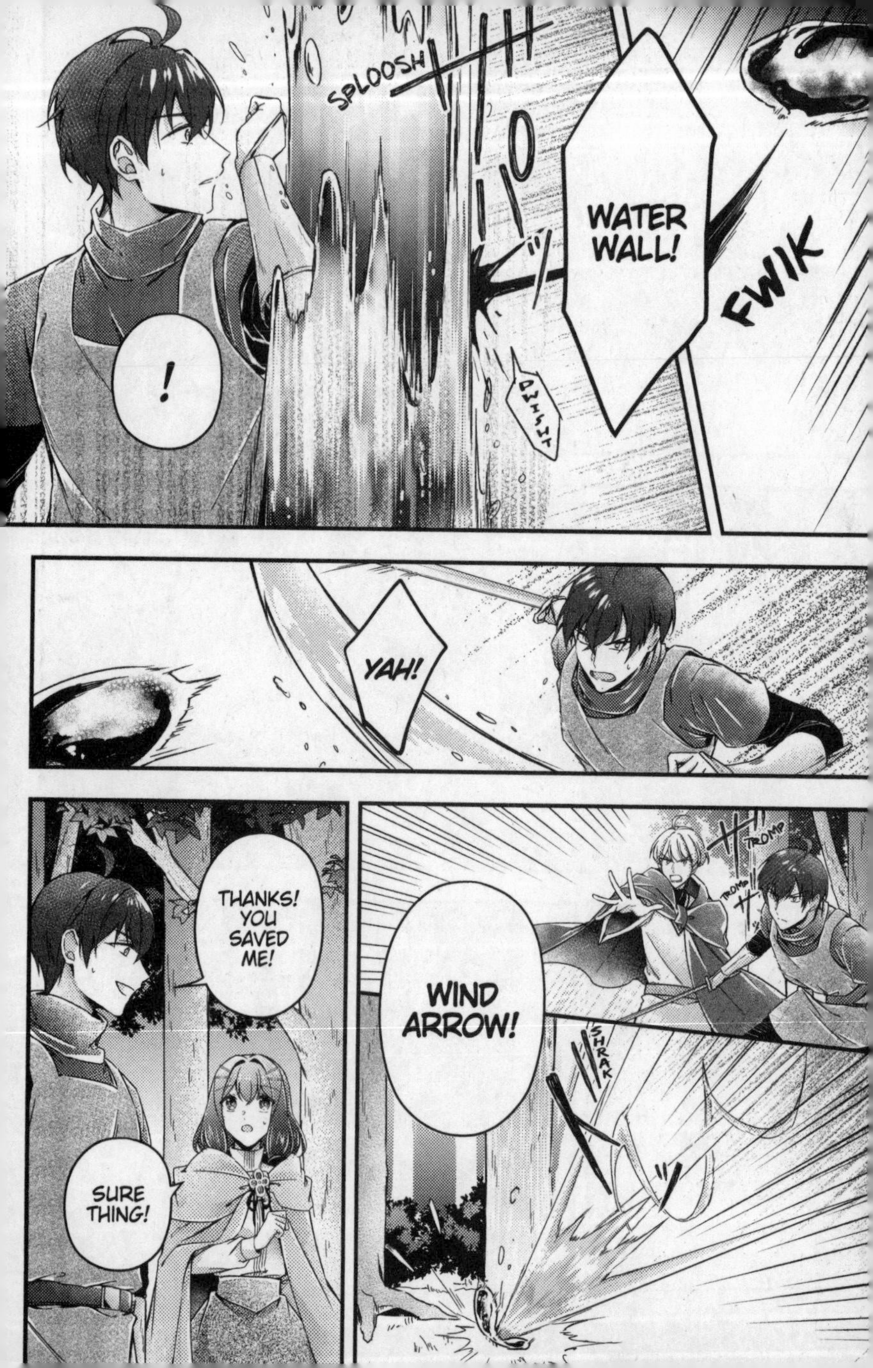
FWIK
WATER WALL!
SPLOOSH
DWISHT
!
YAH!
TROMP
TROMP
WIND ARROW!
SHRAK
THANKS! YOU SAVED ME!
SURE THING!

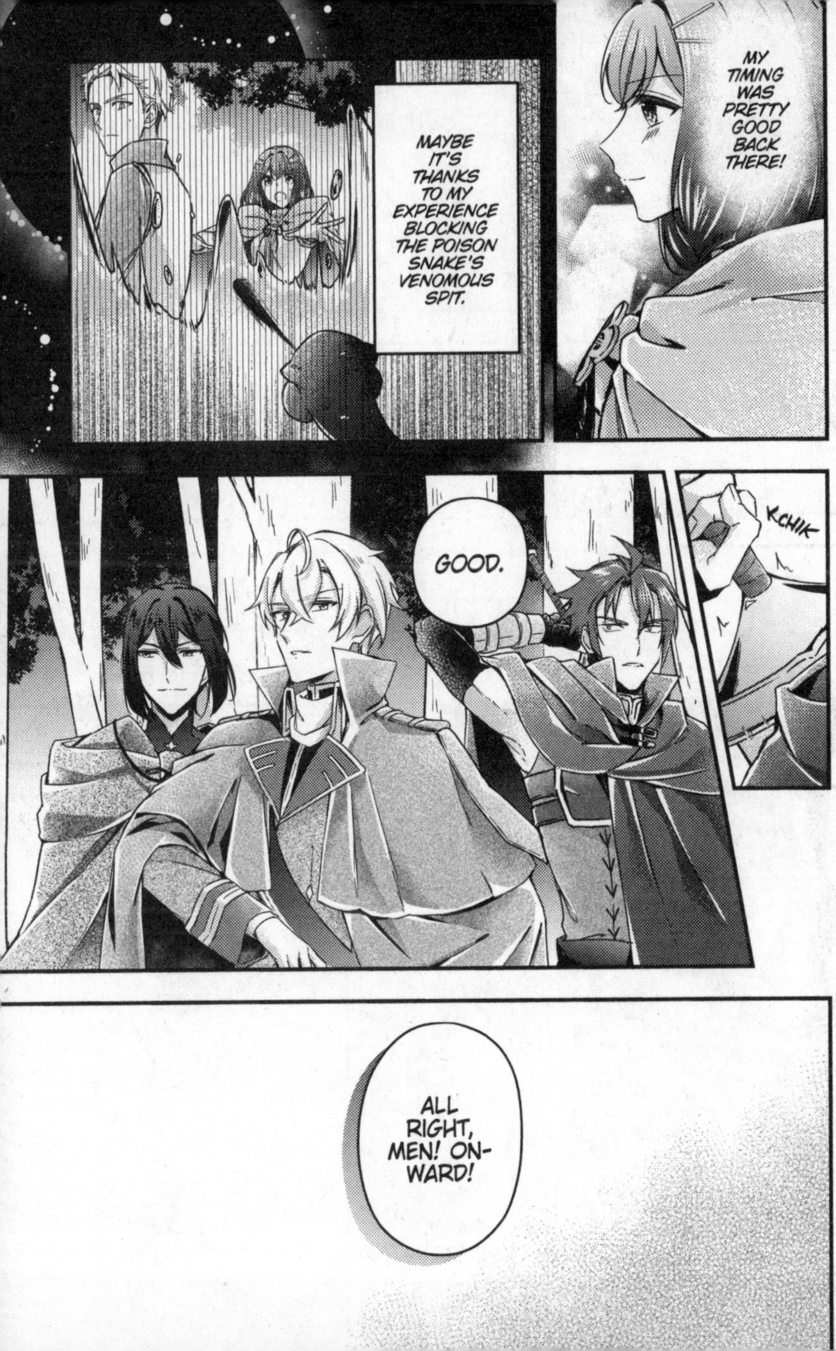
MY TIMING WAS PRETTY GOOD BACK THERE!
MAYBE IT'S THANKS TO MY EXPERIENCE BLOCKING THE POISON SNAKE'S VENOMOUS SPIT.
KCHIK
GOOD.
ALL RIGHT, MEN! ON-WARD!

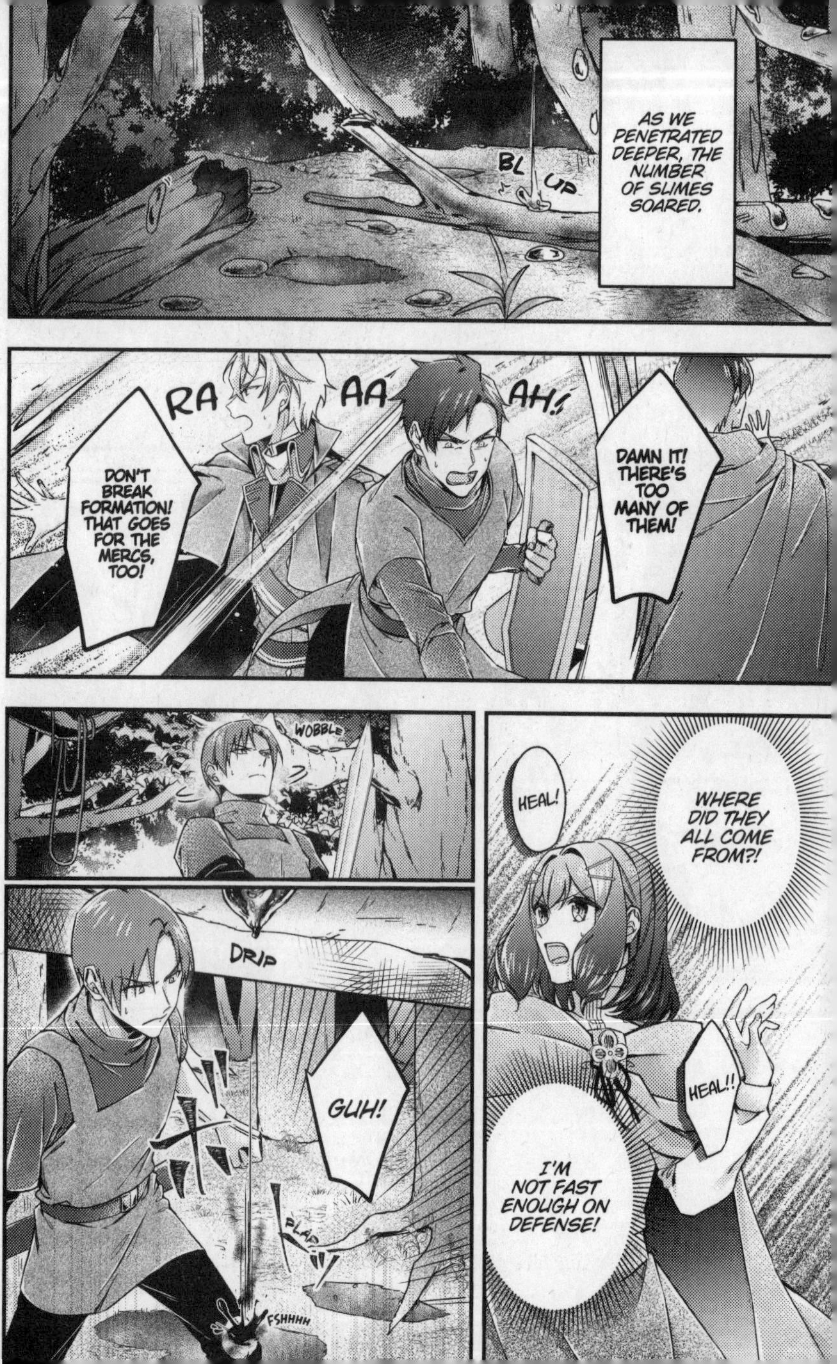
AS WE PENETRATED DEEPER, THE NUMBER OF SLIMES SOARED.
BL UP
DAMN IT! THERE'S TOO MANY OF THEM!
RA AA AH!
DON'T BREAK FORMATION! THAT GOES FOR THE MERCS, TOO!
WHERE DID THEY ALL COME FROM?!
HEAL!
HEAL!!
I'M NOT FAST ENOUGH ON DEFENSE!
WOBBLE
DRIP
GUH!
PLAP
FSHHHH

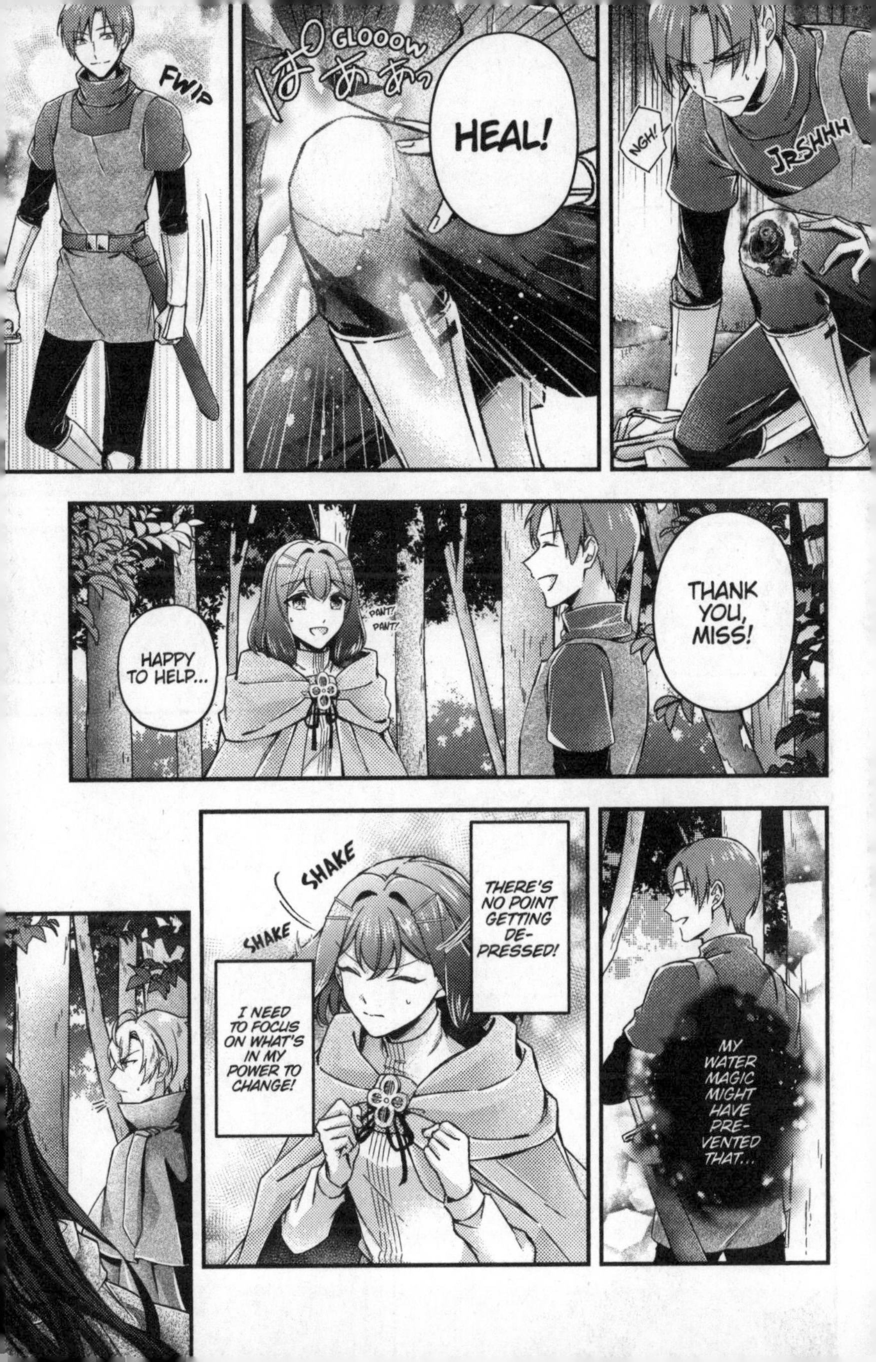
NGH!
JRSHHH
GLOOOW
ぽあぁっ
HEAL!
FWIP
THANK YOU, MISS!
PANT! PANT!
HAPPY TO HELP...
MY WATER MAGIC MIGHT HAVE PRE-VENTED THAT...
THERE'S NO POINT GETTING DE-PRESSED!
SHAKE
SHAKE
I NEED TO FOCUS ON WHAT'S IN MY POWER TO CHANGE!

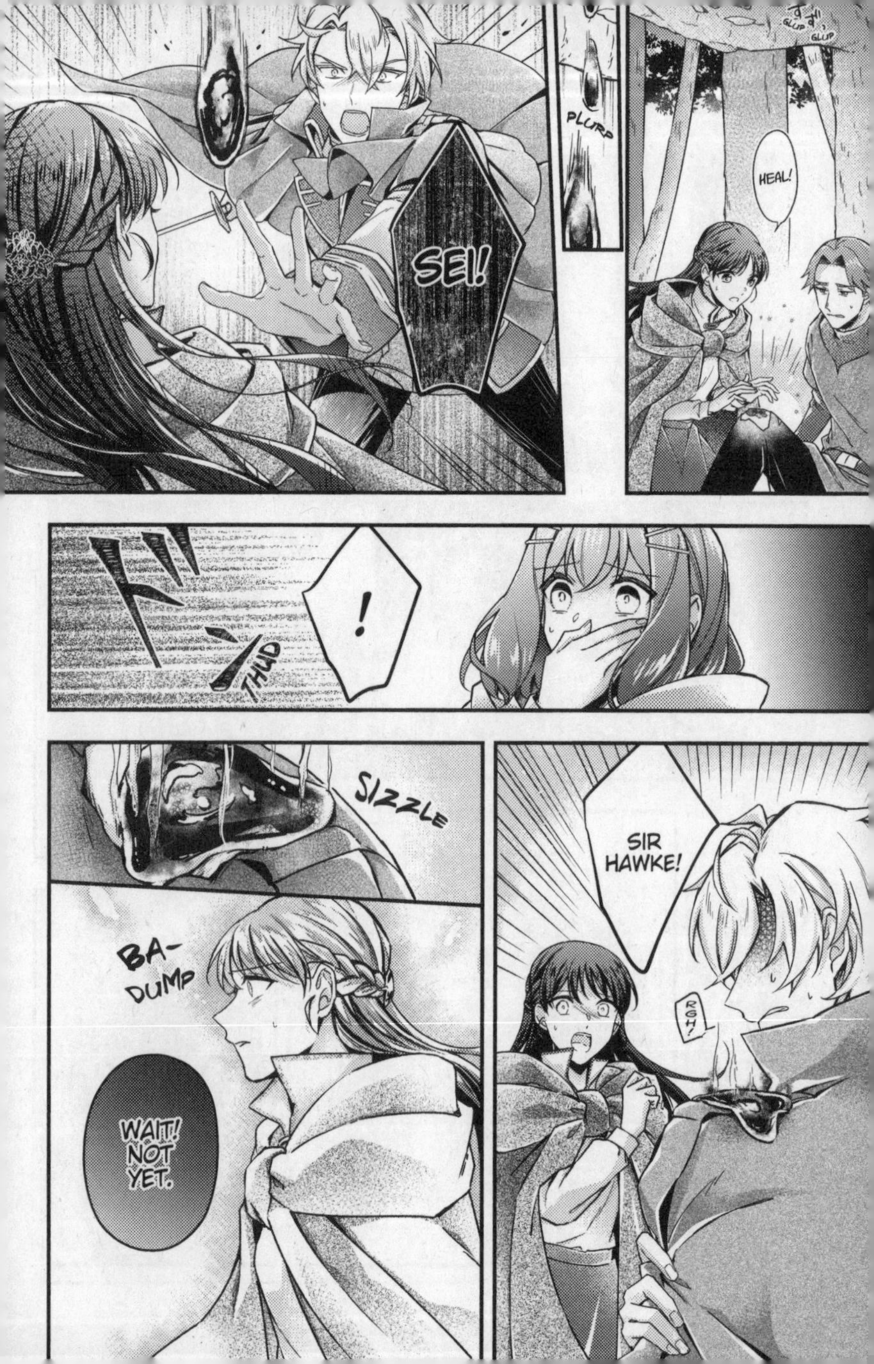
GLUP
GLUP
HEAL!
PLURP
SEI!
!
THUD
SIR HAWKE!
RGH!
SIZZLE
BA-DUMP
WAIT! NOT YET.

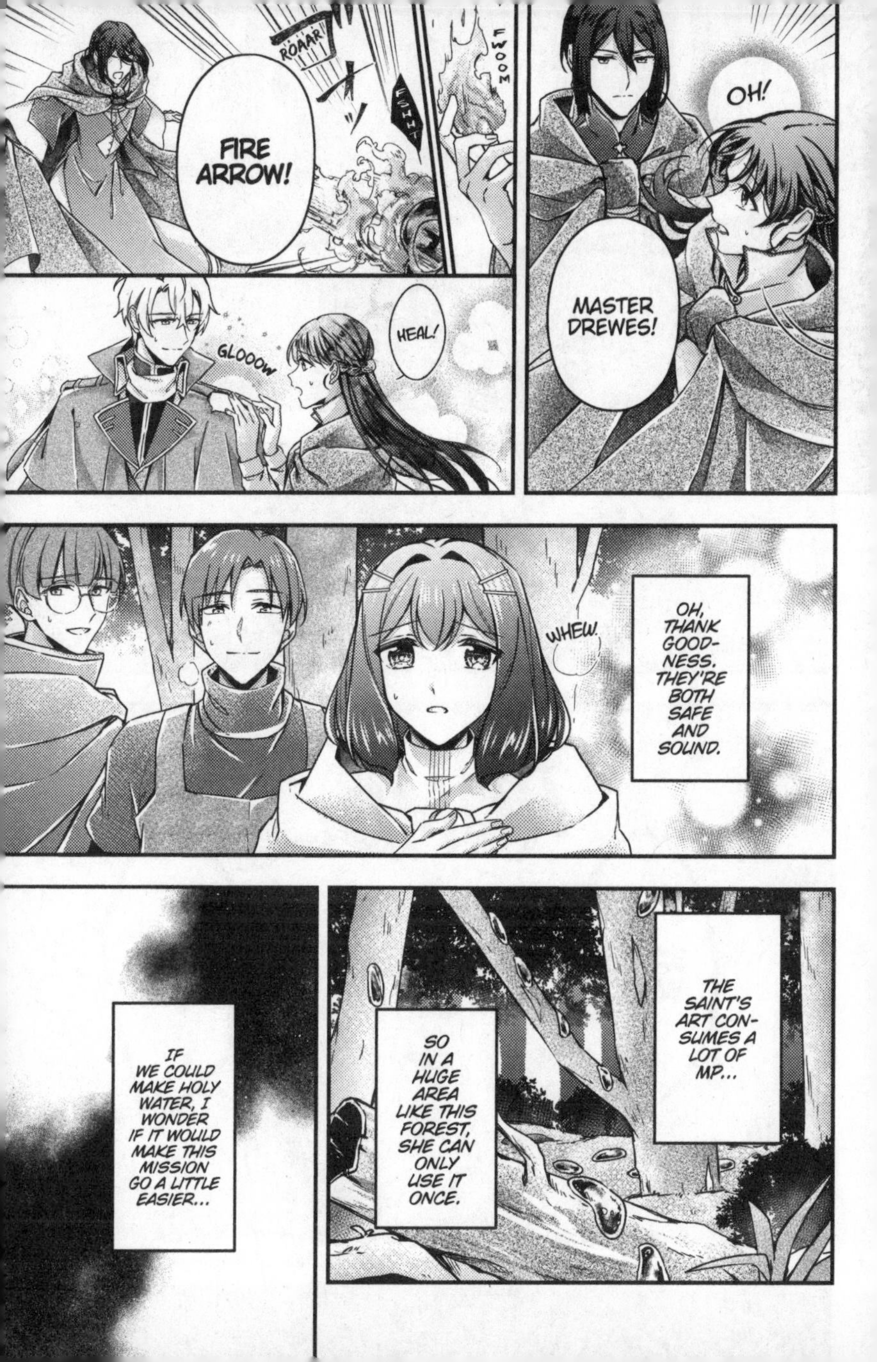

OH!
MASTER DREWES!
ROAAR
FWOOM
FSHHT
FIRE ARROW!
HEAL!
GLOOOW
OH, THANK GOOD-NESS. THEY'RE BOTH SAFE AND SOUND.
WHEW.
THE SAINT'S ART CON-SUMES A LOT OF MP...
SO IN A HUGE AREA LIKE THIS FOREST, SHE CAN ONLY USE IT ONCE.
IF WE COULD MAKE HOLY WATER, I WONDER IF IT WOULD MAKE THIS MISSION GO A LITTLE EASIER...

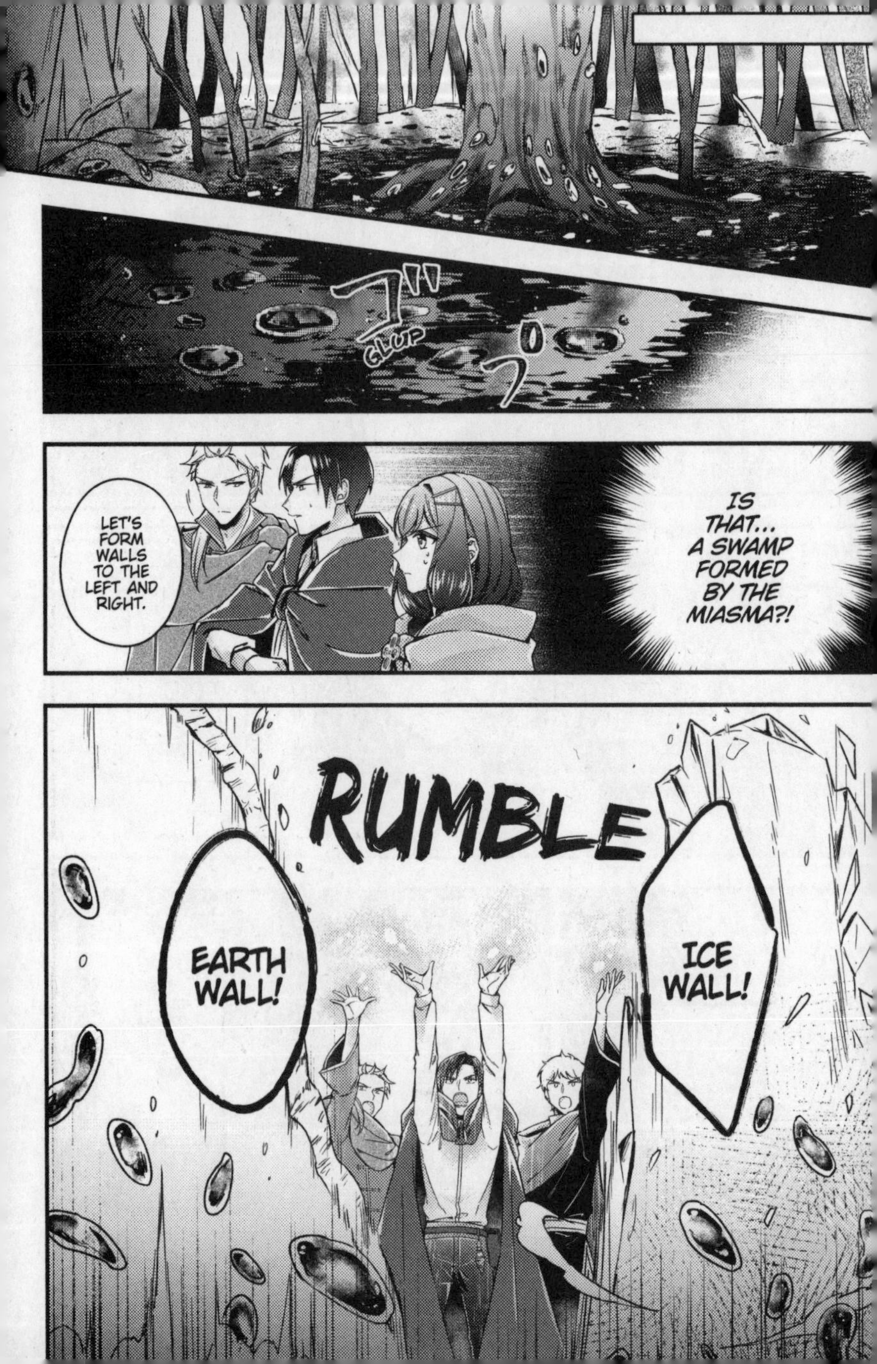
GLUP
IS THAT... A SWAMP FORMED BY THE MIASMA?!
LET'S FORM WALLS TO THE LEFT AND RIGHT.
RUMBLE
ICE WALL!
EARTH WALL!

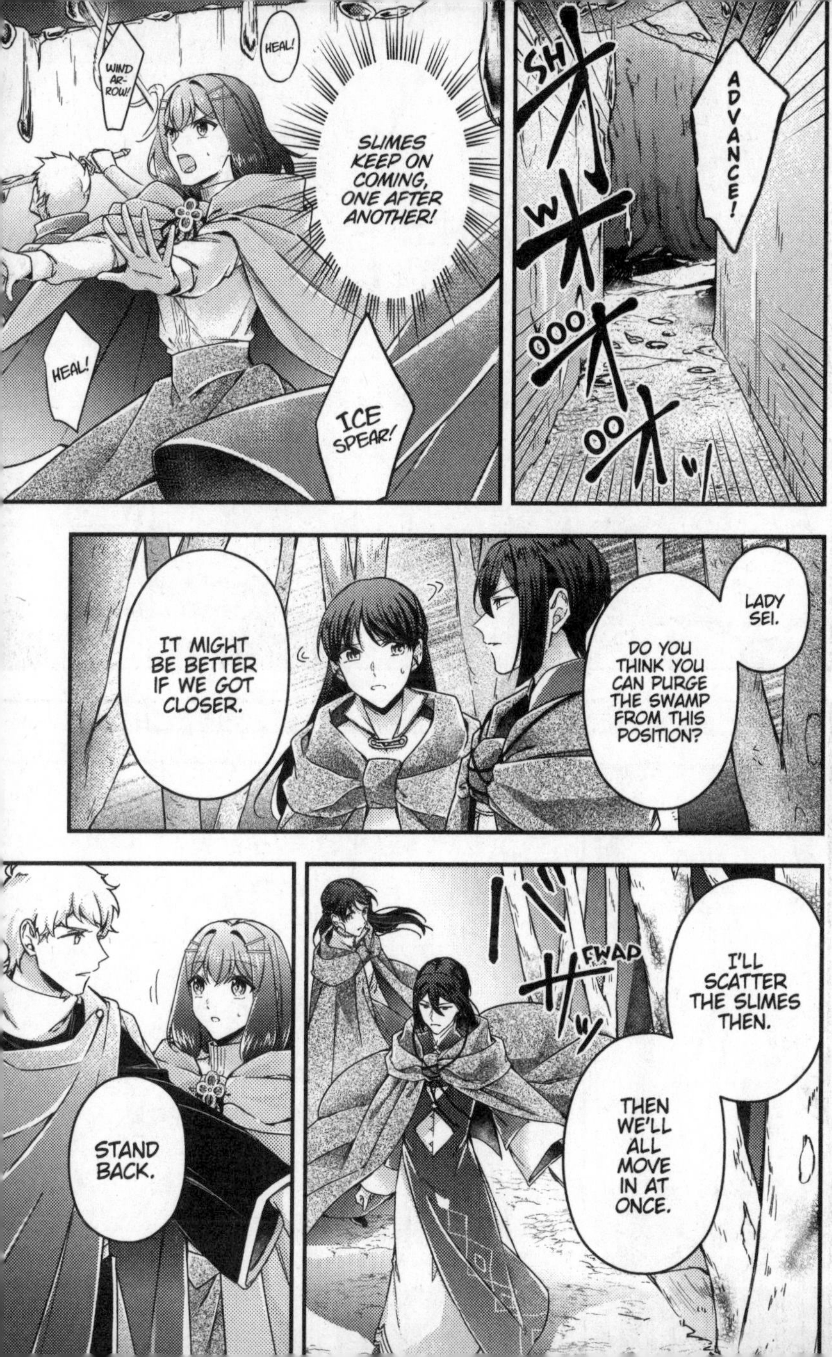
ADVANCE!
SH
W
OOO
OO
HEAL!
WIND AR-ROW!
SLIMES KEEP ON COMING, ONE AFTER ANOTHER!
HEAL!
ICE SPEAR!
LADY SEI.
DO YOU THINK YOU CAN PURGE THE SWAMP FROM THIS POSITION?
IT MIGHT BE BETTER IF WE GOT CLOSER.
FWAP
I'LL SCATTER THE SLIMES THEN.
THEN WE'LL ALL MOVE IN AT ONCE.
STAND BACK.

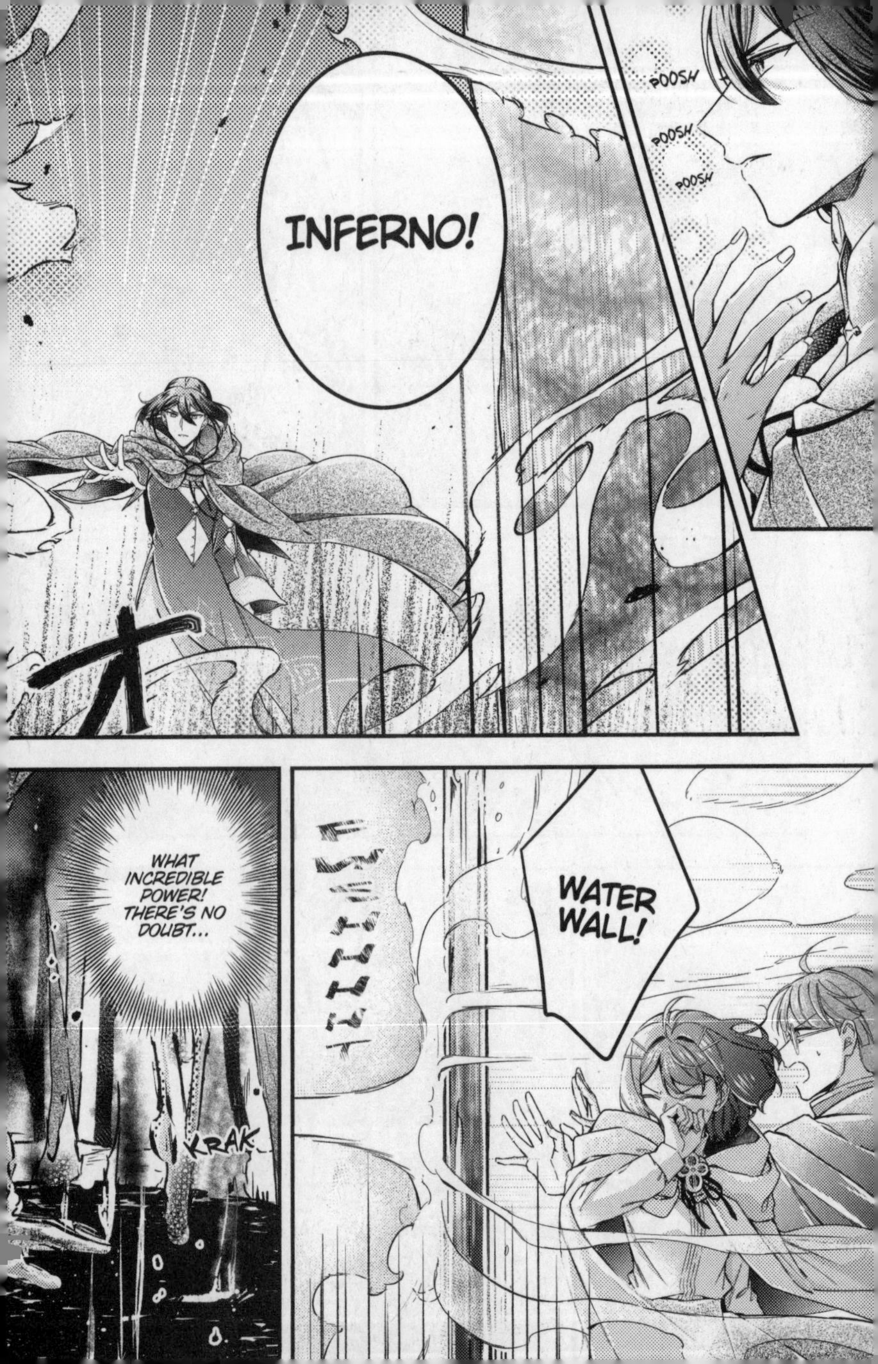
POOSH
POOSH
POOSH
INFERNO!
WATER WALL!
WHAT INCREDIBLE POWER! THERE'S NO DOUBT...
KRAK

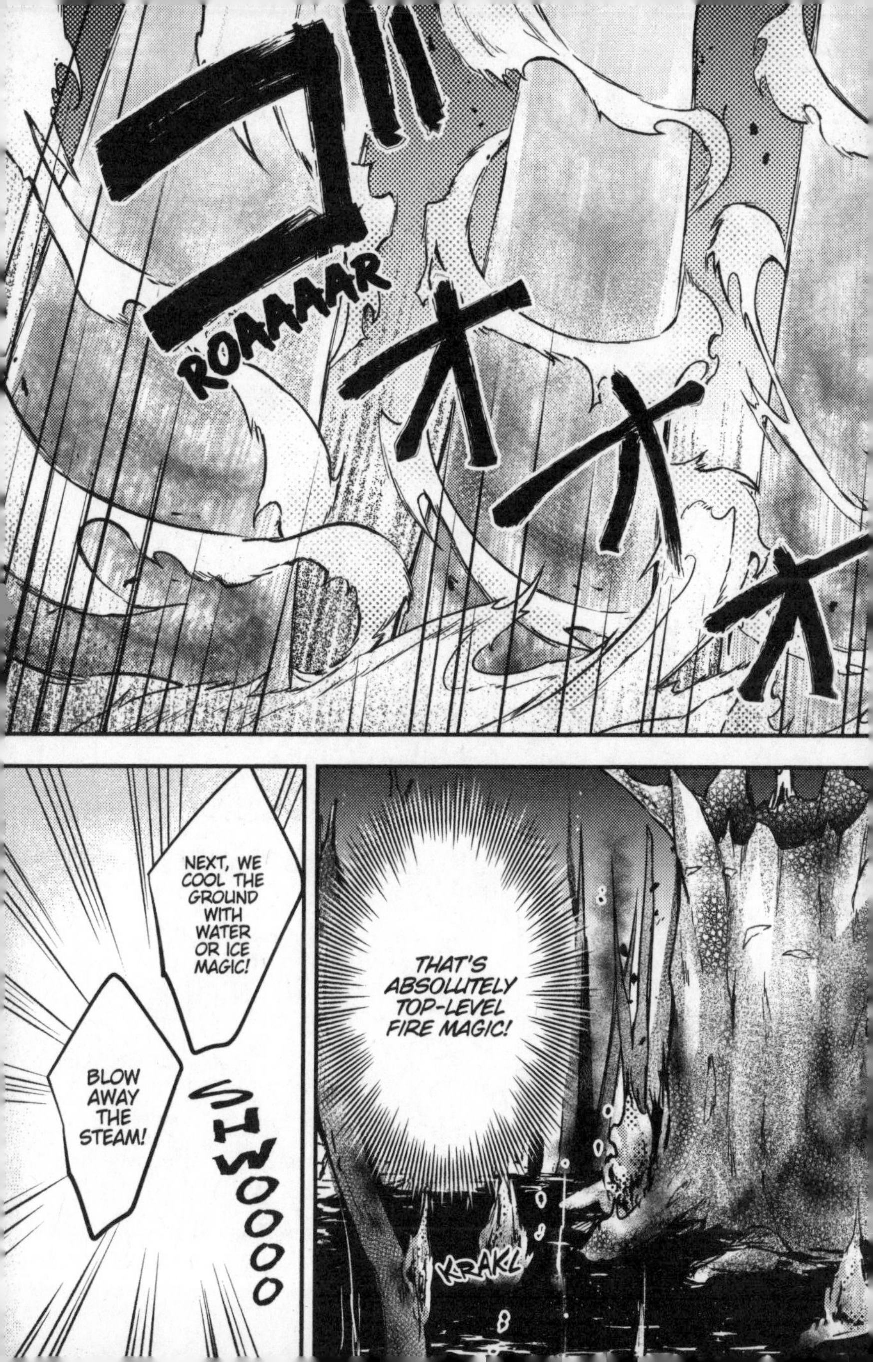
ゴオオオ
ROAAAAR
THAT'S ABSOLUTELY TOP-LEVEL FIRE MAGIC!
KRAKL
NEXT, WE COOL THE GROUND WITH WATER OR ICE MAGIC!
BLOW AWAY THE STEAM!
SHWOOOOO

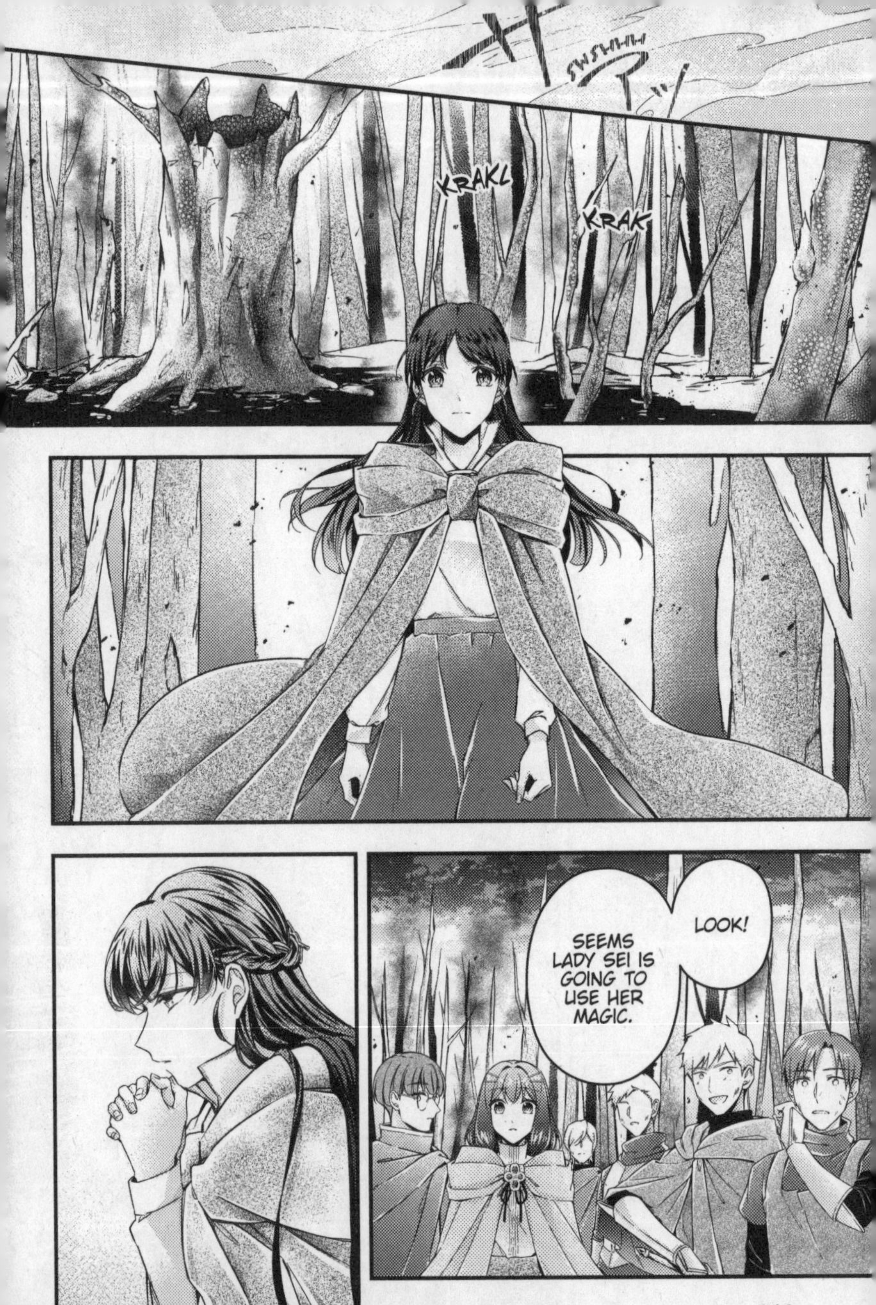
SWSWHH
KRAKL
KRAK
LOOK!
SEEMS LADY SEI IS GOING TO USE HER MAGIC.

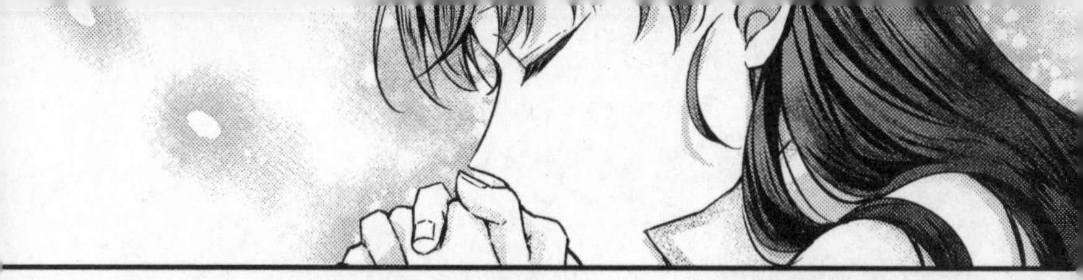

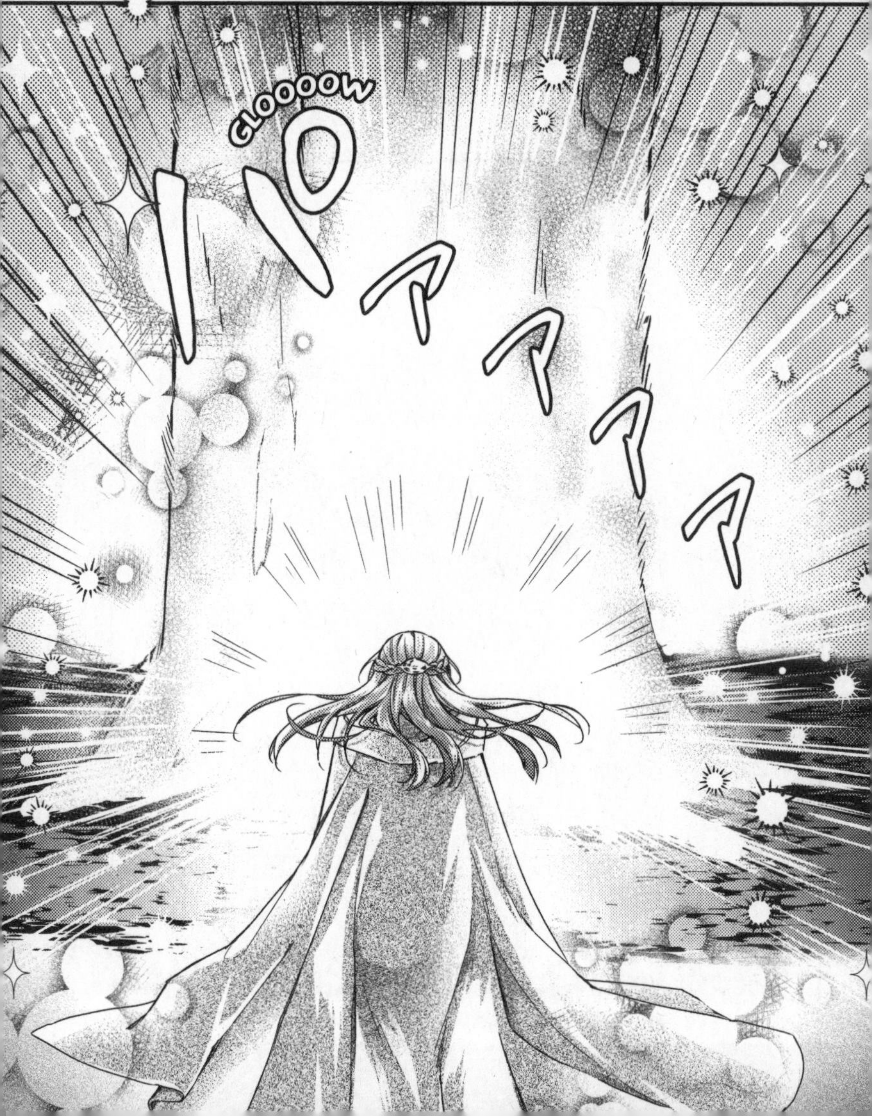
GLOOOOW
パァァァァ

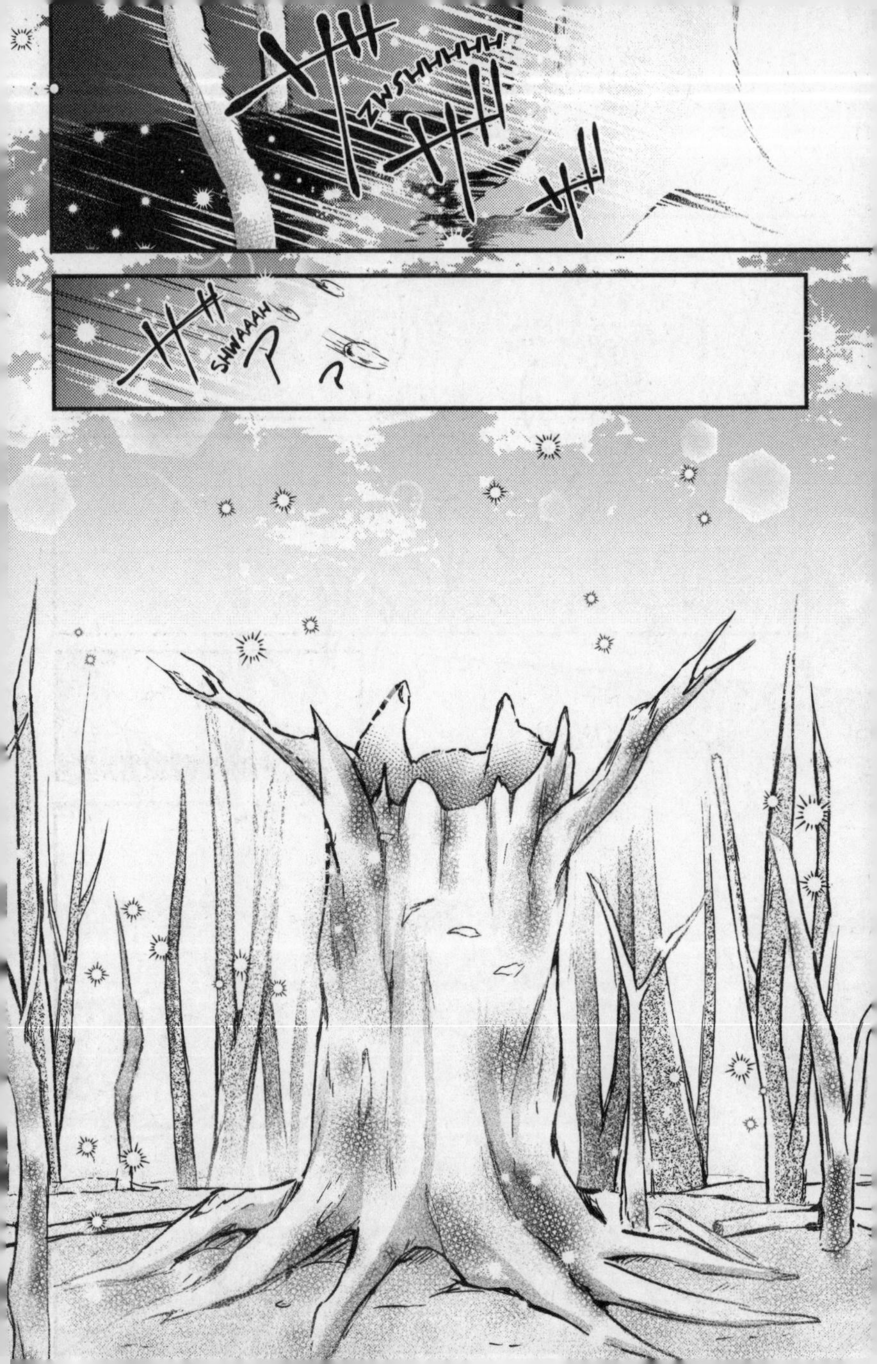
ZWSHHHHH
SHWAAAH

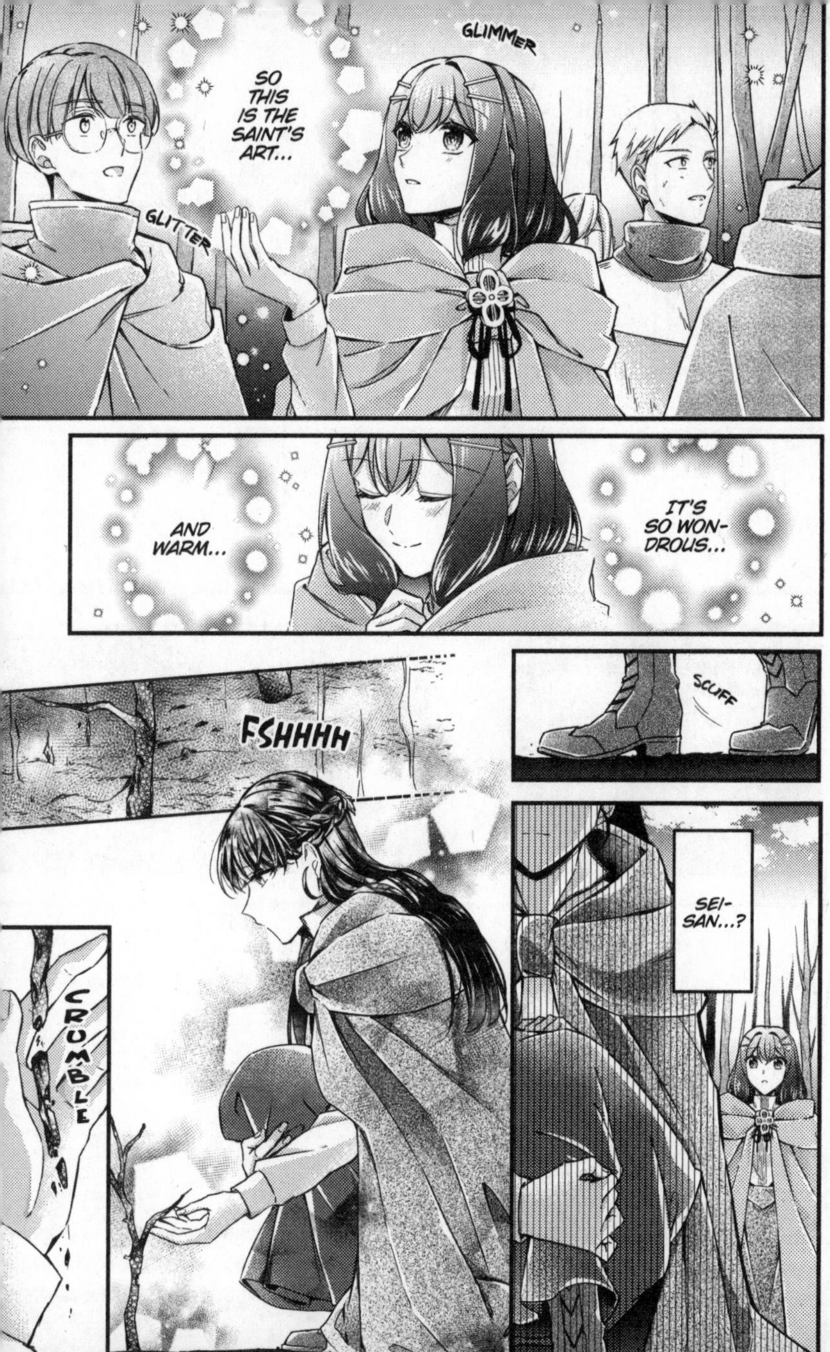
GLIMMER
SO THIS IS THE SAINT'S ART...
GLITTER
IT'S SO WON-DROUS...
AND WARM...
SCUFF
FSHHHH
SEI-SAN...?
CRUMBLE

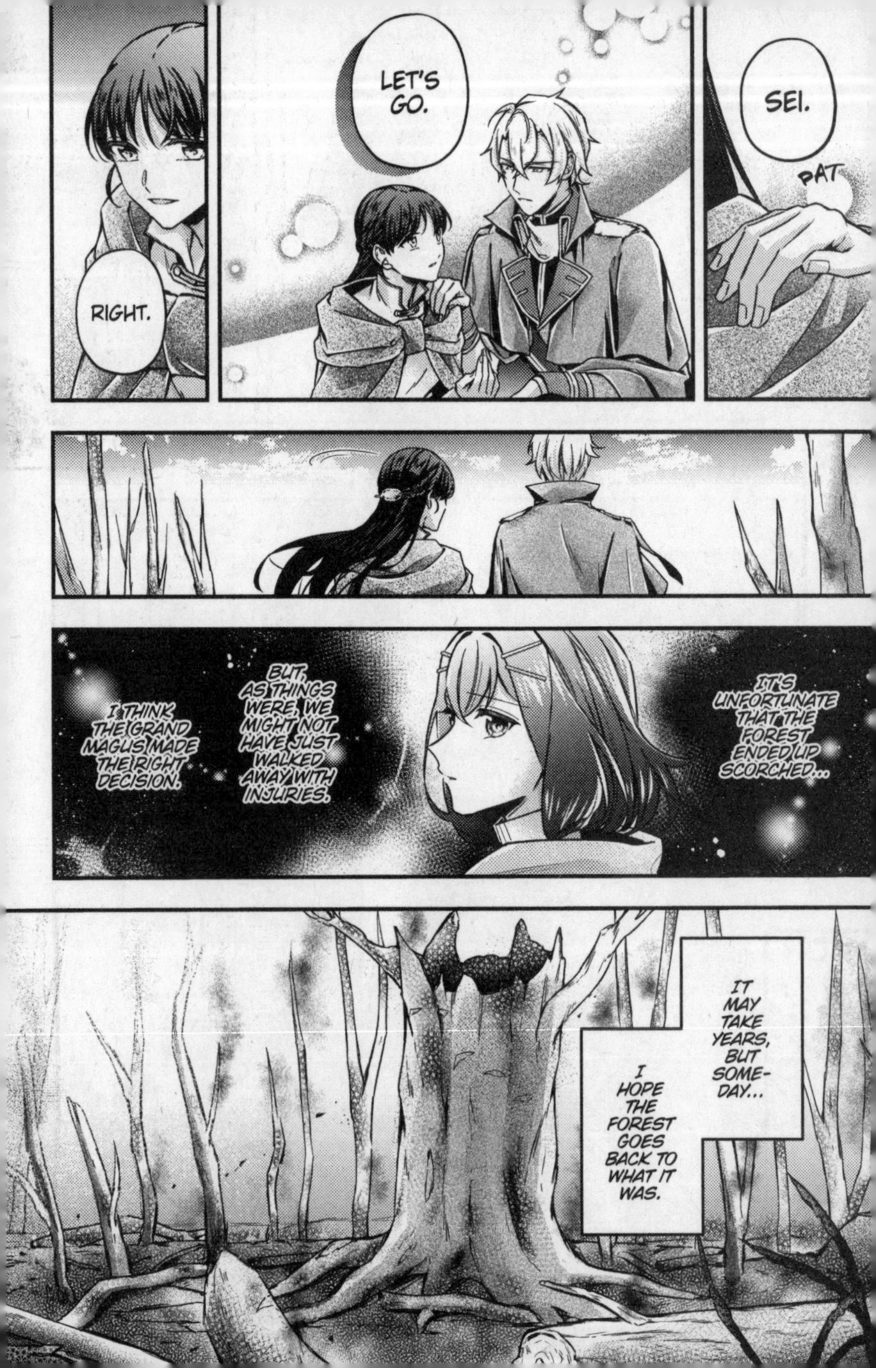
SEI.
PAT
LET'S GO.
RIGHT.
IT'S UNFORTUNATE THAT THE FOREST ENDED UP SCORCHED...
BUT, AS THINGS WERE, WE MIGHT NOT HAVE JUST WALKED AWAY WITH INJURIES.
I THINK THE GRAND MAGUS MADE THE RIGHT DECISION.
IT MAY TAKE YEARS, BUT SOME-DAY...
I HOPE THE FOREST GOES BACK TO WHAT IT WAS.

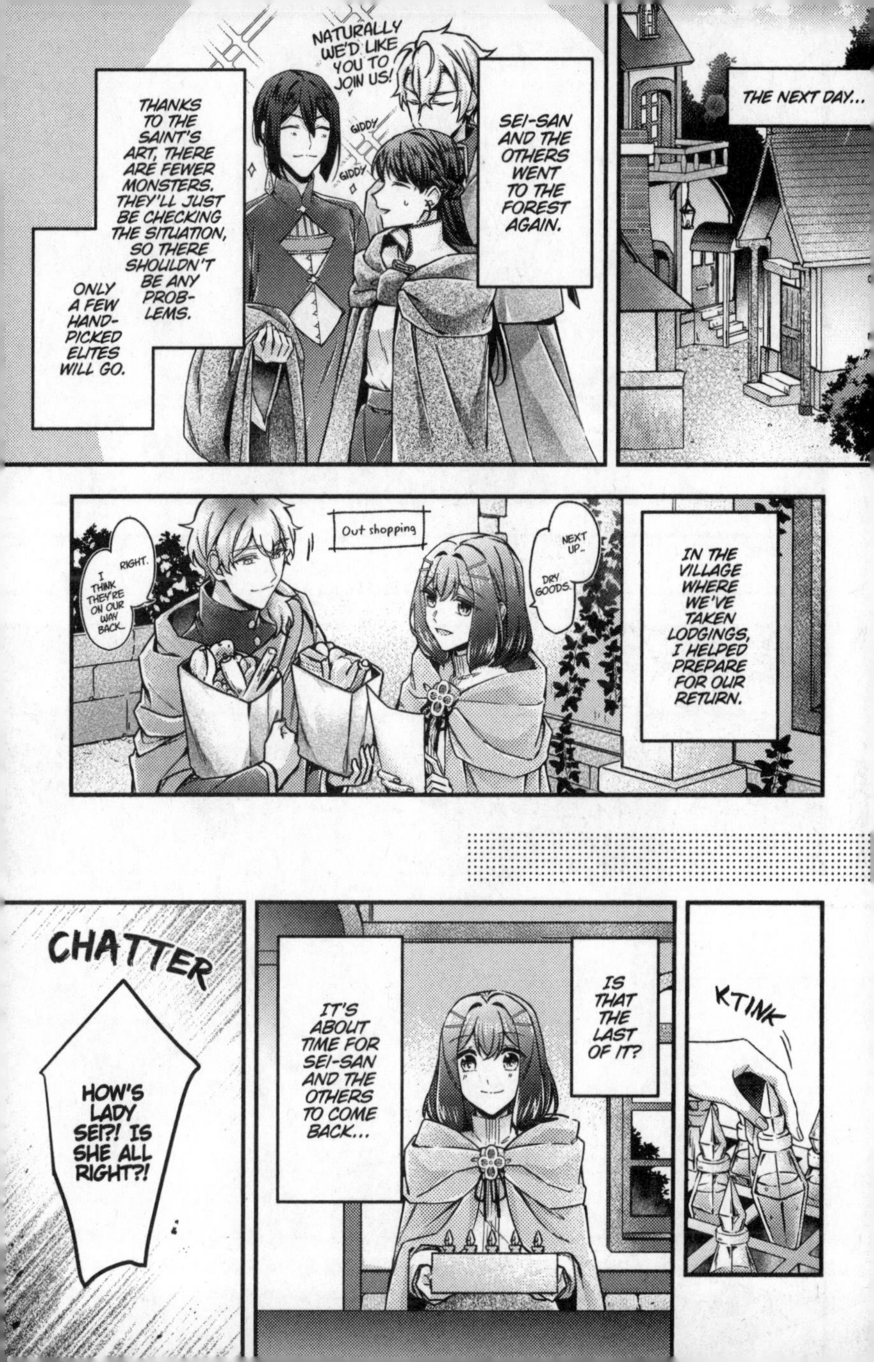
THE NEXT DAY...
SEI-SAN AND THE OTHERS WENT TO THE FOREST AGAIN.
NATURALLY WE'D LIKE YOU TO JOIN US!
GIDDY
GIDDY
THANKS TO THE SAINT'S ART, THERE ARE FEWER MONSTERS. THEY'LL JUST BE CHECKING THE SITUATION, SO THERE SHOULDN'T BE ANY PROB-LEMS.
ONLY A FEW HAND-PICKED ELITES WILL GO.
IN THE VILLAGE WHERE WE'VE TAKEN LODGINGS, I HELPED PREPARE FOR OUR RETURN.
NEXT UP... DRY GOODS.
Out shopping
RIGHT. I THINK THEY'RE ON OUR WAY BACK.
KTINK
IS THAT THE LAST OF IT?
IT'S ABOUT TIME FOR SEI-SAN AND THE OTHERS TO COME BACK...
CHATTER
HOW'S LADY SEI?! IS SHE ALL RIGHT?!

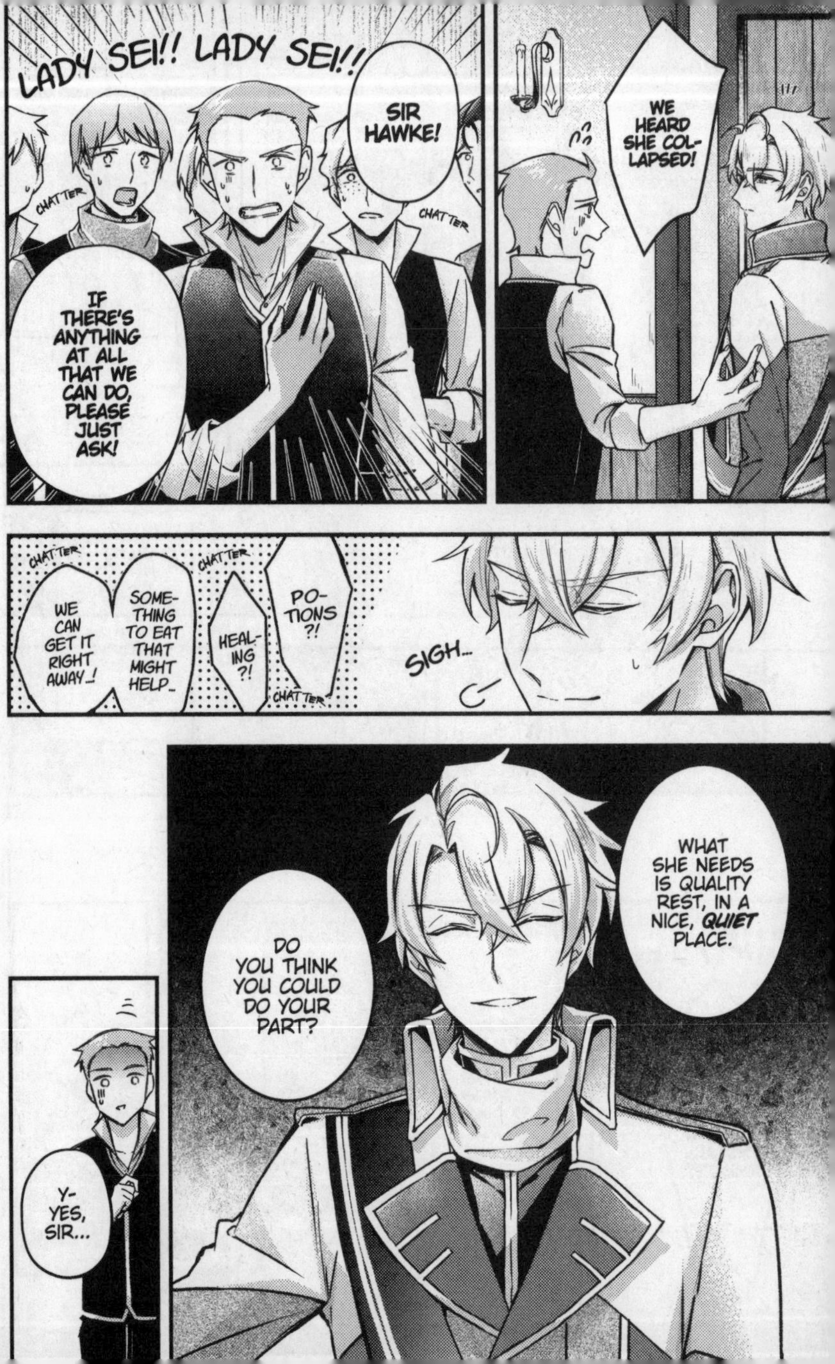
WE HEARD SHE COLLAPSED!
LADY SEI!! LADY SEI!!
SIR HAWKE!
CHATTER
CHATTER
IF THERE'S ANYTHING AT ALL THAT WE CAN DO, PLEASE JUST ASK!
SIGH...
CHATTER
POTIONS?!
HEALING?!
CHATTER
SOMETHING TO EAT THAT MIGHT HELP...
CHATTER
WE CAN GET IT RIGHT AWAY...!
WHAT SHE NEEDS IS QUALITY REST, IN A NICE, QUIET PLACE.
DO YOU THINK YOU COULD DO YOUR PART?
Y-YES, SIR...

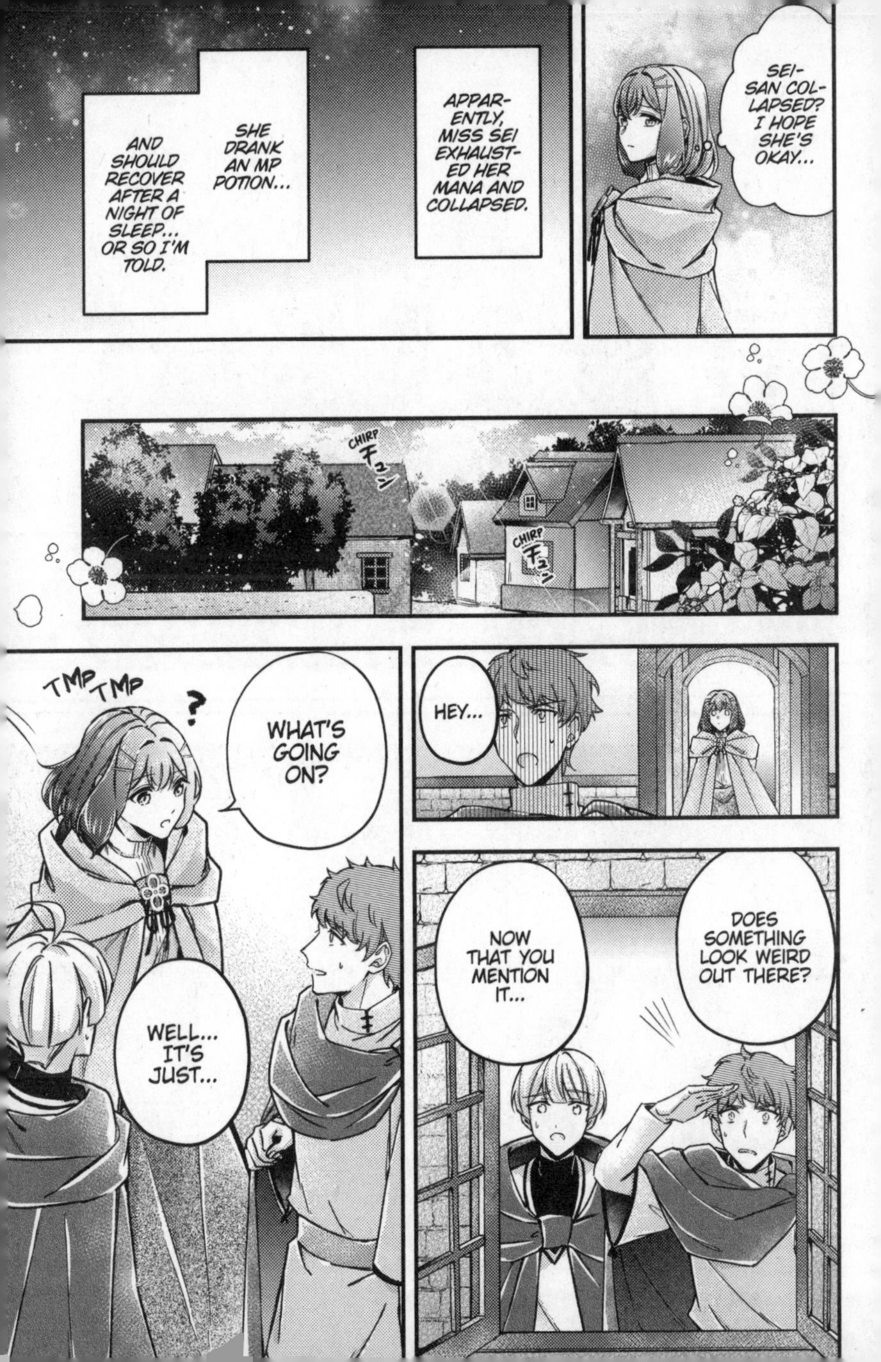
SEI-SAN COLLAPSED? I HOPE SHE'S OKAY...
APPARENTLY, MISS SEI EXHAUSTED HER MANA AND COLLAPSED.
SHE DRANK AN MP POTION...
AND SHOULD RECOVER AFTER A NIGHT OF SLEEP... OR SO I'M TOLD.
CHIRP チュン
CHIRP チュン
HEY...
DOES SOMETHING LOOK WEIRD OUT THERE?
NOW THAT YOU MENTION IT...
TMP TMP
?
WHAT'S GOING ON?
WELL... IT'S JUST...

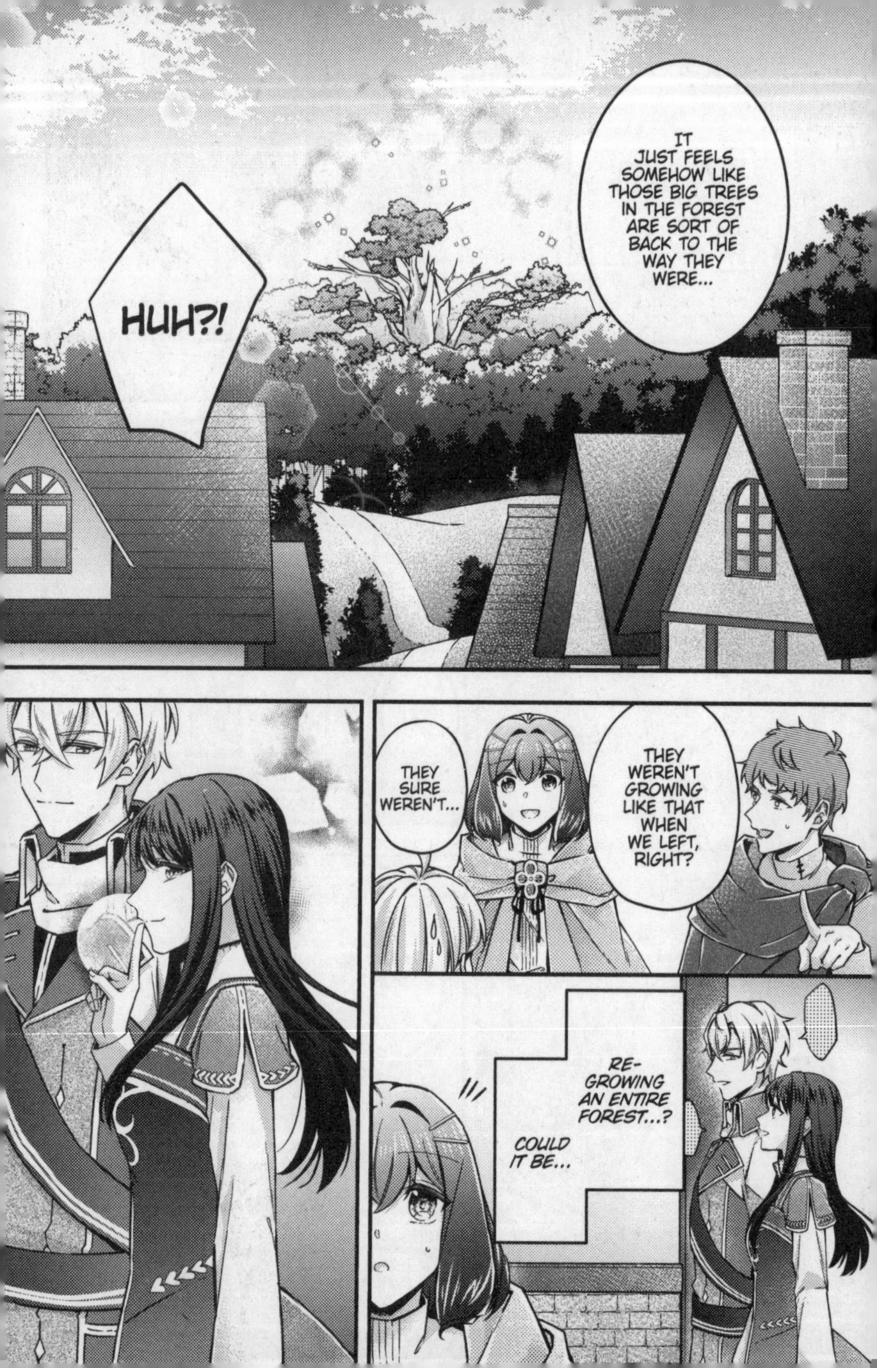
IT JUST FEELS SOMEHOW LIKE THOSE BIG TREES IN THE FOREST ARE SORT OF BACK TO THE WAY THEY WERE...
HUH?!
THEY WEREN'T GROWING LIKE THAT WHEN WE LEFT, RIGHT?
THEY SURE WEREN'T...
RE-GROWING AN ENTIRE FOREST...?
COULD IT BE...

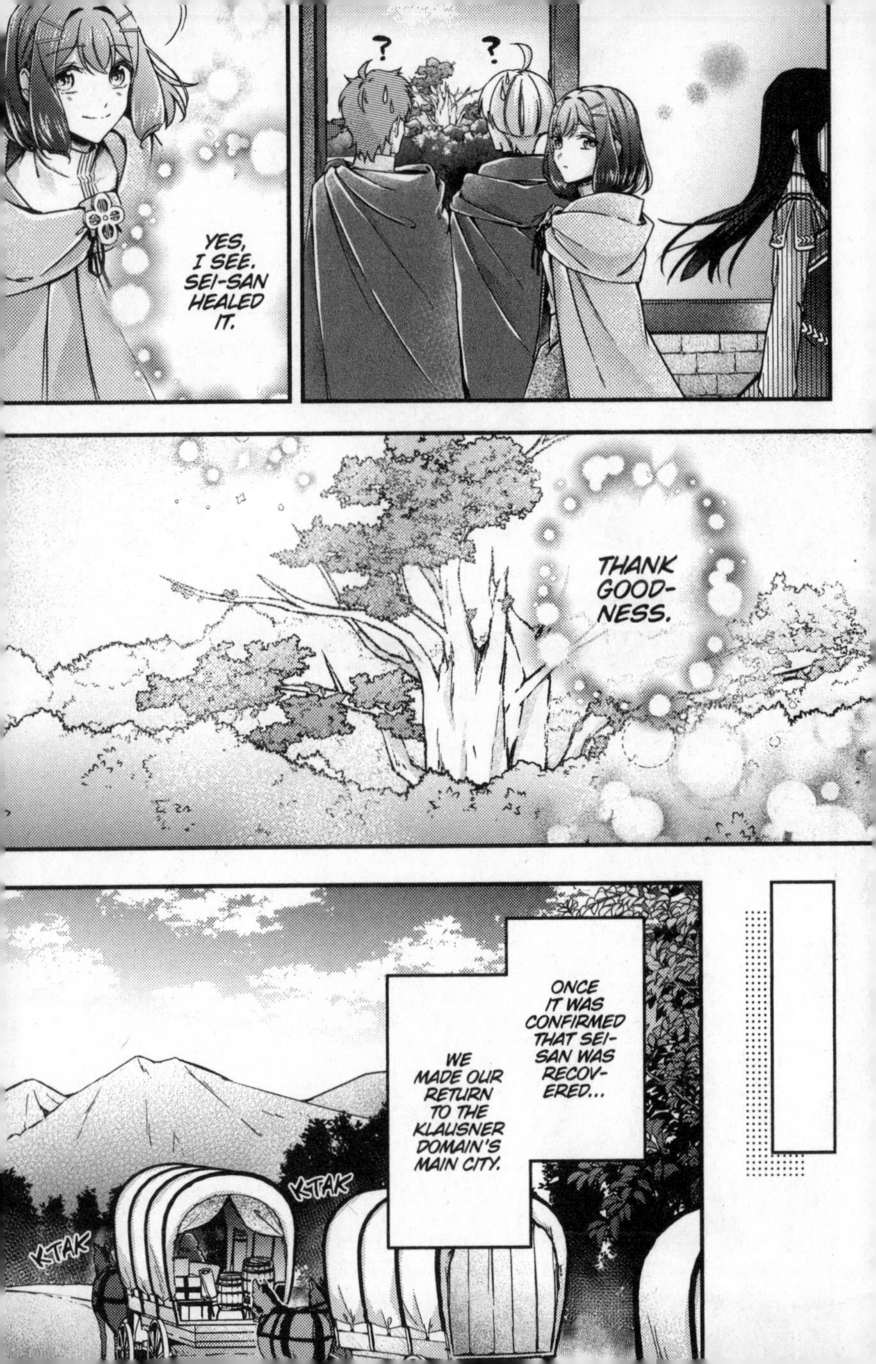
?
?
YES, I SEE. SEI-SAN HEALED IT.
THANK GOODNESS.
ONCE IT WAS CONFIRMED THAT SEI-SAN WAS RECOVERED...
WE MADE OUR RETURN TO THE KLAUSNER DOMAIN'S MAIN CITY.
KTAK
KTAK

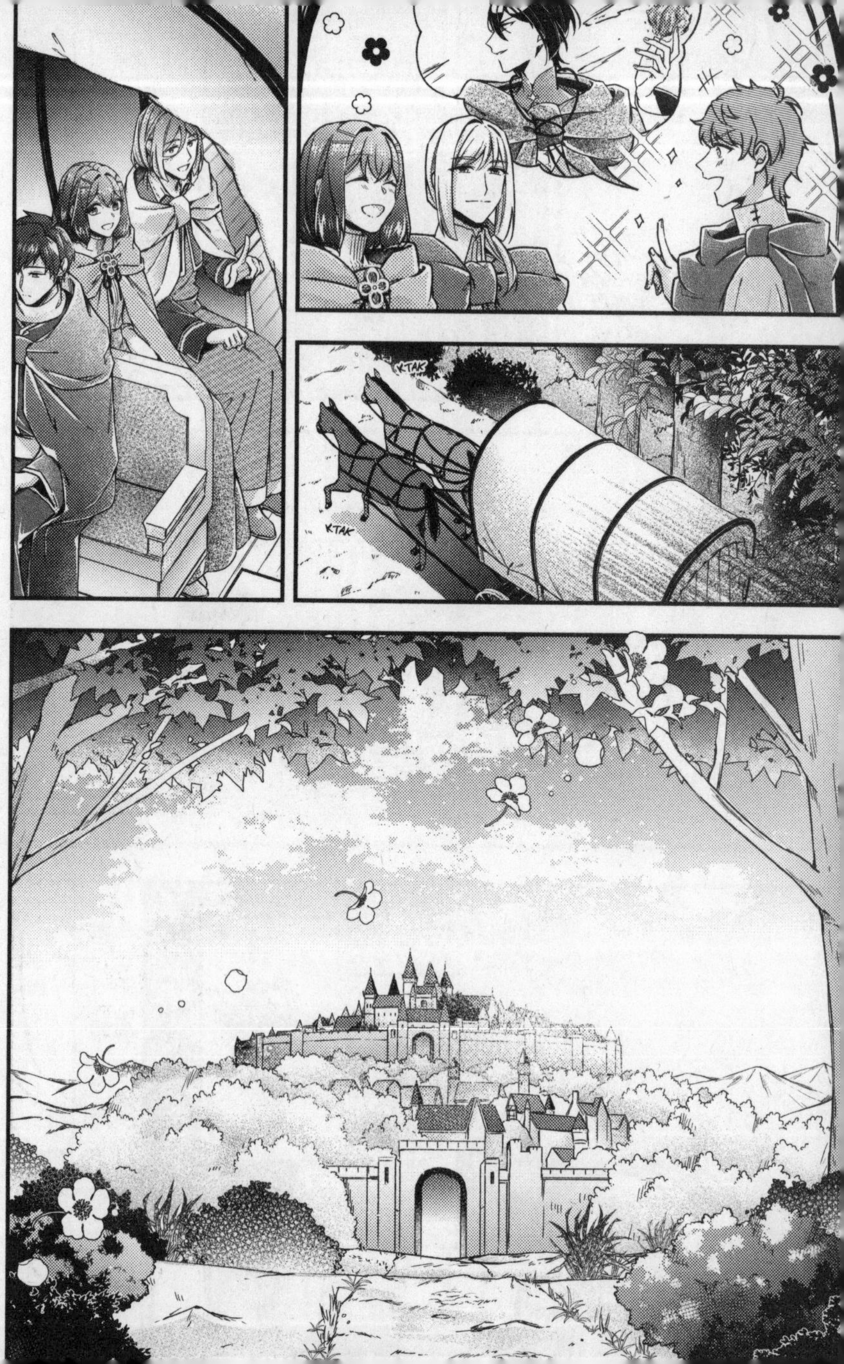
KTAK
KTAK

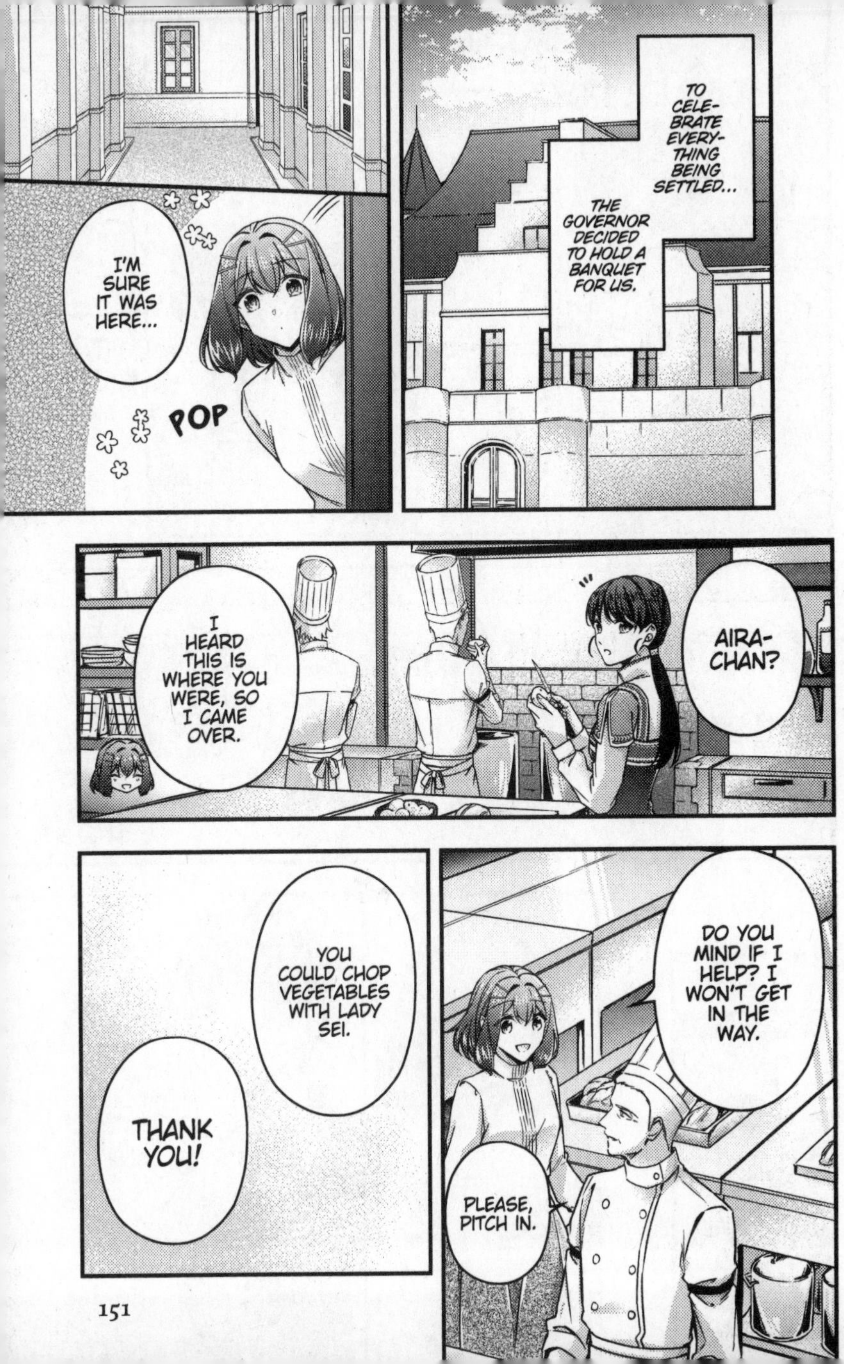
TO CELEBRATE EVERYTHING BEING SETTLED...
THE GOVERNOR DECIDED TO HOLD A BANQUET FOR US.
I'M SURE IT WAS HERE...
POP
AIRA-CHAN?
I HEARD THIS IS WHERE YOU WERE, SO I CAME OVER.
DO YOU MIND IF I HELP? I WON'T GET IN THE WAY.
PLEASE, PITCH IN.
YOU COULD CHOP VEGETABLES WITH LADY SEI.
THANK YOU!

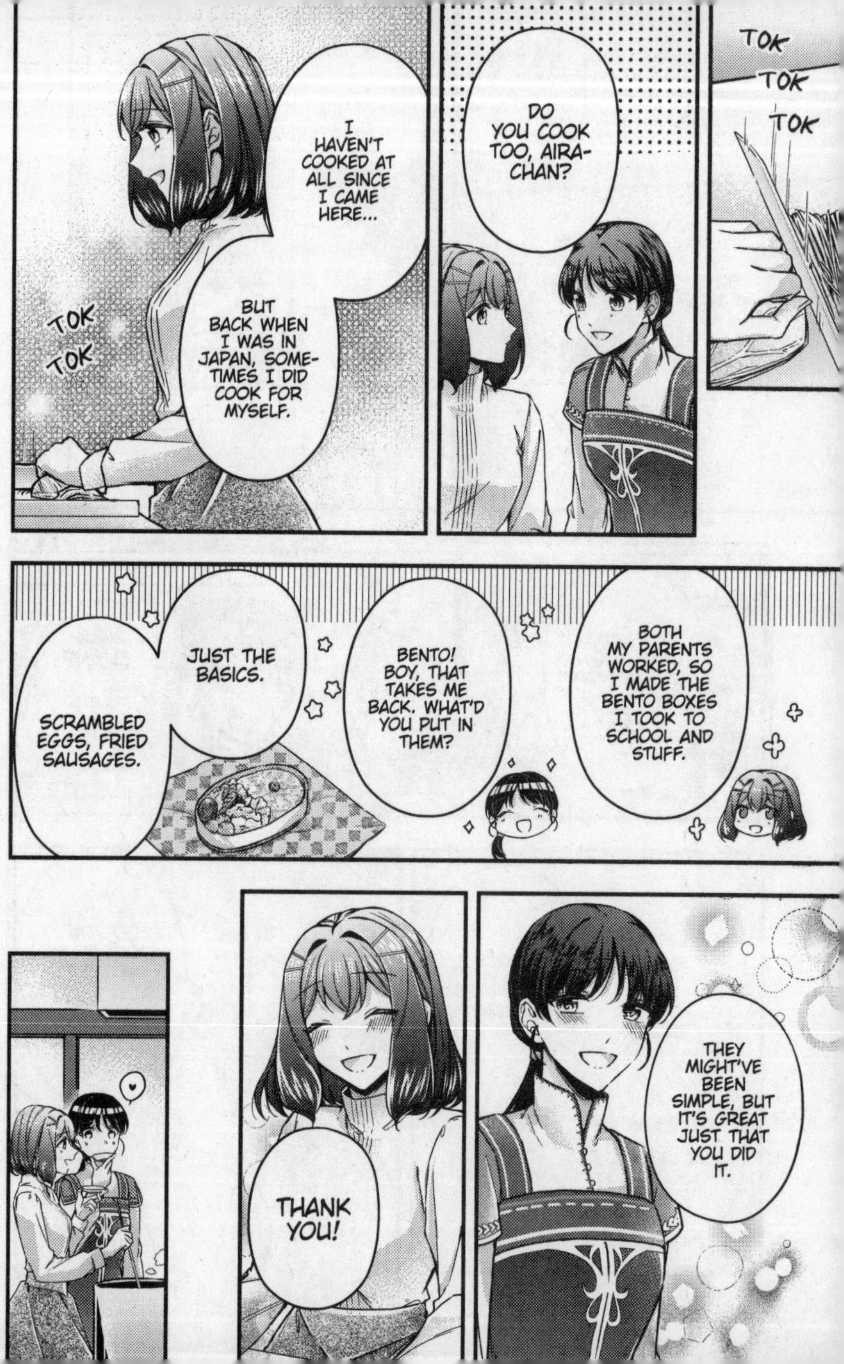
TOK
TOK
TOK
DO YOU COOK TOO, AIRA-CHAN?
I HAVEN'T COOKED AT ALL SINCE I CAME HERE...
BUT BACK WHEN I WAS IN JAPAN, SOMETIMES I DID COOK FOR MYSELF.
TOK
TOK
BOTH MY PARENTS WORKED, SO I MADE THE BENTO BOXES I TOOK TO SCHOOL AND STUFF.
BENTO! BOY, THAT TAKES ME BACK. WHAT'D YOU PUT IN THEM?
JUST THE BASICS.
SCRAMBLED EGGS, FRIED SAUSAGES.
THEY MIGHT'VE BEEN SIMPLE, BUT IT'S GREAT JUST THAT YOU DID IT.
THANK YOU!

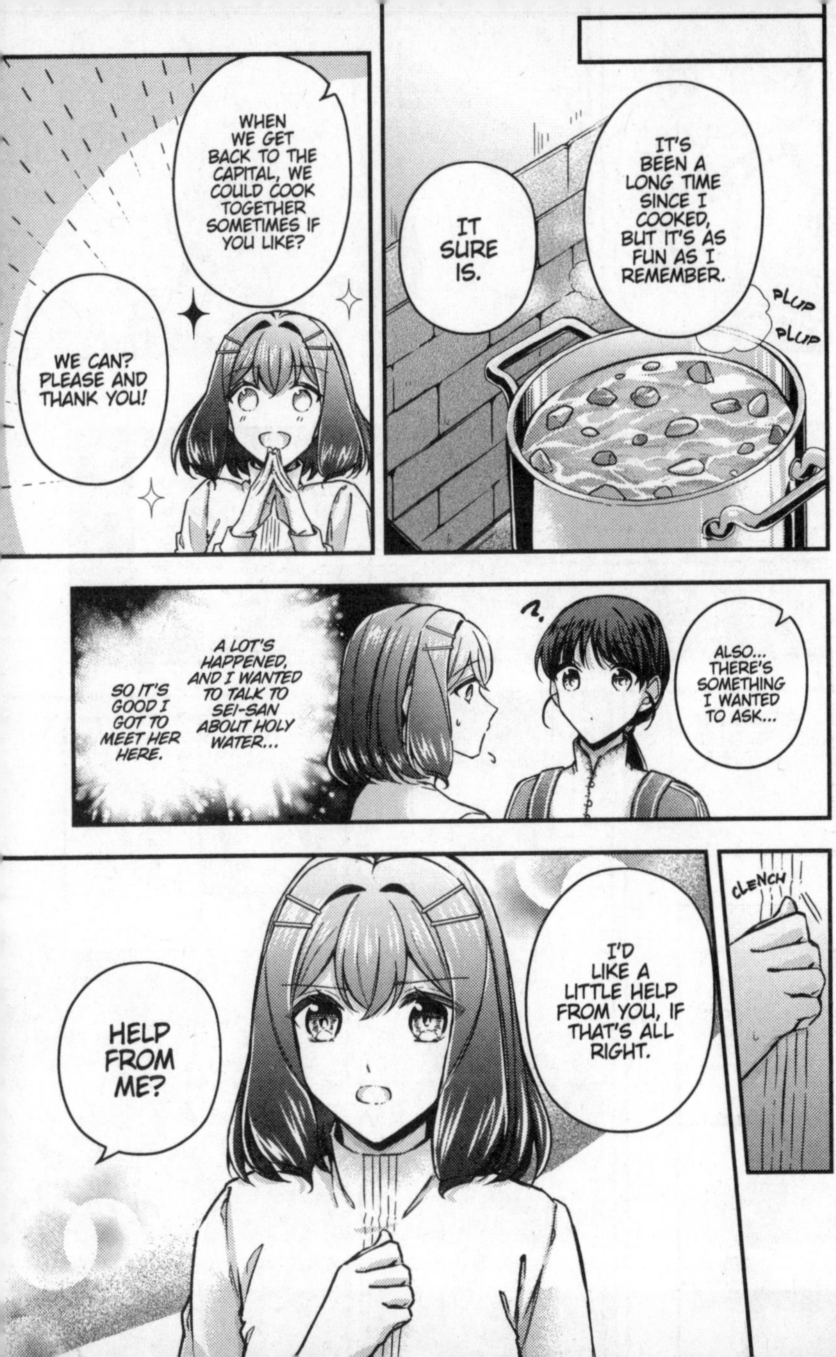
IT'S BEEN A LONG TIME SINCE I COOKED, BUT IT'S AS FUN AS I REMEMBER.
PLUP PLUP
IT SURE IS.
WHEN WE GET BACK TO THE CAPITAL, WE COULD COOK TOGETHER SOMETIMES IF YOU LIKE?
WE CAN? PLEASE AND THANK YOU!
ALSO... THERE'S SOMETHING I WANTED TO ASK...
?
A LOT'S HAPPENED, AND I WANTED TO TALK TO SEI-SAN ABOUT HOLY WATER...
SO IT'S GOOD I GOT TO MEET HER HERE.
CLENCH
I'D LIKE A LITTLE HELP FROM YOU, IF THAT'S ALL RIGHT.
HELP FROM ME?

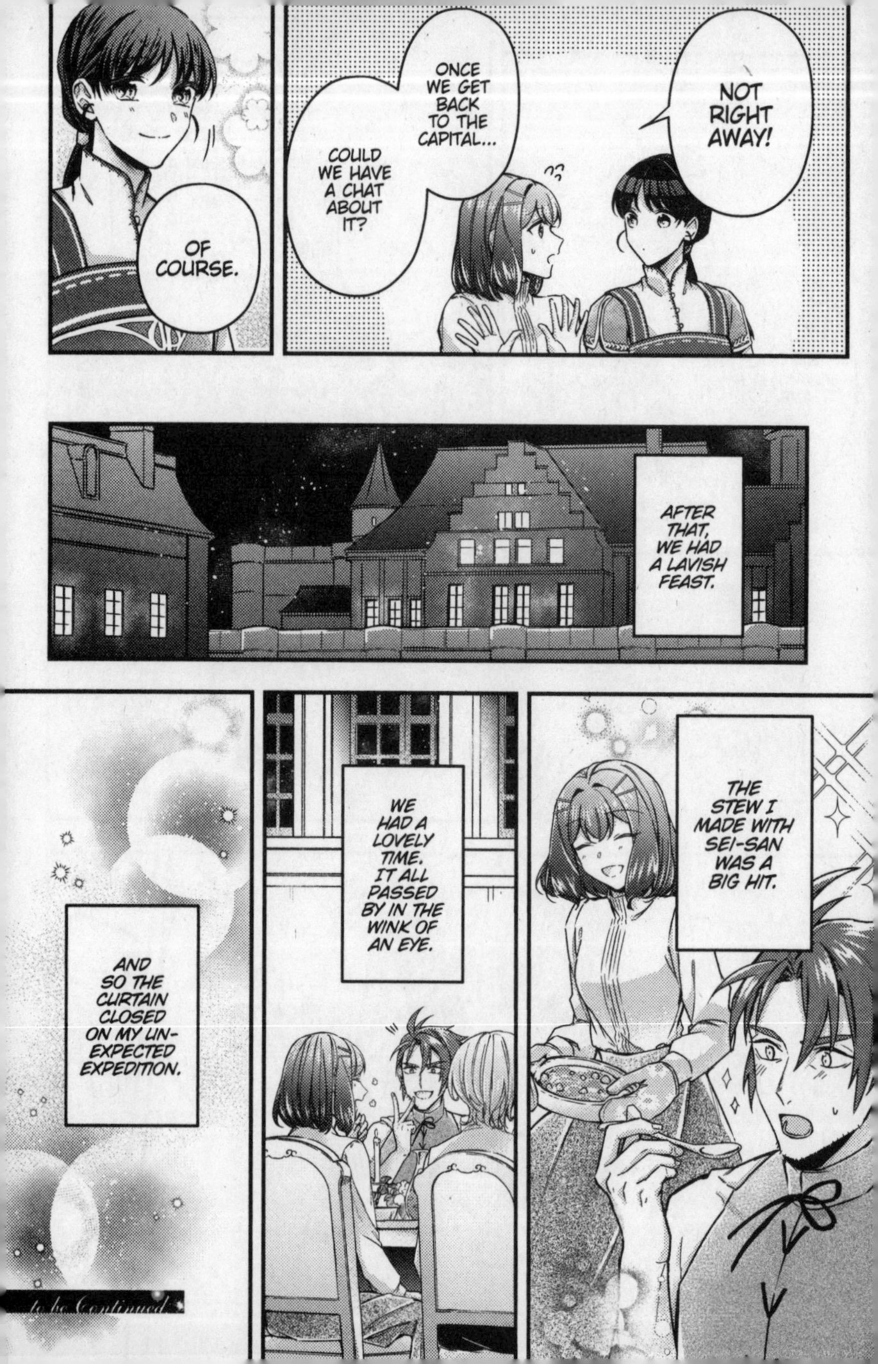
NOT RIGHT AWAY!
ONCE WE GET BACK TO THE CAPITAL...
COULD WE HAVE A CHAT ABOUT IT?
OF COURSE.
AFTER THAT, WE HAD A LAVISH FEAST.
THE STEW I MADE WITH SEI-SAN WAS A BIG HIT.
WE HAD A LOVELY TIME. IT ALL PASSED BY IN THE WINK OF AN EYE.
AND SO THE CURTAIN CLOSED ON MY UN-EXPECTED EXPEDITION.
to be Continued

The **Saint's**
Magic Power is
Omnipotent
The Other Saint

The Saint's Magic Power Is Omnipotent Original Creator's Comment

Thank you very much for picking up *The Saint's Magic Power Is Omnipotent: The Other Saint,* Volume 2. I'm the original creator of this series, Yuka Tachibana. Thanks to you, our spin-off series has also now reached Volume 2. I must express my gratitude first to our constant readers, and also to Aoagu-sensei (who handled the spin-off), the editors in charge, and everyone else involved. Thank you, truly.

Here in Volume 2, Aira-chan finally joins the Royal Magi Assembly. Did you enjoy the scenes of life at the Magi Assembly? That didn't get much treatment in the main story. As I was checking the work, the animated expressions which Ao-sensei drew on Aira-chan's face made me swoon every time. That bright smile that makes it seem like flowers are dancing in the background is just precious. As I checked the work, when that smile appeared, I couldn't help but giggle. It truly is precious. Ao-Sensei, thank you always for the lovely Aira-chan.

And it's not just her. The other characters are abundant with expression too. Personally, the one that made a strong impression on me is the intelligent, glasses-wearing Archmagus of the Royal Magi Assembly, Erhard. When I was writing the novels, I pictured him as the sort of person who doesn't have much variation in expressions. But Erhard in the spin-off has quite a varied range, and it's very fun to observe him. Unlike Aira-chan, his scowling face is the one that leaves the biggest impression. Could you say it looks like he's fallen to the dark side? Something about Erhard's glare when he's dressing down the Grand Magus really made an impression on me.

Finally, I would like to once again thank everyone who picked up this volume. I hope you continue to enjoy these tales centered around Aira-chan in the world of *The Saint's Magic Power Is Omnipotent.* Until next time.

Yuka Tachibana

Afterword

Hello, this is Aoagu.
Thank you very much for picking up this book.

Volume 2! At this stage we've roughly caught up to the events of light novel Volume 4 through Aira's perspective. It's been a mad dash, but having the opportunity to draw scenes I liked from the novels and main manga series has been very fun. Thank you always to series creator Yuka Tachibana-sensei and character designer Yasuyuki Syuri-sensei.

Next volume, we'll begin to branch off more from the light novels. I will do my best to bring you even more of the wonder of the world of *The Saint's Magic Power Is Omnipotent*, so I truly hope you enjoy it.

Aoagu

Special Thanks

Original Creator Yuka
Tachibana-sensei
Illustrator Yasuyuki Syuri-sensei
Assistant Mikimo Nezumi-sama
Everyone in editorial

The Saint's Magic Power is Omnipotent

The Other Saint

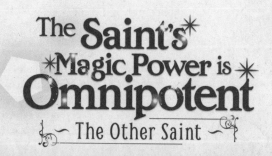

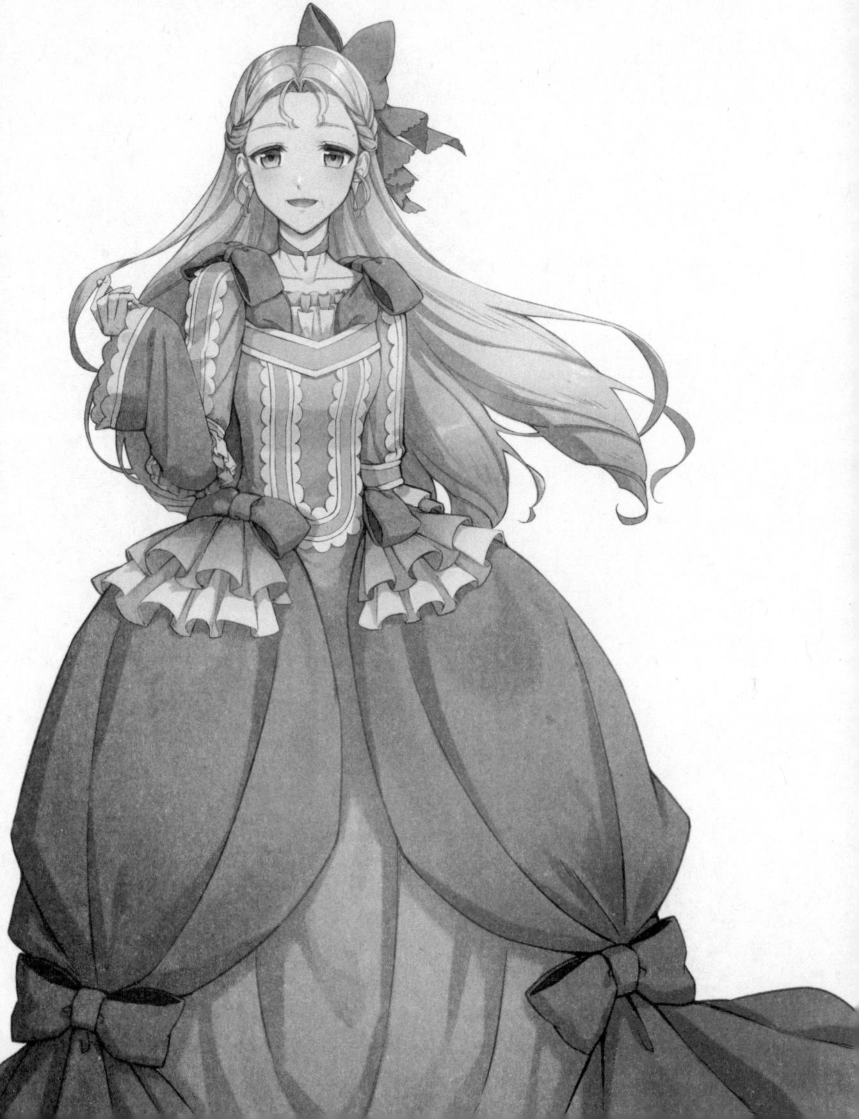

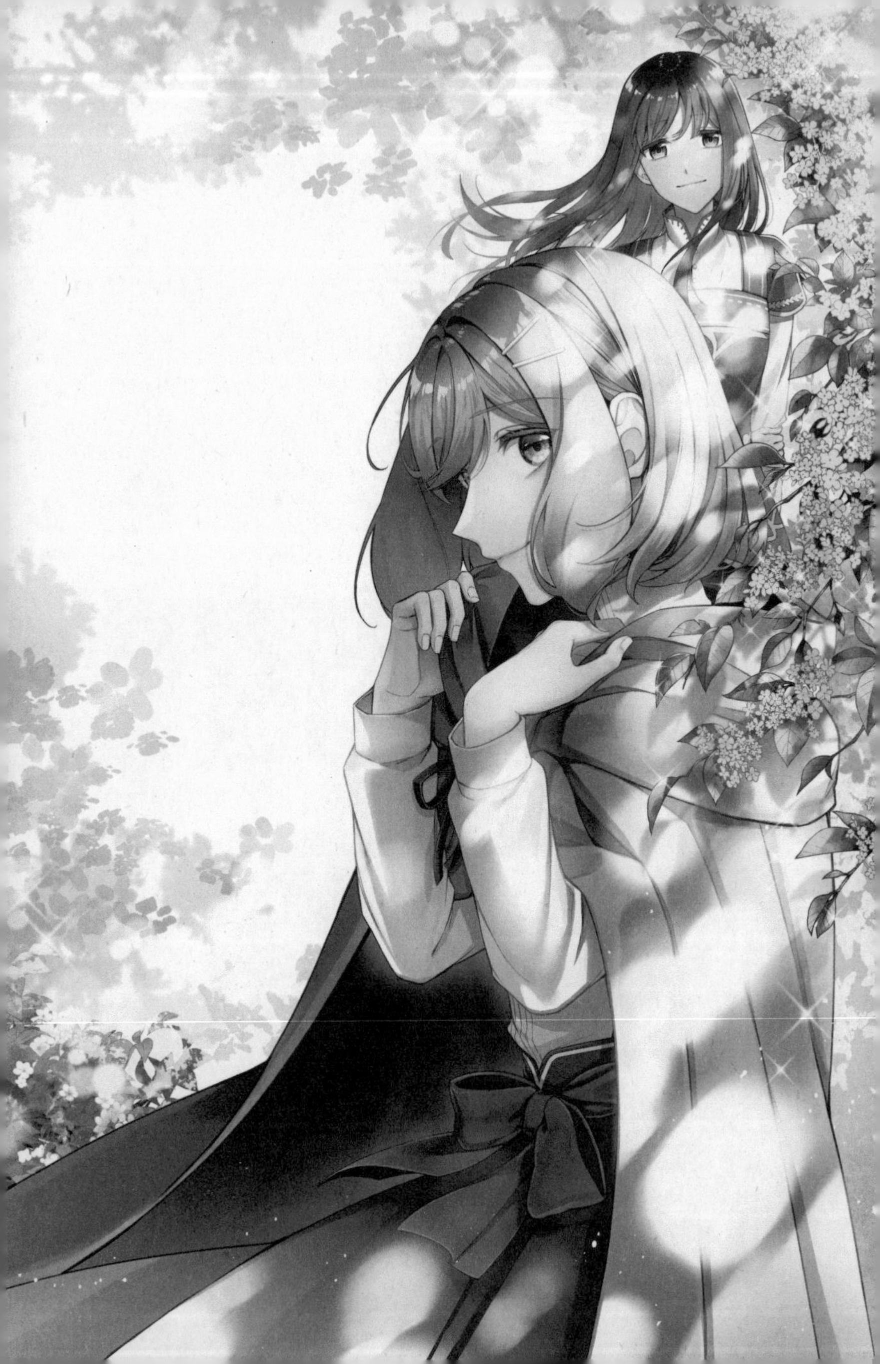

The **Saint's** *Magic Power is* **Omnipotent**

The Other Saint

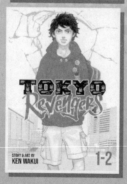

SEVEN SEAS ENTERTAINMENT PRESENTS

The Saint's Magic Power is Omnipotent — The Other Saint —

story and art by **AOAGU**   original story by **YUKA TACHIBANA**   character design by **YASUYUKI SYURI**

TRANSLATION
Kumar Sivasubramanian

LETTERING
Jennifer Skarupa

COVER DESIGN
Nicky Lim

LOGO DESIGN
George Panella

PROOFREADER
Danielle King

SENIOR EDITOR
J.P. Sullivan

PRODUCTION DESIGNER
Christina McKenzie

PRODUCTION MANAGER
Lissa Pattillo

PREPRESS TECHNICIAN
Melanie Ujimori
Jules Valera

EDITOR-IN-CHIEF
Julie Davis

ASSOCIATE PUBLISHER
Adam Arnold

PUBLISHER
Jason DeAngelis

SEIJO NO MARYOKU HA BANNO DESU ~MO HITORI NO SEIJO~ Vol.2
©Aoagu 2021
©Yuka Tachibana, Yasuyuki Syuri 2021
First published in Japan in 2021 by KADOKAWA CORPORATION, Tokyo.
English translation rights arranged with KADOKAWA CORPORATION, Tokyo.

Seven Seas press and purchase enquiries can be sent to Marketing Manager Lianne Sentar at press@gomanga.com. Information regarding the distribution and purchase of digital editions is available from Digital Manager CK Russell at digital@gomanga.com.

Seven Seas and the Seven Seas logo are trademarks of Seven Seas Entertainment. All rights reserved.

ISBN: 978-1-63858-730-9
Printed in Canada
First Printing: May 2023
10 9 8 7 6 5 4 3 2 1

READING DIRECTIONS

This book reads from *right to left*, Japanese style. If this is your first time reading manga, you start reading from the top right panel on each page and take it from there. If you get lost, just follow the numbered diagram here. It may seem backwards at first, but you'll get the hang of it! Have fun!!

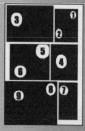

Follow us online: www.SevenSeasEntertainment.com